The Amazing

REVELATION

of St. John
And
The End of Planet Earth

EXPLAINED FOR EVERYONE

By: Shuford Jones, Jr.

Copyright – © 2018 – Shuford Jones, Jr.

ISBN 9781732698703

Fair Hope Publishing
A Division of
Shuford Jones LLC
www.shufordjones.com

Cover Design: Melody Simmons Graphics

TABLE OF CONTENTS

Appendices

Our Purpose in This Book

It is not the purpose of this book to be exhaustive in interpreting Revelation. Rather the desire is for the reader to develop a clear view of the meaning and timeline of Revelation. John's understanding of events, both in the Old Testament and the New Testament, will be in focus as they are connected to the images in Revelation. In Revelation, these events or prophecies do not necessarily have the same interpretation as in their original setting because John has received an altogether new understanding of ancient prophecies not previously explained in Scripture. We will collect these prophecies and trace them into the fuller understanding through the revelations to St. John.

Scripture

The scripture in this book is carefully adapted from the King James Version. We use the term **Easy KJV** to identify these Scriptures. Sentences have been arranged according to today's structure where possible. Difficult passages have been explained where appropriate. Words such as **thee, thine, ye, reigneth, sayeth, searcheth**, and many others have been changed to the current word usage. This is to facilitate the reader's study while strictly maintaining the true and accurate meaning. The reader is encouraged to use the translation of his or her choice along with this book. The greater purpose is to understand the wonderful truth of God's inspired message and to make the appropriate application to our own lives under Christ.

Keys to This Book

- **Book and scripture Chapters numbers are identical.**
- **Most Chapters have a brief Snapshot of what to expect.**
- **Scriptures are the KJV adapted as noted above.**
- **Select Sections to provide additional information for the reader are inserted within many chapters.**
- **The book is straight forward and clear without attempting to discuss the many ideas put forth in history.**
- **Each of the 22 Chapters and the over 400 verses is discussed in this book.**
- **Special reference is made to Old Testament passages that John would know, and that are similar but not identical with Revelation.**

Special Appreciation

This book is the result of extensive encouragement from my fa0mily, friends, and church congregation members in pastorates where I taught the Revelation of John. I am grateful to each of them. I would like express special appreciation to thank Mrs. Carol Jenkins, a long time associate, for reading and rereading the manuscript and providing many excellent suggestions and corrections. The book is better because of her time and expertise. I am grateful for seminary students in my classes at NOBTS that helped me clarify my own vision and understanding. I am certainly thankful for the guidance of our Lord and Savior Jesus Christ as He led me, I believe, into a deeper understanding of the book of Revelation that is about Him from start to finish. Revelation is certainly the Jesus Book. Throughout we find the Lamb of God that was slain. Our hope is in Him, as is our faith. Our salvation is through the shedding of His blood. Amen.

Dedication

This book is dedicated to my outstanding professors: Dr. Clyde Francisco, Dr. Dale Moody, Dr. George Beasley-Murray, Dr. J. J. Owens, Dr. Frank Stagg, Dr. Wayne Ward and many others. I remember having some of these men teach in the churches I served as pastor. There were conversations on Revelation that lasted well past mid-night in our home and other times in the day. Whatever I share in the book, I owe to them from their investment in me; and "though dead, they yet speak." God richly blessed my studies at SBTS as well as post-graduate studies at Fuller Theological Seminary. I pay tribute to the memory of these outstanding scholars who loved God's word and instilled in me the thoughts that will be found in this book.

BEFORE YOU START!

TO UNDERSTAND APOCALYPTIC SCRIPTURE YOU NEED TO HAVE FIVE BASIC ABILITIES

YOU NEED THE ABILITY TO DEEPLY UNDERSTAND POWERFUL SYMBOLS

Symbols portray magnificent reality. You cannot read a single chapter in Revelation without great numbers of symbols coming into use. The symbols frequently have more than one meaning.

YOU NEED A VIEW OF THE OLD TESTAMENT WHERE THE DEEP ROOTS OF APOCALYPTIC SCRIPTURES LIE

Not a single major section of Revelation exists apart from a counterpart in the Old or New Testaments.

YOU NEED TO HAVE THE GIFT OF AN OPEN MIND

Many people approach apocalyptic books, such as Revelation and Daniel, with preconceived notions. You must allow the Scripture to speak for itself. The logical means of Scripture interpretation is to understand one passage in light of another. You interpret Scripture **by Scripture.**

YOU NEED THE ABILITY TO FLEX YOUR MIND TO COMPREHEND THE MANY MAGNIFICENT PANORAMAS

YOU WILL FIND BROAD PICTURES IN THESE APOCALYPTIC BOOKS. They look at history over the course of many thousands of years. They sum up long periods in brief sections. You need to look down on the portrait of the activity of God in all of history, not just in our time.

YOU MUST SENSE THE INTERPRETATIVE POWER OF THE HOLY SPIRIT

You will come to a passage you just don't know how to interpret. This is where the Holy Spirit comes in. God has provided the Holy Spirit to guide us through the unknown and the unexplained.

"But, the counselor, the Holy Spirit, whom the Father will send in my name, will teach you all things, and will remind you of everything I have said to you" (John 14:26).

That's how God sent the Scripture to us—not with the wisdom of men, but the wisdom of the Holy Spirit.

The Amazing Revelation
Of St. John Clearly Explained
THNGS YOU SHOULD KNOW
Who Wrote Revelation and When?

Revelation was written about 69 or 70 AD because the Temple in Jerusalem is still standing (11:1-3). Some scholars disagree on this, and they look toward a date around 90 AD. The author is a man named John. He is saturated in the Old Testament as is obvious throughout the book. He does not identify himself as one of the original Apostles, but rather as a prophet (22:9; cf. 1:3; 22:7, 10, 18, and 19). It is definitely written by John who wrote the gospel, the three letters, and then Revelation. It was most likely taken down by a secretary as John dictated. This explains why the Greek is very different from the Greek in which John wrote the gospel and the letters. It is the most beautiful and descriptive language in the Bible relating to Jesus Christ (cf. 1:8, 12-16).

We see the hand of John clearly. The slain Lamb of God is mentioned 28 times. It is the Lamb slain before the foundation of the world (13:8).

A Special Type of Scripture Known as Apocalyptic

Apocalyptic is a kind of writing using symbols as in Daniel. We have seven churches (1:4, 11) representing all of the churches of Asia, and even the whole world. The Greek word for Church, **"Ecclesia,"** occurs twenty times in Revelation. There are seven spirits (v. 4), the Spirit of God as He is known in all of His attributes. There are seven golden candlesticks (vs. 12, 13, and 14) which are the seven churches (cf. v. 20). These seven churches are called lampstands, not candles. Christ is the absolute light. We are to hold Him up. Thus He said: **"You are the light of the world."** There are seven stars: the angels or messengers of the seven churches (cf. v. 20). They are the pastors of the churches. The seven stars are in the right hand of the risen Christ, the hand of authority. Christ holds His ministers in His hand.

10

A Special Note on Understanding Revelation

Christians in John's day, much as some believers in our day, had difficulty understanding the concepts of future attacks by Satan, as well as the glorious concept of heaven. God chose John to receive special visions that imparted these often difficult and also wonderful times and events.

When I was a small child, my parents took me to see a medical specialist in what was then one of the tallest buildings in Atlanta on Peachtree Street. We entered the spacious lobby and someone directed us to the elevators. I had never entered an elevator and did not know how such devices worked. There was an operator who inquired "What floor?" My mother told him the floor we had been directed to, and he moved a lever to the floor number. When we reached the floor he opened the door and we exited the rectangular compartment. I was amazed at what I saw. Floors were stacked one upon another and there was a window. When I looked out we were high above the city and the view was truly amazing. I could see all the surrounding streets and buildings. Traveling to the building, I could only see the street we were driving down. It was a great revelation.

John was permitted to see much more than my limited view. God allowed him to see amazing and wonderful views called visions. They revealed the persecutions of the world, the evil attacks of Satan and his partners, the work of Christ as the Lamb of God, the final judgment to come upon the world, the punishment of the wicked and unrepentant, and the reward of the saved in the blessed heaven prepared for believers.

John writes with special pictures to explain his visions. For example the picture of Christ in Chapter 1 illustrates His divine and glorious power. The picture of Christ as a slain Lamb pictures His death for sinners as the sacrificial Lamb of God. In Chapter 12, John shows us the great red dragon that he identifies as Satan. People have historically looked at the idea of dragons as fire-breathing beasts that bring great harm and destruction. Satan is spreading his evil intention throughout the world. The two beasts in Chapter 13 represent two individuals who will appear in time and bring unrelenting harm upon the people of earth. They can only be described as **"beasts."**

The abyss in Chapters 9 and 20 represents a fearful bottomless pit. From the pit John sees awesome evil rising to harm the earth (chap. 9). In Chapter 20, he reveals Satan being chained in the bottomless pit God has prepared to contain him for a thousand years.

Revelation is a Prophecy

The book is called a prophecy (1:3). The letters to the seven Asian congregations are little prophetic pronouncements. Sometimes these are called oracles. Revelation is composed in little paragraphs.

Epistles

The letters to the churches are epistles. An epistle is a letter of instruction sent to God's people in a particular place. They begin and end like a letter. You can compare Rev. 2:1-3 with 2 Thes... 1:3-5. The book of Revelation is written to a group of Christians who needed the kind of guidance, instruction, and help that the book gives just like the letters of Paul. They were facing a severe problem: Why were God's people suffering such terrible persecutions?

After dealing with the immediate concerns, Revelation goes far beyond any historical situation in the first century. John was in exile on Patmos—a rock island about 5 miles by 10 miles on the Aegean Sea, and it was on the Lord's Day, Sunday (1:10). Verse 9 seems to indicate that it was written down at a later date.

A Brief Outline of the Four Visions

The key to the visions is the statement: **"I was in the Spirit"** (1:10; 4:1; 17:3; 21:9).

1. The First Vision: **"The Menorah"** (1:9-3:22)
2. The Second Vision: **"The Great Tribulation"** (4:1-16:21)
3. The Third Vision: **"The Mystery of Babylon"** (17:1-21:8)
4. Fourth Vision: **"The New Jerusalem and the Bride of Christ"** (21

ST. JOHN'S
REVELATION
"THE BEGINNING"
CHAPTER ONE

Chapter 1

ALIVE FOREVER!

First Words Rev. 1:1-8

Prologue

^{Rev 1:1} **The Revelation of Jesus Christ, which God gave to him, to show his servants things which must shortly come to pass; and he sent and signified it by his angel to his servant John: ² Who bares record of the word of God, and of the testimony of Jesus Christ, and of all things that he saw.**

Commentary

Revelation is often referred to as an "unveiling." The word **"revelation"** is common in scripture. From the revelation of Nathan who delivered a "revelation" to David (2 Sam. 7:17); to the revelations to Daniel (Dan. 10:1); to the revelation to Habakkuk (Hab. 2:2-3); to the revelation to Simeon as he held the infant Jesus (Luke 2:32) we are shown how God reveals Himself to His servants and prophets. Paul uses the term six times (in the NIV) and eight times (KJV). Peter looks forward to the revelation of Christ.

1 Pet. 1:13 Therefore *get your* mind *ready, and think soberly,* and *fix your* hope on the grace *that is yours* at the revelation of Jesus Christ.
(EKJV)

Paul concludes Romans, in part, as follows:
Rom. 16:25 Now to him that *has the power to hold you* in accordance with the gospel I have preached *regarding* Jesus Christ, and according to the <u>revelation</u> of the mystery, which was kept secret since the world began. (EKJV)

However, not one of these ever experienced a revelation such as John received on the Island of Patmos. He says that **"God gave him"** this revelation **"to show his servants what must soon take place"** (1:1). There are two testimonies here: (1) **the testimony of what John saw;** and (2) **the testimony of Jesus Christ.** Both are valid and reveal God's eternal gospel of truth and good news for the saved. The method of receiving was by the witness of an angel sent for this expressed purpose. John therefore writes here: **"John: ²Who gives testimony..."** What did he see? He saw **"the word of God and the testimony of Jesus Christ"** (1:2).

The Amazing Drama Played Out Before John's Eyes

He saw it as a divine drama played out against the background of both heaven and earth. It was so real that he felt he was present in the throne room of God and the Lamb. What John received was too glorious for adequate human understanding, and yet John explains this revelation in majestic spiritual terms. Through him, we are enabled to visualize the final end of the earth, the judgment of mankind, the return of Christ in immaculate glory, the doom of Satan and his evil associates, and the glory, joy, beauty and indescribable future of the heaven God has prepared and Jesus summons us to experience through faith. In verse 3 John issues a blessing (or beatitude) as follows:

Rev. 1:3 **Blessed is *the one* that reads, and *those* that hear the words of this prophecy, and keep those things that are written in it: *because* the time is *near.*** (EKJV)

We should read and adopt this just as it is written. First, the blessing is to **"the one who reads *aloud* the words of this prophecy..."** Reading aloud permitted others to hear and engage in the prophecy. Books were scarce and copied by hand. John felt that there wasn't time to reproduce these words. It was imperative to get them into the minds and hearts of people as quickly as possible. Next he says: **³ Blessed is *the one* that reads and *those* that hear the words of this prophecy..."** We hear things all day long and they just go through our minds. We are easily distracted. But John charges them to **"keep those things that are written."** By this he means to accept it, act upon it, tell others, and get ready for the return of Christ. Therefore he adds **"because the time is near."** We have the exact same injunction in Rev. 22:10.

Among the last instructions of Jesus are these words:
Matt. 24:32 "Now learn this lesson from the fig tree: As soon as its twigs get tender and its leaves come out, you know that summer is near. ³³ Even so, <u>when you see all these things, you know that it is near, right at the door</u>."

As stated in Mark 1::
Mk.1:15 And *Jesus said*, The time is fulfilled, and the kingdom of God is at hand: repent, and believe the gospel. (EKJV)

The kingdom of God was about to unfold before their very eyes with the coming of Jesus Christ, God's Son. We might add, Jesus began to call disciples in the next verse, and within approximately three years He had completed His earthly ministry, offered His life on the cross as a sacrifice for our sins, and had been raised from the dead by God's power. John certainly understood that God could act in great power instantaneously. But he may also be thinking of the persecution and execution of many within the churches. Certainly the window was narrowly opened. He had also heard the words of Christ **"the desolation is near"** (Luke 21:20) meaning the destruction of Jerusalem and the temple by the Romans in 70 AD. Again, the window was narrowly open for a brief time. But Paul explained this just as we are explaining:

Rom. 13:11 And that, knowing the time, that now *it is* high time to awake out of sleep: for now our salvation *is* nearer than when we believed."

Undoubtedly the time is near with God. Christians held the view that life at best is brief, and then we meet our desired destination if we are in Christ. Salvation is certainly not to be taken lightly, or postponed until another day (cf. 1 Cor. 7:29). Notice that Revelation reports that **the devil's "time is short"** (Rev. 12:12). Who will win the love of this world (Satan or Christ)? Satan never sleeps in his assault upon God's creation. He is always at work to hinder the harvest of the lost. But he has found God to be true to His word and he knows that his end will come before he is ready.

We should always consider that our salvation is close at hand. It is as close as the next second when hundreds the world over will take their last breath. It is as close as God's decision to send Christ and His angels for the gathering of the saints at the last trumpet. Be ready!

Greetings and Doxology

Rev. 1:4 John to the seven churches which are in Asia: Grace and peace to you, from him which is, and which was, and which is to come; and from the seven Spirits which are before his throne;
5 And from Jesus Christ, who is the faithful witness, and the first born of the dead, and the prince of the kings of the earth. Unto him that loved us, and washed us from our sins in his own blood,
6 And has made us kings and priests to God and his Father; to him be glory and dominion forever and ever. Amen. (EasyKJV)

We shall follow up on these seven churches in Chapters 2-3. The greeting expounds the eternal existence of Christ: **"Grace and peace to you, from him which is, and which was, and which is to come ..."** (v.4; also1:8; and 4:8).

Heb. 13:8 Jesus Christ is the same yesterday and today and forever. The greeting is also **"from the seven spirits which are before his throne**..." (v. 4; 3:1; 4:5; 5:6).

First, the seven spirits **are before the throne of Christ**, and thus God the Father (1:4). Then, they are **held in the hands of the risen** Christ (3:1). Seven blazing lamps, representing the seven spirits of God **are before the throne** (4:5). The Lamb who looked as if He had been slain was standing in the center of the throne, **"and he had seven horns and seven eyes"** (the eyes are the spirits of God sent out in the earth).

Rev. 5:6 And *I saw* in the *middle* of *God's throne and the thrones of the four creatures*, and in the middle of the elders, stood a **Lamb as if it had been slain, having seven horns and seven eyes, which are the seven Spirits of God sent forth into all the earth.**

(EKJV)

Old Testament Connection

The greeting from the seven spirits speaks of the seven lamps of

Zech. 4:6 **So he said to me, "This is the word of the LORD to Zerubbabel: 'Not by might nor by power, but by my Spirit,' says the LORD Almighty."**

He is "the First Born from the Dead" (1:5)

Psalm 89 is pronouncing God's blessing upon David when it says:

Ps. 89:27 Also **I will make him my firstborn, higher than the kings of the earth. ²⁸ I will keep my mercy for him for evermore, and my covenant shall stand fast with him.**

David, in the Line of Christ

While David is the focus of this Psalm, Christ is the true **"firstborn"** of the Father and therefore we apply the term to Him who succeeds and exceeds David in glory as God's matchless Son. David was **chosen. "I will make him..."**). But Christ received this honor **by supernatural birth** through the power of the Holy Spirit.

Rom. 8:29 **For whom he did foreknow, he also did predestinate to be conformed to the image of his Son, that he might be the firstborn among many *brothers.*"** (EKJV)

Col. 1:15 **Who is the image of the invisible God, the firstborn of every creature: ¹⁶ For by him were all things created, that are in heaven, nd that are in earth, visible and invisible, whether they *are* thrones, or dominions, or principalities, or powers: all things were created by him, and for him: ¹⁷ And he is before all things, and by him all things consist. ¹⁸ And he is the head of the body,** the church: who is the beginning, the firstborn from the dead; that in all things he might have the preeminence. **(KJV - cf. Heb.1:6; 11:28; 12:23).**

Rev. 1:5 continues, "**...and from Jesus Christ, who is the faithful witness, the firstborn from the dead, and the ruler of the kings of the earth**" (Rev. 1:5). The term **"kings of the earth"** is found nine times in Revelation (KJV; NIV has **"kings"** alone in 6:14). Only on the final occasion in Rev. 21:24 do we find these kings subjected to the Christ, and it says **"they bring their glory and honor into it (the new heaven).** These kings are shown to us as bound with **"chains and fetters"** (Ps. 2:2; and Ps. 149:8). Notice the balance between the second Psalm and the next to the last Psalm. Both psalms indicate the power of Christ over the evil rulers of mankind.

Consider the roles of Jesus as specified in just two verses:

- **From him who is, and who was, and who is to come—**
- **Jesus Christ, who is the faithful witness—**
- **The firstborn from the dead—**
- **The ruler of the kings of the earth—**
- **Who loves us and has freed us from our sins by his blood—**
- **And has made us to be a kingdom and priests to serve his God and Father—**

The Sudden and Unprecedented Appearance of Christ

> **Rev. 1:7 Look! he comes with clouds; and every eye shall see him, and those also which pierced him: and all kindreds of the earth shall wail because of him. Even so, Amen. [8] I am Alpha and Omega, the beginning and the ending, says the Lord, which is, and which was, and which is to come, the Almighty.** (KJV)

Obviously, John is thinking in verse 7 of the prophecy of Christ in His final days before the cross. Universally, every eye of mankind is enabled to see Him in His regal glorious appearing accompanied by His angels. Notice that in this passage as well as the prophecy of Christ in Matthew 24:30 that those who missed the reward of His coming are said to **"wail"** or **"mourn."** Compare Rev. 1:7; 21:4. The KJV **"wail"** is more expressive of the divine truth here.

Matt. 24:30 **And then** *will* **appear the sign of the Son of man in heaven: and then shall all the tribes of the earth mourn, and they shall see the Son of man coming in the clouds of heaven with power and great glory.** (EKJV)

They mourn and grieve because it is too late. Unbelief, procrastination, and worthless priorities have forever denied them what God so freely offered through the sacrifice of His Son Jesus Christ. We should not mourn or grieve as the rest of mankind who do not have the hope of the resurrection.

1Thes. 4:13 **But I would not have you to be** *uninformed,* **brothers, concerning** *those* **that are asleep, that** *you do not have sorrow* **as others that have no hope.** (EKJV)

> ## *Heart of the Present Vision—Rev. 1:9*
> ## The glorious appearing of Christ coming with the clouds

The First Vision
Rev. 1:9-3:22
The Seven Churches
Each vision begins with "I was in the Spirit..."
(cf. 1:10; 4:2; 17:3; and 21:10)

John's Vision of Christ

Rev. 1:9 **I John, who also am your brother, and companion in tribulation, and in the kingdom and patience of Jesus Christ, was on the isle that is called Patmos, for the word of God, and for the testimony of Jesus Christ.**

10 I was in the Spirit on the Lord's day, and heard behind me a *loud* voice, like a trumpet,

11 Saying, I am Alpha and Omega, the first and the last: and, Write what you see in a book, and send it to the seven churches which are in Asia; to Ephesus, and to Smyrna, and to Pergamum, and to Thyatira, and to Sardis, and to Philadelphia, and to Laodicea. (KJV: Also see: Rev. 1:6; 5:10; 12:10; and 2 Peter 1:11.)

John is in close relationship and fellowship with the seven churches of Asia. He is known to them as indicated in verse 9: **"John, your brother and companion in the tribulation..."** He shares in the **"kingdom"** to which the suffering is a prelude, if not a prerequisite for believers in that day. We further have the kingdom explained in Rev. 11:15.

John was on the small isle of Patmos when he received the vision. It was a place of exile for numerous reasons. Yet, in this obscure, desolate, and isolated place God opens up His heaven for John to see the great events of the end time. He indicates that his exile is **"for the word of God and the testimony of Jesus Christ."** John's writings, and no doubt his preaching, gave precise and compelling power to the gospel of Christ. In verse 10, we read: **"I was in the Spirit on the Lord's day ..."** No doubt John had already opened his heart, as was customary, and in that moment God opened His divine revelation to John.

He immediately **"heard behind *(him)* a *loud* voice, as of a trumpet."** Then he addresses the letter to the churches: and each is named. Thus, the initial message is opened to these seven churches with very specific messages to each one. Some receive praise while others receive condemnation.

REMARKABLE ATTRIBUTES OF
THE RISEN LORD
FROM JOHN'S VISION IN REVELATION 1

I am the Alpha and Omega (1:8; 21:6; 22:13)

Seven golden lampstands (1:12, 13; 1:20; 2:1; also: 11:4; Zech. 4)

Someone like a son of man among the lampstands (1:13)

Dressed in a robe reaching down to his feet with a golden sash around his chest (1:13; Dan. 7:9; Isa. 6:1; Mt. 17:2; Rev.6:1; 7:9, 13, 14; 15:6; 19:13,16; 22:14; also cf. "sins" Isa. 1:18)

His hair was like wool, as white as snow (1:14; Dan. 7:9)

His eyes were like blazing fire (1:14; 2:18; 19:12; 2 Thes. 1:7)

His feet were like fine brass burned in a furnace (1:15; 17; 2:18)

His voice was like the sound of rushing waters (1:15; 14:2; 19:6)

In his right hand he held seven stars (1:16; 1:20; 2:1; 3:1)

Coming out of his mouth was a sharp double-edged sword (1:16; 2:12, 16; 19:15, 21; Ps. 149:6)

His face was like the sun shining in all its brilliance (1:16; 10:2; Mt. 17:2)

HIS IDENTITY: I am the first and the last (1:17; cf. Rev. 2:8; cf. Rev. 22:13) "I am the Alpha and the Omega, the First and the Last, the Beginning and the End."

I am the living one (1:18)

I was dead and now I am alive forever and ever (1:18).

I hold the keys of death and Hades (1:18; 6:8; 20:13-14; "the Abyss" 9:1; 20:1).

He answers the mystery of the seven stars and the seven lampstands (1:19).

John's Thrilling Vision of the Risen Christ
(Rev. 1:12-20)

Rev. 1: 12 And I turned to see the voice that spoke with me. And having turned, I saw seven golden candlesticks; 13 And in the middle of the seven candlesticks one like the Son of man, clothed with a *robe* down to the foot, and a golden *sash across his chest.* 14 His head and his hairs were white like wool, as white as snow; and his eyes were as a flame of fire; 15 And his feet like fine brass, as if they were burned in a furnace; and his voice was like the sound of many waters. 16 And in his right hand he had seven stars: and out of his mouth preceded a sharp two-edged sword: and his countenance was like the sun shining in his strength.
17 And when I saw him, I fell at his feet as dead. And he laid his right hand upon me, saying to me, Fear not; I am the first and the last: 18 I am he that lives, and was dead; and, behold, I am alive for evermore, Amen; and have the keys of hell and of death. 19 Write the things which you have seen, and the things which are, and the things which shall take place after this; 20 The mystery of the seven stars which you saw in my right hand, and the seven golden candlesticks. The seven stars are the angels of the seven churches: and the seven candlesticks which you saw are the seven churches. (KJV)

DESCRIPTION OF THE RISEN CHRIST
FROM THE SEVEN LETTERS OF REVELATION 2-3
(Follows on the Next Page)

TO THE CHURCH IN EPHESUS—FIRST LETTER
Rev. 2:1 "These are the words of him who holds the seven stars in his right hand and walks among the seven golden lampstands."
Seven Stars: 1:16; 1:20; 2:1; 3:1
Walking among the seven golden lampstands: 1:12; 1:20; 2:1

TO THE CHURCH IN SMYRNA—SECOND LETTER
2:8 "These are the words of the one who is the First and the Last, who died and came to life again."

23

The First and the Last: Rev. 1:17; 2:8; 22:13
Who died and came to life: Rev. 20:4—the martyrs came to life.

TO THE CHURCH IN PERGAMUM—THIRD LETTER
2:12 "These are the words of him who has the sharp, double-edged sword."
The Double-Edged Sword: 1:16; 2:12; 2:16; 19:15, 21; Ps. 149:6

TO THE CHURCH IN THYATIRA—FOURTH LETTER
2:18 "These are the words of the Son of God, whose eyes are like blazing fire and whose feet are like burnished bronze."
Eyes are like blazing fire: 1:14; 2:18; 19:12; 2 Thes. 1:7
Feet like burnished bronze: 1:15; 2:18; see also Ezek. 1:7; Dan. 10:6

TO THE CHURCH IN SARDIS—FIFTH LETTER
3:1 "These are the words of the one who holds the seven spirits of God and the seven stars."
Holds the seven spirits: 1:4; 3:1; 4:5; 5:6
Holds Seven Stars: 1:16; 1:20; 2:1; 3:1

TO THE CHURCH IN PHILADELPHIA—SIXTH LETTER
3:7 "These are the words of the one who is holy and true, who holds the key of David. What he opens no one can shut, and what he shuts no one can open."
The One who is holy and true: Rev. 3:7; 6:10
Who holds the key of David: Isa. 22:22
What he opens no one can shut: Isa. 22:22; Rev. 3:7, 8
What he shuts no one can open: Isa. 22:22; Rev. 3:7, 8

TO THE CHURCH IN LAODICEA—SEVENTH LETTER
3:14 "These are the words of the Amen, the faithful and true witness, the ruler of God's creation."
The Amen: Rev. 3:14; 2 Cor. 1:20

Faithful and true witness: Rev. 3:14; 19:11
The ruler of God's creation: Rev. 4:11; Col. 1:15; "all
things" Mt. 15:27; Luke 10:22; Jn. 13:3; Eph. 1:10, 22;
Col. 1:16, 20; Heb. 1:2

The Voice Behind Him and
the Seven Golden Lampstands

John turned **"to see the voice that was speaking."** In verse 15 John tells, **"his voice was like the sound of rushing water"** (or mighty water). When he turned he saw an astonishing figure standing **"among the** *(seven golden)* **lampstands"** (vs. 12-13). In verse 20 we are told that the seven golden lampstands are the seven churches. Thus, the figure is with His churches in their tribulation and their ordeal. John recognized that the figure **"was someone like the son of man"** (cf. Dan. 7:13 below).

Dan. 7:13 **"I saw** *a vision* **in the night, and, I looked,** *one* **like the Son of man came with the clouds of heaven, and he** *approached* **the Ancient of days, and they** *led* **him before** *his presence***."** (Easy KJV)

Matt. 24:30 **"Then will appear the sign of the Son of Man in heaven. And then all the peoples of the earth will mourn when they see the Son of Man coming on the clouds of heaven, with power and great glory. 31 And he will send his angels with a loud trumpet call, and they will gather his elect from the four winds, from one end of the heavens to the other."**
Matt. 26:64 **"You have said so,"** Jesus replied. **"But I say to all of you: From now on you will see the Son of Man sitting at the right hand of the Mighty One and coming on the clouds of heaven."** (See also: Acts 7:56 where the Son of Man is standing in honor of Stephen; and Rev. 14:14 where the Son of Man comes with a golden crown and a sharp sickle to harvest the earth.) To John He bears the representation of a man, but He is much more than a man. There are 37 references to the Son of Man in Matthew alone.

His Robe and His Hair

He is **"dressed in a robe reaching down to his feet and with a golden sash..."** giving the appearance of a priest or prophet. His **"hair...was as white as wool, as white as snow..."** We are immediately led to think of a God-like figure with human features (head, body, legs, feet, etc.). Those in the church at Sardis who are

25

"worthy" will **"walk with** (Him) **dressed in white."** The church of Laodicea is counseled to buy **"white clothes to wear..."** (3:18).

The twenty-four elders seated on thrones surrounding the heavenly throne were dressed in white (4:4). Those who had been martyred for the sake of Christ were given white robes (6:11). In the great multitude that could not be numbered, each one was wearing a white robe (7:9).They came out of the great tribulation and their robes were white because they had **"washed them in the blood of the Lamb"** (7:14).The figure like **"a son of man"** comes seated on a white cloud (14:14). The Christ comes riding on a white horse to wage war on the kingdom of the beast (19:11), and He is followed by the armies of heaven all riding white horses and dressed in fine white linen (19:14).We are shown the great white throne (20:11).

His Blazing Eyes
"His eyes were like blazing fire..." There is a burning, piercing focus of the eyes of the One who sees all and judges rightly. [15] **And his feet like fine brass, as if they had been burned in a furnace..."** We are reminded of the figure in Daniel 10:6ff. His eyes are like blazing fire and his feet were like glowing bronze as if He had walked from the hot blaze. His voice was discussed in a previous paragrap

The Stars in His Right Hand
"In His right hand He held seven stars..." (v. 16). In verse 20 we are told that the seven stars are the **"angels** (or pastors/messengers) **of the seven churches."** Also compare Rev. 2:1 and 3:1.

The Sharp Double-edged Sword
And **"out of his mouth *there came* a sharp doubled-edged sword ..."** (v. 16). The double-edged sword is first located in Psalm 149:6 where the saints join together in the final battle of history, and the doubled-edged sword is the single instrument of victorious defeat for the wicked. The purpose of the sword is to bring vengeance upon the evil kings and nations. Vengeance is the assigned prerogative of the Son of God. Christ will appear:

2 Thes. 1:8 In flaming fire taking vengeance on them that know not God, and that *do not obey* the gospel of our Lord Jesus Christ:

The **"Sword of the Spirit, which is the word of God"** completes the believer's armor (Eph. 6:17). In Hebrews we see both the sword and the eyes of God:
Heb. 4:12 For the word of God is quick, and powerful, and sharper than any two-edged sword, piercing even the dividing of soul and spirit, and of the joints and marrow, and is a discerner of the thoughts and intents of the heart. ¹³ Neither is there any creature that is not *plain and clear* in his sight: but all things are *uncovered* and opened to the eyes of him with whom we *have* to give account." (Easy KJV)

The sword **"out of his mouth *there came*"** (Rev. 19:15, 21) is the instrument of victorious battle over the unrepentant nations as we saw in Ps. 149:6. The word of God is sufficient to overcome every wicked and evil attitude and action, and release mankind from the domination of Satan.

His Face Like the Sun
"His *face* was like the sun *shining* in *its strength*" (v. 16). What a magnificent and stirring vision! But it is also awesome and fearful so that John falls down before the one in his vision.

The Touch of Christ and John's Reaction
Text: Rev. 1:17-18
¹⁷ And when I saw him, I fell at his feet as dead. And he laid his right hand upon me, saying to me, *Do not be afraid*; I am the first and the last:" *(See Rev. 2:8; and 22:13).*

¹⁸ I am *he* that lives and was dead; and, *now*, I am alive for evermore, Amen; and I have the keys of hell and of death. (EKJV)
Rev. 22:13 I am the Alpha and the Omega, the First and the Last, the Beginning and the End.

He is before all things and He is after all things. He was here before the beginning and He will be here after the consummation of all things. He who held the seven stars holds His people in the eternal future of God.```

In the midst of a shocking and fearful vision, the right hand of the Christ touches him to comfort him. The Christ is alive: **¹⁸ I am *the*** one that lives and was dead; and, *now*, I am alive for ever-more!" (See Rev. 2:8). The One who lives gives life eternal because He holds **"the keys of hell and of death"** (v. 18). In Rev. 20:13-14 death and Hades belch up the dead they are holding. Death cannot hold Him or those who belong to Him.

This Section can be used as a study in churches.

Select Section

Two Extremities: The Alpha and Omega
Revelation 1:8; 21:6; 22:13

Rev. 1:8 **I am Alpha and Omega, the beginning and the ending, says the Lord, which is, and which was, and which is to come, the Almighty.**

Rev. 21:6 **And he said to me, It is done. I am Alpha and Omega, the beginning and the end. I will give to him *who is thirsty to drink from* the fountain of the water of life freely.** (EKJV)
Rev. 22:12 **Behold, I am coming soon! My reward is with me, and I will give to everyone according to what he has done.** [13] **I am the Alpha and the Omega, the First and the Last, the Beginning and the End.**

Three times the Risen Lord Jesus Christ is referred to in Revelation as **"the Alpha and the Omega"** (Rev. 1:8, 21:6; 22:12). In both the first and the final visions He is so affirmed. He is the great **"I Am." He is "the same yesterday, today, and forever."**
Rev. 1:7 **Look, he is coming with the clouds...**
We are made aware of the awesome appearance of the person of the living Christ (Rev. 1:12-16). And John says: This one **"is the Alpha and Omega."** In the New Testament—the Greek, Alpha is the first letter and Omega is the last letter. We find this statement in the first chapter of Revelation and the final chapter.

HIS DAZZLING APPEARANCE

He stands in the midst of his churches (1:13). He stands with His churches. He addresses His message to His churches (1:11). He holds the seven stars in his hand (1:16). He explains the mystery of the seven lampstands and the seven stars in verse 20. The seven stars are the angels (messengers or pastors) of the seven churches.

We recognize Him from the Scriptures

He **"was someone like —the son of man."** (v. 13; cf. Ezek. 1:26, Dan. 7:13, 10:16; Rev. 14:14).

Dan. 7:13 **I saw visions in the night, and, behold, one like the Son of man came with the clouds of heaven, and came to the Ancient of days, and they brought him near** *to him.* [14] **And** *he* **was given dominion, and glory, and a kingdom, that all people, nations, and languages, should serve him: his dominion is an everlasting dominion,** *that* **shall not pass away, and his kingdom** *is one* **that shall not be destroyed. (Easy KJV)**

Rev. 14:14 **I looked, and there before me was a white cloud, and seated on the cloud was one like a son of man with a crown of gold on his head and a sharp sickle in his hand.** (EKJV).

He was **"dressed in a robe reaching down to his feet"** (Rev. 1:13). There was a golden sash around his **chest** (Rev. 1:13). Babylon is the nation we know as Iraq. Daniel stood there on the banks of the Tigris River (Dan. 10:4). He saw the figure like the Son of man with a golden belt. In Revelation it is a **"golden sash."** Read Rev. 15:6 where angels of the seven plagues are dressed in similar fashion. His head and hair **were white like wool**, as white as snow (Rev. 1:14). In Daniel 10:6 this was the appearance of the Ancient of Days. His eyes were **like blazing fire** (Rev. 1:14). His feet were **"like fine brass, as if they had been burned in a furnace."**
(1:15). His voice was like **"like the sound of** *rushing rapids* **of water."** (Rev. 1:15). I have gazed at Niagara Falls many times and listened to the sound of millions of gallons of water plunging over the brink of the falls and crashing below.

In his right hand **He held seven stars** (Rev. 1:16). He is holding his pastors. Out of his mouth came **a sharp double-edged sword**

(Rev. 1:16). **"His face was like the sun shining in all its strength"** (Rev. 1:16). John says: **"When I saw him, I fell at his feet as though dead,"** (Rev. 1:17) so obvious was His deity.

HIS DELIBERATE AUTHORITY

Rev. 1:17 **And when I saw him, I fell at his feet as dead. And he laid his right hand upon me, saying to me, Fear not; I am the first and the last:"** (See Rev. 2:8; and 22:13).

18 **I am he that lives, and was dead; and, behold, I am alive for evermore, Amen; and have the keys of hell and of death."** (KJV)

He possesses the everlasting authority given Him by His Father. He places the right hand of authority upon John and encourages him not to be fearful. The sword that comes from His mouth is the insignia of final authority and victory (cf. Rev. 19). The church should take note of the sword and His everlasting authority.

Rev. 2:16 **Repent; or else I will come to you quickly, and will fight against them with the sword of my mouth.** (KJV)

The purpose of the sword is to fight the final war of the earth with the evil kings and nations of earth. Please see further comments at Rev. 19:15 in this commentary.

Rev. 19:15 **Out of his mouth comes a sharp sword with which to strike down the nations. "He will rule them with an iron scepter." He treads the winepress of the fury of the wrath of God Almighty.** 16 **On his robe and on his thigh he has this name written:**
KING OF KINGS AND LORD OF LORDS.

Remember that sign placed above the cross?
Luke 23:38 **There was a written notice above him, which read: THIS IS THE KING OF THE JEWS.**

God has given Him absolute authority. In his left hand he holds **"the keys to hell and death"** (Rev. 1:18). The one who can open the seals of the locked book can also unlock the doors of death. This is a tremendous encouragement to John and the churches that are entering terrifying persecution. The martyrs are dying because they will not renounce their Savior.

HIS DEFINITIVE ANNOUNCEMENT

Rev. 1:19 **"Write the things that you have seen, and the things which are, and the things which shall be hereafter..."** (KJV)

Notice the assurance—**"Don't be afraid!"** (Rev. 1:17). He is the One **"who is, and who was, and who is to come, the Almighty"** (1:8). He is revealing: **"what you have seen, what is now and what will take place hereafter"** (1:19).

God set apart our Lord with awesome responsibility for those who have been saved by faith in His death and resurrection. Therefore, He is completely trustworthy in every sense. He explains the mysteries of the present. There is tribulation and suffering ahead. They must not shrink back. In this vision, they will see the end of Satan. They will see the blessedness of the martyrs and saints (Rev. 14). The will see Satan bound, loosed and then destroyed (Rev. 20). They will see the amazing and indescribable beauty of the New Jerusalem. Revelation assures us that He is coming! He is coming! He is to bring the saved home and to judge the nations and the unrepentant.

Select Section Ends Here

A Command: Write Down the Vision
The Stars and Lampstands Explained

Text: Rev. 1:19
¹⁹ **Write the things which you have seen, and the things which are, and the things which shall be after this. ²⁰ The mystery of the seven stars which you saw in my right hand, and the seven golden candlesticks. The seven stars are the angels of the seven churches: and the seven candlesticks which you saw are the seven churches.**
The message to be written down contains **"what is now and what will take place hereafter"** It is important that we understand this distinction as the revelation unfolds. Throughout prophecy we must discern what is for that present moment and what is yet to come.

Chapter 2

HELD IN HIS HANDS, Part 1

Revelation 2

Snapshot of Chapters 2-3

What is contained in Chapters 2-3? The chapters contain seven messages known as letters to seven specific New Testament era churches in Asia Minor. The seven churches have different problems, positive and negative attitudes, and sinful conditions that must come to repentance. They represent the extremes of churches throughout the world. We should always analyze our own ministries and congregations to make sure that we truly belong to Christ in every way and that we are fulfilling His mission until He comes. The risen Christ calls upon them to repent of their sin and disobedience. He commends when they have acted obediently, and He chastises them for their disobedience and sin. He issues stern warnings to them to change in an era when they should be focused on spiritual matters.

TO THE CHURCH IN EPHESUS

FIRST LETTER (Rev. 2:1-7)

Text: Rev. 2:1-7

^{Rev. 2:1} "Unto the angel of the church of Ephesus write; These things says he that holds the seven stars in his right hand, who walks in the middle of the seven golden candlesticks;
² I know your works, and your labor, and your patience, and how you cannot bear those who are evil: and you have tested those that say they are apostles, and are not, and have found them false: ³ And have endured, and had patience, and have labored for my name's sake, and have not grown weary. ⁴ Nevertheless I have something against you because you abandoned your first love.

⁵ Remember therefore how far you have fallen, and repent, and do the first works; or else I will come to you quickly, and will remove your lampstand from its place, unless you repent. ⁶ But you have this in your favor, that you hate the deeds of the Nicolaitans, which I also hate. ⁷ He that has an ear, let him hear what the Spirit is saying to the churches; To him that overcomes I will give to eat of the tree of life, which is in the midst of the paradise of God."

Background of the Church in Ephesus

The largest number of Christians, at that time, was in the Church in Ephesus. It was Paul's longest ministry. Both John Mark and Timothy ministered there. There were two temples to Caesar located in Ephesus. Tradition has it that Mary the mother of Jesus went there in her later life. It was the largest city in that part of the world. When it says that the Lord held the churches in His hand, it could be a happy thought or it might make you think twice. When He holds them in His hand He sustains them in their needs. He also has the power to discipline them. Christ walks in their midst seeing them and strengthening them.

Ephesus was the greatest of the ministries of Paul. He continued there longer than at any of the other places where he planted the gospel. That place saw a great movement of God. Read in Acts what mighty works the Holy Spirit accomplished in Ephesus.

^{Acts 19:8} And he went into the synagogue, and spoke boldly for the period of three months, disputing and persuading the things con-

33

cerning the kingdom of God. [9] But when those that *had* different *views* were *firmly opposed,* and did not believe, but spoke evil things concerning that Way in front of the multitude, he left them, and separated the disciples, disputing daily in the school of a person named Tyrannus. [10] And this continued for the period of two years; so that all those that lived in Asia heard the word of the Lord Jesus, both Jews and Greeks. [11] And God performed astounding miracles through the hand of Paul. (EKJV)

But a disturbance was started and some people spread rumors and finally this great spiritual work of Paul's ended and he left town. It was not God's desire that Paul leave. It was the opposition to his ministry. So to five of the seven: the church at Ephesus, and the church at Pergamum, and the church at Thyatira, and the church at Sardis, and the church at Laodicea, the Risen Christ commands that they repent.

- **Ephesus** has fallen from the heights and become **"loveless"** (2:4-5).
- **Pergamum** has been **infiltrated with immorality** (2:16).
- **Thyatira** harbored **a Jezebel**—an evil and despicable person—like Jezebel (2:22).
- **Sardis** was a dying church and already she was at the point of death (3:3).
- And we all know about **Laodicea**—she was indifferent, lukewarm, uncommitted (3:19).

Select Section Inserted Here
Commentary on Ephesus Continues After This Section

Select Section

A COMPLETE TURNAROUND: REPENTANCE

The Risen Christ walks among His churches but He holds His pastors in His hands. Here is an awesome reminder that He will never abandon them. He is walking among His churches to inspect them and to evaluate them. He says to the church in Ephesus: **"REPENT!"**

Somehow we expect the Risen Christ to be resting, not laboring over His churches. He endured the cross, despised the shame and was seated at the right hand of the Father. This place of authority is certainly portrayed in the great book of Revelation.

When we go to heaven, we cease from our labors, but Christ is still carrying out His divine role. Remember He is the judge of the universe. The day is coming when His enemies will bow before Him in submission. But the Day of Judgment is also coming when the wrath and fury of God will fall upon unrepentant mankind. This scene in Chapter 2 prepares us to understand that judgment always begins with the household of God (cf. Rev. 14:6 ff.—**the hour of judgment"**).

THE CHURCH IS CLEARLY GOD'S HOUSEHOLD

Paul alerts us in 1Timothy 3:14 that judgment begins with the house of God. 1 Peter 4:17 affirms the same thought :
1 Pet. 4:17 **For the time *has* come that judgment must begin at the house of God: and if it first begins with us, *what will be the outcome* of those that do not obey the gospel of God? [18] And if the righteous scarcely are saved, *what hope is there for* the ungodly and the sinners? (Easy KJV)**

It is so easy to come to the place where we feel that because we had an experience with Jesus that there is nothing else that we can suffer. Nothing could be further from the truth. It is possible to adopt the belief: "Once repentant always repentant." It is not that they may lose their <u>position</u> in Christ, but they may lose their <u>place</u> in the world and bring shame and humiliation to their Lord. These churches are told again and again to **"repent."**

THERE ARE MORE WARNINGS TO COME

So the Risen Christ in this startling passage surely warns His churches. And to five of the seven He warns them in no uncertain terms that they must repent or face dire consequences. The idea of churches repenting is seldom preached but strongly proclaimed in the Word. It is certain that Christ finds no joy in judging His churches.

Consider the joy of the heavenly relationship and the welcome He received upon His ascension. But remember, His work continues until the rapture. The term "rapture of the church" is never used in Scripture. The Bible speaks of the gathering up of believers, and we understand this to be the rapture (1 Thes. 4:17). We understand what we mean, but the world can easily misunderstand us. The term rapture is a theological term, not a biblical term. But the rapture or catching up of believers is based upon actual salvation, not church membership.

It is almost beyond belief that the church could become so faithless since this book is dated within a few decades following Christ's resurrection. And here in Chapter 2 we are immediately faced with the divine call of the eternal Christ to the first church on the list to repent.

WHAT DOES HE MEAN BY HAVING FALLEN FROM THE HEIGHTS?

It is not to lose one's balance. It means to regress. It means to lose one's place, position, and reputation. They no longer loved Christ with their initial fervor. And they no longer loved one another in the same way. The loss of love is a tragic consequence.

The question arises: Why do we need to repent? We need to repent because of sins against God and against our fellow human beings.

Personal Repentance

There is personal repentance and there is corporate repentance. What is repentance? Repentance is a genuine turning to God from wrong and sin. We see a vivid picture of masses of people turning in personal repentance under the preaching of John the Baptist much as we have witnessed the same experience under Billy Graham.
Mark 1:4 John baptized in the wilderness, and preached the baptism of repentance for the *forgiveness* of sins.
n Luke 24 the resurrected Christ is speaking:

Luke 24:45 **Then he opened their minds, that they might understand the scriptures,** 46 **And said to them, Thus it is written, and was necessary for Christ to suffer, and to rise from the dead the third day:** 47 **And that repentance and forgiveness of sins should be preached in his name among all nations, beginning at Jerusalem."**

Who Should Repent?

Everyone should repent. Paul expressed this in Acts 20:

Acts 20:20-21 **"...I have showed you, and have taught you** *openly,* **and from house to house,** 21 **Testifying both to the Jews, and also to the Greeks** *(the need to have)* **repentance toward God, and faith toward our Lord Jesus Christ."** (EKJV)

2 Pet. 3:9 **The Lord is not slow in keeping his promise, as some understand slowness. He is patient with you, not wanting anyone to perish, but** *(fully desiring)* **everyone to come to repentance.** (EKJV)

Repentance is the result of godly sorrow:
2 Cor. 7:10 **For godly sorrow** *produces* **repentance that** *leads to* **salvation** *and no regret:* **but the world's sorrow results in** *(eternal)* **death.** (EKJV)

How often should I repent? We should repent as often as we realize that we have sinned. What will repentance accomplish? Repentance restores your relationship with God.

Corporate Repentance

Solomon's great message in 1 Kings 8 is a classic on what it means to repent.

1 Kings 8:46 **If they sin against you, (for there is no one that does not sin,) and you are angry with them, and hand them over to the enemy, so that they carry them away captives unto the land of the enemy, far or near;** 47 **Yet if they have a change of heart in the land where they were carried captives, and repent, and make supplication unto you...and say: We have sinned, and have done wrong, we have committed wickedness;** 48 **And so turn to you with all their heart, and with all their soul, in the land of their enemies, that led them away captive, and pray unto you toward their land, which you gave to their fathers, the city which you hast chosen, and the house which I have built for your name:** 49 **Then hear their prayer and their supplication in heaven your dwelling place, and maintain their cause,** 50 **And forgive your people that have sinned**

against you, and all their transgressions that they have transgressed against you, and have compassion before the enemy who carried them captive, that they may have compassion on them: [51] For they are your people, and your inheritance, that you brought out of Egypt, from the midst of the furnace of iron..." (Easy KJV)

HOW DOES A CHURCH REPENT?

You go back to where you began. Solomon reminded them of Egypt and the iron-smelting furnaces. Jesus preached repentance in every place.

Mt. 11:20 **Then Jesus began to denounce the cities in which most of his miracles had been performed, because they did not repent.**

The Book of Acts has many references to the urgent imperative need to repent.

Acts 3:19 **"Repent, then, and turn to God, so that your sins may be wiped out, that times of refreshing may come from the Lord, [20] and that he may send the Christ, who has been appointed for you—even Jesus."**

Go back to the cross and the empty tomb where love was kindled at the first. Return to the feet of the Risen Christ and renounce the self-righteousness that has led to your fall.

WHAT DOES HE MEAN WHEN HE WARNS THEM?

Rev. 2:5 **"If you do not repent, I will come to you and remove your lampstand from its place."**

The lampstand in Zechariah was the symbol of the anointing of the Holy Spirit. To remove the lampstand is to remove the church. To remove the lampstand is to remove the church's place and voice in the world. The seven lampstands in Rev. 1:20 are **the seven churches.**

Rev. 1:20 **"The mystery of the seven stars that you saw in my right hand and of the seven golden lampstands is this: The seven stars are the angels of the seven churches, and the seven lampstands are the seven churches."**

One of the remarkable accounts in the Old Testament is the reforms and revivals under young king Josiah. It is well worth your time to read 2 Kings 22-23 to understand how God, for example, removed evil practices. God requires repentance prior to conversion leading to salvation.

Select Section on Repentance Ends Here

> ## Heart of the Present Vision
> ## Rev. 2-3
> **The Glorious Risen Christ—the Lamb of God who laid His hand upon John—is walking among and watching His churches and His ministers in their obedience and disobedience. He is the Alpha and Omega, the Beginning and the End, and the Savior of His Church.**

Rev. 2:1-7
TO THE CHURCH IN EPHESUS HE COMMANDS:
Unto the angel of the church of Ephesus write; These things says he that holds the seven stars in his right hand, who walks in the midst of the seven golden candlesticks...

Text: Rev. 2:2-3
Rev. 2:2 **I know your works, and your labor, and your patience, and how you cannot bear those who are evil: and you have tested those that say they are apostles, and are not, and have found them false: ³ And have endured, and had patience, and have labored, for my name's sake and have not grown weary.**

He knows their works (deeds), their toil and their endurance (patience). The evil men in their midst are Gnostics who do not believe in the flesh and blood death of Jesus. Hence, this was a very disturbing heresy. The church at Ephesus would not tolerate this promiscuous evil. He observes that they **"have not grown weary."** They have continued in the faith (2:3). But they have deserted the love they were known for at the first (2:4). They had fallen from the height of their first experience. Their love for God and for one another had grown cold. But now the warning comes—
Text: Rev. 2:5

39

^{Rev. 2:4-5} **Nevertheless I have *something* against you because you have left your first love. ⁵ Remember therefore, *how far* you have fallen, and repent, and do the first works; or else I will come to you quickly, and will remove your *lampstand* from its place, unless you repent.** (EKJV)

He warns them to **"do the first works."** Do the work of love (2:5). Here He calls upon them to repent. Christians need to repent. He makes an exceedingly grave statement: "I will remove your lampstand." This means that it will cease to exist as a church. A church can still have the building and the membership roll, but Christ will not own it. This is seen in Ezekiel 8 (cf. Chapters 8-11) where the glory of God left the Temple. This means that the temple loses all significance. Love is a fruit of the spirit, and this fruit is absent in Ephesus.

They may be orthodox but dead. Paul means this when he writes to the church at Ephesus concerning "**speaking** (or maintaining) **the truth in love**" (Eph. 4:15). This letter points to the colossal importance of love to the Lord as a trait in His people. The risen Lord is speaking through the Spirit: "**He that has an ear let him hear what the Spirit says to the churches.**" If God applies the Scriptures to your heart, then accept it and change.

Christ reprimands each of these churches. He warns each of them. The past good we have done does not replace the wrong or evil or immoral acts we commit later. Ephesus was once a great church.

Text: Rev. 2:6-7
⁶ But you have this in your favor, that you hate the deeds of the Nicolaitanes, which I also hate. ⁷ He that has an ear, let him hear what the Spirit is saying to the churches; To him that overcomes I will give to eat of the tree of life, which is in the midst of the paradise of God."

The one who conquers will continue to the end and will be given of the tree of life to eat. The **"tree of life"** is the sign of eternal life. Where is it? It is in the midst of the paradise of God. The restoration of the Garden of Eden is in view as also in Revelation 22:1-5. In Genesis, a flaming sword blocked the way to the tree of life, but he who overcomes will find it forever available. Unless a person becomes grossly unspiritual, we have no way of telling who sincerely belongs to Christ until the end. Those who begin the journey but never finish their road perhaps did not have a genuine experience with Christ.

Someone said: "A faith that fizzles before the finish had a fatal flaw from the first." Our relationship with Christ should grow sweeter as our walk gets closer to the Lord. The risen Christ will reward them, but He will also judge them. We decide the outcome.

TO THE CHURCH IN SMYRNA
(Rev. 2:8-11)—THE SECOND LETTER

Rev. 2:8 And unto the angel of the church in Smyrna write; These things says the first and the last, who died, and is alive; 9 I know your works, and tribulation, and poverty, (but you are rich) and I know the blasphemy of those who say they are Jews, and are not, but are the synagogue of Satan. 10 Fear none of those things which you will suffer: listen, the devil will cast some of you into prison, that you may be tried; and you shall have tribulation ten days: be faithful unto death, and I will give you a crown of life. 11 He that has an ear let him hear what the Spirit says to the churches; He that overcomes shall not be hurt in the second death. (KJV)

It becomes evident to the reader that these letters are not equal in length. The letter to Smyrna is only four verses. Christ identifies Himself as the one who is **"the first and the last, who died, and is alive"** (2:8). Literally He said: "I became dead, and I became alive." The Lord has conquered death. This is most encouraging to those under persecution.

The risen Christ says: **9 "I know your works, and tribulation, and poverty, (but you are rich)"** Tribulation is the better word here, and speaks to the great suffering of the church. Smyrna was poor by the world's standards (v. 9), but rich by God's standards. This church is the opposite of the church in Laodicea who claimed to be rich, but in fact they were poor (3:17).

"I know the blasphemy of *those that* say they are Jews, and are not, but are the synagogue of Satan" (v. 9, EKJV).

41

They were nationalistic Jews, but because they rejected Christ and fought His church, they have fallen into Satan's trap just as the Jewish leaders did before the cross. The word here can mean slander or blasphemy. It may be slander against the church, but it is **blasphemy** against God and His Son. These false Jews were verbally destroying the church, and inciting others to join them. Slander destroys the reputation and heaps abuse on people by insidious and hateful attacks on good people.

In such cases, fear can overwhelm people. But Christ says: **[10]** **"Fear none of those things which you will suffer."** He did not promise that they would not suffer. Rather, He affirmed that suffering would mark their existence. In verse 9 we have **"a synagogue of Satan"** and in verse 10 what the **"devil"** is going to do to them. He has certain freedom just as he entered into attacks on Jesus on earth to bring about His death. **"Listen, the devil will cast some of you into prison, that you may be tried; and you shall have tribulation ten days"** (v. 10). **"Ten days"** is a limited period of time.

Their suffering will come to an end, but it will be intense during this brief period. Therefore, Christ says the **"devil"** is doing his worst **"to test"** them. He encourages them: **"Be faithful** (even) **unto death."** Some of them will be tortured and they will die. Christians everywhere faced this tribulation, and Christians in our world are often slaughtered today (Iraq, Syria, Africa, and many other places).

The test is to see how long they can hold out for Christ. How would you and I do in the same situation? But He gives them a promise: **"and I will give you a crown of life"** (v. 10). What the world denies you Christ will give you in full measure. Death through torture earned them the coveted **"victor's crown"** (some translations) of life. They will not experience the second death as do those who do not repent. The **"second death"** is eternal death (cf. 20:6, 14; 21:8). Christians don't talk so much about going to heaven. Rather, they look forward to being with Christ the Lord.

TO THE CHURCH IN PERGAMUM
(Rev. 2:12-17)—THE THIRD LETTER

Text: Rev. 2:12

Rev. 2:12 **And to the angel of the church in Pergamum write; These things says he who has the sharp double-edged sword.**

Pergamum was the capital of Asia Minor. There were two temples of emperor worship there.

His Sharp Double-edged Sword

The sword is the sharp doubled-edged sword (2:12) mentioned in Rev.1:16; 19:15. It was the Roman sword used in battle that had enormous advantages for the slaughter of many people. The sword could be swung right and left, up and down. It was the sword that threatened the Christians of that day (cf. 2:16). Read Ps. 149:6ff; and Rev. 19:15ff for more on the sword.

Satan's Throne Is in Their Midst (v. 13)

Text: Rev. 2:13

Rev. 2:13 **I know your works, and where you live, even where Satan** *occupies his* **seat: and** *you fully* **hold my name, and have not denied my faith, even in those days when Antipas was my faithful martyr, who was slain among you, where Satan lives.** (Easy KJV)

"I know where you live," says the living Christ. Every church faces difficulties, but for these Christians, faith was tested to the limits. He commends them: **"You remain true to my name."** They had faced the martyrdom of a man named Antipas referred to as **"my faithful witness (or martyr)"** implying that he went to a martyr's death still holding publicly to the name of Jesus.

The title **"faithful witness"** was Christ's own title from Rev. 1:5. This is the only reference in scripture to this particular believer named Antipas. He **"was put to death in your city—where Satan lives."** Antipas may have been the first person persecuted and executed for failure to engage in emperor worship.

Pergamum was filled with pagan worship. Probably, though, **"where Satan has his throne"** refers to the prominence of worship of the Roman Emperor. The snake god may also remind them of the figure of Satan as a serpent. Their persecution resulted from Satan in the heart of the Romans. Believers and their adversary lived in the same city.

Charges Against the Church

Ephesus was the city of intolerance. Pergamum was the city of tolerance. They tolerated wicked, false and divisive doctrines. Paganism and immorality were rampant. The question of Christians is: "How can believers be responsible in this world, and yet not be of it?" Despite the faith of many, there are charges against **"some"** because they have caused the church to become spiritually lax against the pagan influences. Yet there were sins that threatened the very life of the church.

Text: Rev. 2:14-15

^{Rev. 2:14} **But I have a few things against you, because you have those that hold the doctrine** *(or teaching)* **of Balaam, who taught Balak to cast a stumbling block before the children of Israel, to eat things sacrificed to idols, and to commit sexual immortality. ¹⁵ So you also have those that hold the doctrine of the Nicolaitanes, a practice I hate.** (EKJV)

Pergamum was a city where the serpent was worshiped. Asclepius was the serpent god of healing. The serpent is still the symbol of the medical profession today. In Rev. 2:14 his first charge against the church regards those **"who hold to the doctrine of Balaam."** Balaam and the Nicolaitans (v. 15) were people conquerors. We recognize the name of Balaam from the Old Testament (Num. 22-24; also 25:1-3; and 31:16). Israel played the harlot (Num. 25:1ff). The chief sin mentioned is **"sexual immorality."** The term may be used of being unfaithful to God as well.

We know from the Corinthian church that food offered to idols could be purchased in the marketplace cheaply, or it might be consumed in a feast in a pagan temple. These new believers had come out of paganism and would have many ties to those who participated in pagan worship. They went into the pagan temples for a cheap meal, but thereby they compromised their faith. They had no Christian example to follow other than Paul.

Repent Now

Like Ephesus, they are called upon to **"repent"** (v. 16). Only a few had entered into this sin, but Christ commands the entire church to repent because the church had accepted those who followed a false doctrine.

Text: Rev. 2:16
Rev. 2:16 **Repent; or else I will come to you quickly, and will fight against them with the sword of my mouth.**

The word **"come"** (v. 16) used here is ***"parousia"*** in the Greek. It is the same word used for the final coming of Christ. Here, He means He will come presently in His role as judge. The word of God searches out even our motives. The One who searches out also has the heart of compassion that feels for His people. Verse 17 is the same refrain spoken to all seven churches: **17 He who has ears, let him hear what the Spirit says to the churches.**

The **"sword of my mouth"** (v. 16) is the same sword from the mouth of Christ in the great final battle recorded in Revelation 19:15 (also see Psalm 149). Infidelity to God will not go unpunished.

Rev. 19:15 **And out of his mouth goes a sharp sword, that with it he should smite the nations: and he shall rule them with a rod of iron: and he treads the winepress of the fierceness and wrath of Almighty God.**

Text: Rev. 2:17
Rev. 2:17 b **To him that overcomes I will give to eat of the hidden manna, and will give him a white stone, and on the stone *is written a new name that no one knows except the one* that receives it.** (EKJV)

Look at the terms used in verse 17b. The opportunity is for the church to experience victory in the midst of an evil world dominated by despicable tyrants. The term **"hidden manna"** implies the bountiful banquet table of God in heaven. Manna was the supernatural food of the wilderness. Manna was not seen in the Old Testament until God revealed it and poured it out bountifully. To receive a **"white stone with a new name written on it"** (cf. Isa.62:2; Rev. 3:12) is to have a new identity in eternal life. The **"white stone"** was used to cast an anonymous vote. In the ancient world, anonymity was the real security.

TO THE CHURCH IN THYATIRA
(2:18-29)—FOURTH LETTER

Text: Rev. 2:18

^{Rev. 2:18} **And to the angel of the church in Thyatira write; These things says the Son of God, who has eyes like a flame of fire, and his feet are like fine brass.**

The longest letter was written to the least known and important church and city. God does not value a church based upon size or its sense of importance.

The phrase **"Son of God"** is only found here in Revelation. There are notes of the connections of additional verses to these descriptions that form the beginning of each of the letters. Here we have **"who has eyes like a flame of fire, and his feet are like fine brass."** For the above characteristics of Christ see Dan. 10:6. They describe His splendor and strength.

The next thoughts (v. 19) express praise for their growth. However, there is a woman who has declared herself a prophetess, but her message was not from God. She is teaching extremely immoral concepts.

Text: Rev. 2:19-20

^{Rev. 2:19} **I know your works, and love, and service, and faith, and your patience, and your *latter* works are *greater* than the first. ²⁰ Notwithstanding I have a few things against you, because you permit that woman Jezebel, who calls herself a prophetess, to teach and to seduce my servants to commit *sexual immorality*, and to eat things sacrificed to idols. ²¹ And I gave her *time* to repent of her <u>sexual immorality</u>; and she *would* not repent.** (Easy KJV)

Facing Their Charges
- They **"tolerate that woman Jezebel."**
- She **"calls herself a prophet (prophetess)."**
- **"She misleads my servants into sexual immorality."**

Christ likens her to Jezebel, the evil wife of Ahaz in the Old Testament. Jezebel stands for the epitome of evil. She is evil, a false teacher, unrepentant and obstinate in the face of spiritual correction. Christ says, **"I gave her time to repent."** (See the full section on repentance prior to the commentary of the first letter.) She has no desire to repent. And worse, the church is tolerating this instead of correcting the problem and removing her from her place of dominance over weak believers who lack spiritual maturity.

Her immoral teaching is identified in verse 20 above. Therefore, the risen Christ announces:

Text: Rev. 2:22
Rev. 2:22 **Behold, I will cast her into a sickbed, and those that commit adultery with her into great tribulation, *unless* they repent of their *ways*.** (EKJV)

To be cast into a bed of suffering is a play on words for the place where she committed her immorality. She has misled others and is incorrigible in her insistence that she be allowed to teach this immoral false doctrine.

Therefore, those who have adopted her false beliefs will share her intense suffering **"unless they repent of their *ways*."** For her followers to repent they must denounce what they have been taught and repent of what they have been a part of. People do not enter the final suffering alone. They take others with them. This is the strategy of Satan.

Text: Rev. 2:23
Rev. 2:23 **And I will *strike* her children *dead*; and all the churches shall know that I am he who searches the minds and hearts: and I will *repay* every one of you according to your works.** (EKJV)

Her children could be the offspring of her adultery, or this may mean those who have followed her teachings and example and have become enamored with her sexual perversity. Christ says: **"I am he who searches hearts and minds..."** He knows us and He knows where our hearts are focused. Notice that Christ says, **"I will repay every one of you according to your works."** They each will pay the penalty and a severe one at that, for the false doctrine they have accepted rather than the light of Jesus revealed to them.

Text: Rev. 2:24-25
Rev. 2:24 **But I say to the rest of you in Thyatira, you who are not practicing this doctrine, and who have not known, *as they say, the deep secrets* of Satan; I will not put any other burden upon**

you. ²⁵ But what *you* have already *attaine*d hold that *firm* until I come. (EKJV)

The **"deep secrets"** of Satan represent the Gnostic teaching which was very prevalent at that time. These false teachers implied that they had deeper knowledge than others and could reveal ultimate truth. They had no conscience regarding evil.

Text: Rev. 2:26-28

Rev. 2:26 **And the one that overcomes,** *and keeps my will* **to the end, I will give him power over the nations:** ²⁷ **And he shall rule them with an iron rod** *(or scepter);* **as the vessels of a potter shall they be broken to shivers: even as I received** *authority from* **my Father.** ²⁸ **And I will give him the morning star.** ²⁹ **Whoever has ears, let them hear what the Spirit says to the churches.** (Easy KJV)

To be victorious is to conquer in a world where evil is present and persistent. To do His will is to keep the faith and hence be victorious in a world where sin is rampant. To be given **"power over the nations"** is to share the rule of Christ given Him by His Father. This refers to the millennium reign of 1000 years (Rev. 20:4). **"I will also give him the morning star."** Christ is the **"morning star"** (Rev. 22:16). To be victorious and to overcome is to have the presence of Christ, **"the morning star."**

Chapter 3

HELD IN HIS HAND
Part 2

TO THE CHURCH IN SARDIS
(Rev. 3:1-6) FIFTH LETTER

Text: Rev. 3:1-2
Rev. 3:1 "**And unto the angel of the church in Sardis write; These things says he that has the seven Spirits of God, and the seven stars; I know your works, that you have a reputation that you are alive, but you are dead.** ² **Wake up, and strengthen the things that remain, that are ready to die: for I have found your works incomplete before God.**

Sardis was the **"dead"** church. Christ has some major issues with Sardis. First, he declares: **"I know your works..."** (v. 1). **"You have a reputation that you are alive, but you are dead"** (v.1). They earned the most serious denunciation (3:1-2). Christ identifies Himself to this church as He **"that has the seven spirits of God and the seven stars"** (v. 1). Remember that while **"angels"** might mean actual angels, it is our understanding that the term represents the pastors of the churches who certainly need encouragement in a most difficult and challenging responsibility and calling.

They have a good name, but in reality they are like a corpse in a mortuary. He knows the deeds of his churches although others may not be so informed. Their deeds are hidden from the general public. The shame in many churches is found in secret and unconfessed sins. He tells them that no matter what other people may see, He knows for a fact that they are dead. He calls upon them to [2] **"Wake up, and strengthen the things that remain, that are ready to die"** (v. 2). There is still the possibility of life. They are just barely hanging on as far as God is concerned. Jesus continues: **"for I have found your works incomplete before God"** (v. 2). Their deeds are incomplete. God had an expectation, but they simply did not fulfill it. Many believers, on the other hand, devote themselves to service for God in order to complete their calling, and to champion the mission of the Lord in a world that desperately needs to know God.

Sardis was a city that could only talk about their best days in the past. They were, what some call, a has-been city. Sardis was built on a mountain top, and it was virtually impregnable. Yet, twice it had been taken. How surprised many people will be when Christ returns. Jesus warns them that He may come as a thief in the night—without warning. For coming as a thief see Rev. 16:15; Mt. 24:43; Luke 12:39; 1 Pet. 4:15; 2 Pet. 3:10.

Text: Rev. 3:3
Rev. 3:3 **Remember therefore, what you have received and heard, and *hold on to it*, and repent. If you fail to watch, I will come *to* you as a thief, and you will not know what hour I will come upon you.**
Sardis was known because it was the first place to dye wool. There is this thought that since they are so much in the business of beautiful garments, that they have the best, but Jesus says to them:

Text: Rev. 3:4
Rev. 3:4 **You have a few names even in Sardis who have not soiled their clothes; and they will walk with me in white: for they are worthy.**

The dye of sin had entered their very souls. Only a few people there have kept themselves in the faith and above the rampant sin. **"They have not soiled** (or defiled) **their clothes."** He does not say in verse 3, "If I come." Rather He says, **"I will come as a thief..."** He will come to their church in judgment, not in joy. But those who have not engaged in faithlessness and sin will be with Him in that day when God confers perfection upon His saints. The promise is that these believers are going to be dressed in the white robes of the resurrected saints. They will be marked as those who have made their robes white by the blood of the Lamb (See Revelation 7:14).

Text: Rev. 3:5
Rev. 3:5 **He that overcomes, *that person will* be clothed in white *clothing*; and I will not blot out his name out of the book of life, but I will confess his name before my Father, and before his angels.** (EKJV)

The picture of the book of life comes from what was known as a citizens' registry. We are registered in heaven. Moses talked about this as did the Psalmist and others. Here we see Jesus as He speaks of the role of those who are citizens of the eternal kingdom of God. He tells them **"I will confess his name** (the name of those who are righteous) **before my Father, and before his angels."** (cf. Mt. 10:32; Luke 12:8). What a wonderful and powerful testimony for those who have been so recorded. The day is coming for them to be presented before God and His angels. The dead church requires repentance, revival and renewal.

TO THE CHURCH IN PHILADELPHIA
(Rev. 3:7-13)—SIXTH LETTER

Text: Rev. 3:7
Rev. 3:7 **And to the angel of the church in Philadelphia write; These things says the one who is holy, the one who is true, the one who holds the key of David, the one that opens, and no one shuts; and shuts and no one opens.**
Philadelphia was located 28 miles southeast of Sardis. The region was subject to earthquakes. Christ refers to Himself as **"holy"** or **"the holy one"** in verse 7. **"Holy One"** is a term for God (cf. Rev. 4:8; 6:10), and the Messiah (Mark 1:24; Luke 4:34; John 6:69). He also refers to Himself as the One who is **"true"** meaning that He is faithful to His promises. **"Holds the key of David"** (v. 7) means to possess the key to David's house and all the promises God made to

51

David concerning the future of his line. **"What he opens no one can shut, and what he shuts no one can open"** means that He has absolute authority to admit or to exclude.

Text: Rev. 3:8
Rev. 3:8 **I know your works: behold, I have set** *(or placed)* **an open door before you, and no one can shut it: for you have a little strength, and yet, have kept my word, and have not denied my name.** (EKJV)

He has **"placed before (them) an open door"** of opportunity. **"I have set before"** is a perfect active indicative in Greek. The door is the gift of Christ to His church. For additional scriptures on **"the open door"** see John 10:7-9; Acts 14:27; 1 Cor. 16:9; 2 Cor. 2:12; Col. 4:3; Rev. 3:20; 4:1. The consistent view of Scripture is that the open door is for a good opportunity for missionary outreach.

Text: Rev. 3:9
Rev. 3:9 **Behold, I will make those who are of the synagogue of Satan, and who say they are Jews, and are not, but lie; behold, I will make them come and** *fall before* **your feet, and** *they will* **know that I have loved you. (Easy KJV)**

When He says, **"I will make them come and fall** (or bow) **down at your feet"** it indicates the ultimate future inclusion and salvation of the Jews (cf. Isa. 60:14; 45:14; 49:23; Ezek. 37:28; 36:23). The church has become true Israel. While this does not picture the salvation of the Jews necessarily, the fact is that the Jews will acknowledge their mistake in denying the Christians a place in the kingdom, and will recognize them to be the beloved of the Lord, and the true Israel.

Text: Rev. 3:10
Rev. 3:10 **Because you have kept** *my command to endure patiently***, I also will keep you from the hour of** *testing* **that will come on** *the whole* **world, to test those that dwell on the earth. (Easy KJV)**

Verse 10 points to the great tribulation **"that is going to come on the whole world to test those that dwell on the earth."** This is not the local tribulation referred to in Rev. 2:10. Because of their faithful obedience, the risen Christ will **"keep (them) from the hour of trial."**

Text: Rev. 3:11

Rev. 3:11 **I am coming soon: hold on to what you have so that no one will take your crown.**

He promises: **"I am coming soon"** (v. 11). Some translations have **"Behold, I come quickly"** (cf. Rev. 22:7). This is the key note of the entire book. **"Hold on to what you have..."** It is so easy to become faint in heart, but believers will hold on and hold tightly to their faith and commitment. The reason is **"so that no one will take your crown."** Compare **"the crown of life"** (James 1:12) and **"the crown of glory"** (1 Pet. 5:4).

Text: Rev. 3:12-13

Rev. 3:12 **To him that overcomes I will make a pillar in the temple of my God, and he will never go out again; and I will write on him the name of my God, and the name of the city of my God, which is new Jerusalem, which is coming down out of heaven from my God: and I will write on them my new name.** [13] **He that has ears let him hear what the Spirit says to the churches.**

"The one who overcomes I will make a pillar in the temple of my God" means a sure place in the eternal city of God. **"He will never go out again."** The promise is continuous, perpetual and eternal. Their place is assured by the Christ who died and came to life. He is going to mark them by writing on them **"the name of my God and the name of the city of my God, the new Jerusalem, which is coming down out of heaven from my God."**

For **"the new Jerusalem"** see Rev. 21:2, 9. He calls the name **"my God"** three times in this brief passage. He **"will also write on them my new name"** which marks them as belonging solely to Him.

These will not bear the mark of the beast.

Rev. 3:13 **Whoever has ears let them hear what the Spirit says to the churches.**

TO THE CHURCH IN LAODICEA
(Rev. 3:14-22)—SEVENTH LETTER

Text: Rev. 3:14   **And to the angel of the church of the Laodiceans write; The One that says these thing is the Amen, the faithful and true witness, the beginning of the creation of God.**

Background

Laodicea was the Zurich of the ancient world. It was a banking center. Three things characterized it: banks and wealth, a famous woolen industry, and a medical school. They raised rare black goats and made wool that was famous. As far as a medical school, Laodicea was famous throughout that world for its eye ointment. There was a famous hot springs near Laodicea. It left a white limestone deposit, and persons who would drink the water would spew it out quickly because it made them sick. This church was neither cold nor hot.

The Problem

Text: Rev. 3:15-16

^{Rev. 3:15} **I know your works, that you are neither cold nor hot: Would that you were cold or hot. ¹⁶ So then because you are lukewarm, and neither cold nor hot, I will spit you out of my mouth.**

The risen Christ tells them **"Would that you were cold or hot."** You can challenge people with commitment to become something better. But a church that is lukewarm rides the fence without commitment.

The Lord would rather have an honest pagan than a hypocritical Christian who is a member of an indifferent congregation. Because they were neither hot nor cold, He will spew them out of His mouth. This is a shocking statement regarding their future. Christ indicates an urgent need for immediate change, but the language implies a soon coming judgment.

Text: Rev. 3:17

^{Rev. 3:17} **Because you say, I am rich, and have gained material wealth, and you believe that there is nothing you need; and you do not know that you are wretched, and miserable, and poor, and blind, and naked:**

They said: **"I am rich; I have acquired wealth and do not need a thing"** (v. 17). This reminds us of the farmer in the parable of Jesus (Luke 12:16ff; cf. Hos. 12:6-8). They were proud, boastful and self-satisfied. They claimed to be rich, but in respect to true riches they were beggars. Jesus charged: **"you are wretched, pitiful, poor, blind and naked."** All the things they boasted of meant nothing in the eyes of God.

Text: Rev. 3:18
Rev. 3:18 **I counsel you to buy gold from me refined in the fire, that you may be rich; and white clothing, that you may be clothed, and that people do not see the shame of your nakedness; and anoint your eyes with *eye* salve, so that you may see."**

The Solution

Come to **"Me"** for real gold. That is the faith that receives the grace of God. For **"gold refined in the fire"** see 1 Cor. 3:13; 1 Peter 1:7; Ps. 12:6; Dan. 11:3. Though they manufacture the finest wool, they need **"clothes to wear, so you can cover your shameful nakedness."** They make a wonderful eye salve, but they need Him to **"anoint your eyes with *eye* salve, so that you may see."**

Text: Rev. 3:19-20
Rev. 3:19 **Those whom I love I rebuke and discipline; so be zealous therefore, and repent. 20 Behold, I stand at the door, and knock: if any one hears my voice, and opens the door, I will come in to him, and will dine with him, and he with me.**

He warns them: **"Those that I love, I rebuke and discipline."** All that He is saying to them is because He loves them. If He did not love them, He would not bother to rebuke them. Jesus knocks on the door of their heart because they are self-excluded from His church. If they will open, He will come in and eat with them and they will enjoy sweet and lasting fellowship.

It is a two-way street: He says **"I will come in to him, and will dine with him, and he with me."** The Lord and the person must have their hearts in agreement. He is ready and waiting, but they are backslidden and reticent to become faithful.

The call is to become victorious in a world that condemns and destroys faith. Consider His promise if they accept His invitation:

Text: Rev. 3:21-22

^{Rev. 3:21} **To him that overcomes I will grant to sit with me in my throne, even as I also overcame, and have sat down with my Father in his throne.**

²² **He that has an ear let him hear what the Spirit is saying to the churches.**

They are so far away, and yet Christ says you can be with me on my throne. What a promise!

CONCLUSION TO THE LETTERS TO THE SEVEN CHURCHES

You will find yourself in one of these churches. The invitation in the final letter may be applied to all. Jesus eternally lives to save, and during the entire church age, He stands at the door of the hearts of His people—the church—knocking to be admitted.

But until His people open the door, He will remain outside, and unless they do open the door, they will remain eternally outside of heaven and the everlasting fellowship shared mutually with Him and His people who have established Him upon the throne of their hearts.

Previewing Revelation 4-7

Revelation 4—The Second Vision
1. The **24 seats/elders** (4:4).
2. **The 4 Creatures/Beasts** (4:6).

Revelation 5—The Book with the Seven Seals
1. The Book is in the hand of **the one seated on the throne** (5:1).
2. There appears a **"Lamb as if it had been slain"** (5:6).
3. The Lamb had **"seven horns and seven eyes which are the seven Spirits of God..."** (5:7).
    1) In providing this explanation, John is revealing a key to understanding the Book.
4. "**10,000 times 10,000 and thousands of thousands of angels"** (5:11).
    1) Rev. 5:13 fulfills Phil. 2:1-11—**"Every knee shall bow...."**

2) The New Song in Rev. 5:9 relates to Psalm 40:1-3.

Revelation 6—The Opening of the First Six Seals

1. **First four seals**—the four horsemen of the Apocalypse (6:1-8).
2. **The fifth seal**—reveals the souls of the martyrs under The altar
3. **The sixth seal**—shows **great destruction** in heaven (the sky, space) and on earth, and explains that this is **"The Great Day of Wrath"** (6:17).

Revelation--7—The 144,000/Seal Number Seven

1. **Four angels hold back the four winds** (7:1).
      1) If the angels loose the winds, then what?
2. **The fifth angel with the seal of God** is ready to seal the earth   (7:2).
3. **The 144,000 sealed** (7:4f.).
4. **An innumerable multitude** (7:9).
      1) These come out of the **Great Tribulation** (7:14).
      2) They are receiving the blessed reward (7:15-17).

A Quick Look at Chapters 4 - 5

Chapter 4—GOD THE CREATOR
Chapter 5—CHRIST THE REDEEMING LAMB

I.   **A DOOR OPENS IN HEAVEN (4:1).**
   1. The open door into heaven is the prelude to the second vision.
      1) Remember the significance of an open door in heaven.

         A. **Ezek. 1:1—"...the heavens were opened, and I saw visions of God.**
         B. **Mark 1:10—"And when he came up out of the water, immediately he saw the heavens opened and the Spirit descending upon him like a dove..."**
         C. **John 1:51—"Truly, truly, I say to you, you will see heaven opened, and the angels of God ascending and descending upon the Son of man."** (KJV)

    2) There are three doors mentioned in Revelation (3-
      4)   (3:8, 20; 4:1).
  2. The key to the four visions (1:10; 4:1-2; 17:3; 21:10).
  3. The voice like a trumpet (4:1).

II.   **JOHN IS PERMITTED TO VIEW THE THRONE IN HEAVEN** (4:2; Cf. Ezek. 1:26-28; Jerusalem temple: 1 Kings 6:1ff; Dan. 7:9ff).
  1. The Great Throne of God (4:2).
  2. The One on the Throne (4:2).
  3. Next we are made aware of beings surrounding the throne (4:3-11).

III.   **THE SIGHTS AND SOUNDS ASSOCIATED WITH THE THRONE (4:5).**
  1. There are flashes of lightning, voices and peals of thunder.
  2. Seven torches or lamps (4:5).
  3. A sea of glass like crystal (4:6).
  4. The four living creatures (4:6; Greek= ***Zoa; Zo-on*** is *singular*).
  5. The activity of the four living creatures or cherubim (4:6-9).
  6. The response of the twenty-four elders (4:9-11).

The Second Vision
Rev. 4:1-16:21
"The Great Tribulation"
Each vision begins with "I was in the Spirit..."
(cf. 1:10; 4:2; 17:3; and 21:10)

Chapter 4

DOORWAY TO HEAVEN

Snapshot of Chapter 4

John is caught off guard for what is about to be revealed. He is in the Spirit and, and while in the Spirit, he is summoned to heaven. His first view is of a throne with someone sitting on it. He never uses the name God or Christ in this vision which is a trait of this apocalyptic book. He also sees 24 additional thrones and we learn that these are occupied by "elders." In addition he meets four creatures—a term in no way meant to minimize their importance. They are just unlike anything he has ever seen before. He will view the glory of the central throne with its grandeur, as well as the sea of glass, and the adoration for God by the elders and the four creatures.

The Throne in Heaven

Text: Rev. 4:1-2

Rev. 4:1 **After this I looked, and, behold, a door was opened in heaven: and the first voice I heard was like *a* trumpet talking with me, *and it said*, Come up here, and I will show you things that must happen after this. ² And immediately I was in the spirit: and, behold, a throne was *set there* in heaven, and one sat on the throne.**

Can you imagine how this vision affected John? He is totally unprepared for what he is experiencing except that he has various guides—usually angels that interpreted the essentials of the experience. Today, we depend upon the Holy Spirit to interpret, guide, and teach us the meaning of the things of God. It is easy for us to be too dogmatic in our response to the Revelation of John, and to miss the primary meaning of these experiences.

The Scriptures have always taught of the throne of God in heaven. The psalmists wrote of it many times. God had two dwelling places: His heavenly throne above all the heavens, and the holy of holies in the temple in Jerusalem where He came to be among His people. Unless God comes to us there is no way that we can understand or comprehend His being and His power.

When John is summoned to **"come up here,"** he is transcending far beyond what any person past or present has experienced. Thus, a door is opened to permit John to go where no man has ever gone. Obviously, he must be **"in the Spirit"** (4:2) in order to receive this experience.

The first sight is the central throne, but quickly he observes twenty-four additional thrones. One tradition is that the elders represent the patriarchs of the Old Testament and the saints of the New Testament. We do not see the Christ immediately. In Chapter 4, verse 11, we see that the praise is to God, who **"is worthy,"** and in Chapter 5, verse 9, it is the Lamb that was slain that is **"worthy."** Each is introduced separately. Each figure on the throne or in its vicinity is identified by description, character or role but never by name. John is left to conclude their identity. For example, it is obvious that the one who sits on the throne in unimaginable glory is the Lord God. The picture of **"the Lamb that was slain"** illustrates the death of Christ for the sins of the world as God's sacrificial Lamb.

The Occupant of the Throne
Text: Rev. 4:3-4
Rev. 4:3 And the appearance of the one that sat on the throne was like a jasper and a sardine stone: and there was a rainbow around the throne, and it looked like an emerald. 4 And twenty-four elders

were seated on thrones *surrounding* the first throne, and they were dressed in white clothes; and they wore golden crowns on their heads. (Easy KJV)

The one sitting on the throne looked **"like a jasper"** (a diamond) **"and a sardine stone"** with a rainbow about the throne, and it looked something like **"an emerald."** The throne is immaculate and beautiful beyond description. John likens the scene to the most beautiful jewels he has ever seen. Surrounding the throne were 24 lesser thrones occupied by elders all dressed in white with gold crowns on their heads.

THE THRONE IN HEAVEN

> - A Door Open in Heaven and the Command issued: "Come up here..." (4:1)
> - John is immediately in the Spirit (4:2)
> - John saw a throne and someone sitting on it (4:2)
> - The figure on the throne had an amazing appearance (4:3)
> - Twenty-four other thrones surround the main throne (4:4)
> - The elders were seated on these thrones (4:4)
> - They were dressed in white and wore golden crowns (4:4)
> - The gold crowns indicated their ruling responsibility (4:4)
> - From the throne came flashes of lighting, rumblings and peals of thunder (4:5)
> - Seven torches blazed before the central throne; representing the seven Spirits of God (4:5)
> - A sea like glass was in front of the throne and it was clear as crystal (4:6)

The Awesome Display of Sights and Sounds

Text: Rev. 4:5

Rev. 4:5 **And out of the throne preceded lightning and thundering and voices: and there were seven torches burning before the throne, which are the seven Spirits of God.**

The lightning and thunder is a sign of God's great power as seen in many of the Psalms.

Ps. 77:17 **The clouds poured out water: the skies sent out the sound of wind: your arrows flashed across the sky.** **[18] The voice of your thunder filled the heaven: the lightning illuminated the world: the earth trembled and shook.** (See Ps. 97:3-5)

The seven lamps of fire represent the Spirit of God. In Rev. 3:1 the risen Christ holds the seven Spirits. Seven represents the completeness of the Spirit. Christ and the Spirit are joined together. The Spirit brings people into a relationship with Christ, and reveals His truth in their hearts.

Text: Rev. 4:6-7

Rev. 4:6 **And before the throne there was a sea of glass like crystal: and in the midst of the throne, and *surrounding* the throne, were four *creatures* with eyes in front and in back. [7] And the first creature was like a lion, and the second was like a calf, and the third creature had a face like a man, and the fourth creature was like a flying eagle. (Easy KJV)**

The Beautiful Crystal Sea Like Glass

Almost casually, John mentions the sea of glass. I believe this crystal sea represents the otherness of God. You do not rush in and approach the throne. We remember that God is altogether holy. In Revelation 15:2 John sees the sea again and it is glowing like fire. Beside the remarkable, beautiful, glowing sea like glass we find those martyrs who have been victorious over the beast and his number and his name. These courageous ones have endured the terror of the reign of Antichrist and now they hold harps preparing to sing. So we have these two pictures. One is in John's first view of heaven and the second follows the great tribulation.

The Four Living Creatures

Also visible to John are four creatures (Greek is zoa; *zo-on* singular where get our words "zoo" and "zoology") and twice John says they had eyes everywhere, both in front and in back (vs. 6 and 8). The many eyes represent their all-seeing and all-knowing capacity. With the many eyes everything is constantly visible to them. Each creature was different: the first **"was like a lion, the second...was like a calf, and the third had a face like a man, and the**

fourth beast was like a flying eagle" (v. 7). A lion is untamed, a calf is domesticated, an eagle soars and represents the greatest of the birds, and man is God's ultimate creation. These four creatures represent the creation of God. Paul illuminates our understanding in Romans 8.

Rom. 8:19 **19 For the earnest expectation of the *creation* waits for the manifestation of the *children of God*. 20 For the creation was made subject to vanity, not willingly, but by reason of him who subjected *it* in hope, 21 Because the *creation* itself also shall be delivered from the bondage of *certain decay* into the glorious liberty of the children of God. 22 For we know that the whole creation groans as in the *pain of birth sounding in one voice* up until *the present time*.**

By creation is meant all of life: animal and human. Everything on earth is **"groaning."** We see this very clearly in the next chapter (Rev. 5).

> Rev. 5:13 **And I heard every creature in heaven, and on the earth, and under the earth, and in the seas, and all that are in them, saying, Blessing, and honor, and glory, and power, to him that is seated on the throne, and to the Lamb forever and ever.** (EKJV)

Here it is for us all to see: **"every creature in heaven and on earth and under the earth, and on the sea, and all that is in them..."** To paraphrase **"and all that is in them"** means the whole universe will be crying out in praise to God. In chapter 5 we will join in this anthem of the universe to the glory of God.
Ezekiel also saw four creatures in visions (Ezek. 1 and 10). In Chapter 10, Ezekiel calls them Cherubim. Cherubim were very familiar in the Old Testament Days.

Perhaps you remember that after the Lord drove Adam and Eve from the Garden of Eden He placed cherubim to guard the entrance

(Gen. 3:24). God commanded Moses to make an ark for the testimony (the Ten Commandments) and to form two cherubim of gold and place them facing one another at opposite ends of the cover of the ark also known as the **"mercy seat"** (Ex. 25:10-22). They were to make curtains for the tabernacle in the wilderness with cherubim woven into the fabric (Ex. 26:1). Also skilled workmen were to make a beautiful curtain of blue, purple and scarlet yarn to hang inside to separate the holy of holies from the rest of the tabernacle (Ex. 26:31; also Exodus 36 and 37).

When the temple was constructed, Solomon made more cherubim and expanded their placement (1 Kings 6-8). In worship, God was considered to reside between the Cherubim (2 Kings 19:15; 1 Chron. 13:6; cf. Ps. 18:10; 80:1; 99:1; Is. 37:16). Isaiah experienced an amazing vision in which he saw the seraphim in the temple and they were living (Isaiah 6).

In Revelation, the four living creatures (or cherubim) not only surround the throne in heaven along with the 24 elders, but they have great responsibility (5:6, 8, 11, 14; 6:1, 3, 5, 6, and 7:2, 11; 14:3; 15:7; and 19:4). In Rev. 15:7 they present the golden bowls of the seven plagues of God's wrath to the angels of the plagues. We see them singing wonderful anthems of praise together with others who surround the throne.

Text: Rev. 4:8-11

Rev. 4:8 **And each of the four** *creatures* **had six wings; and they had eyes** *front and back*: **and they do not rest day and night, saying, Holy, holy, holy, LORD God Almighty, who was, and is, and is to come.** [9] **And** *when those* **creatures give glory and honor and thanks to him that sat on the throne, which lives forever and ever, (Easy KJV)**

[10] **The** *twenty-four* **elders fell down before him that sat on the throne, and worshiped him that lives forever and ever, and cast their crowns before the throne, saying,**
[11] **You are worthy, O Lord, to receive glory and honor and power: for you have created all things, and for your pleasure they are and were created.** (EKJV)

At all times they are saying: **Holy, holy, holy, LORD God Almighty, which was, and is, and is to come"** (4:8), a phrase used three other times of Christ (Rev. 1:4, 8; 3:10). And when they say these marvelous words of praise, the 24 elders also bring praise to the One seated on the throne, and they cast their crowns before the throne in a beautiful act of submission to our God. To be granted a crown is a coveted achievement, but to the twenty-four elders, their crowns are joyfully surrendered to the One who sits on the great throne of heaven. We should find ourselves caught up in this scene of glorious praise, and even in this moment lift our voices in joyful and blessed praise to the Lord God and the Lamb.

SS

Select Section

THIS THING ABOUT SEVEN

The number seven has great significance in scripture being found 394 times in the word (but not always of significance). The number represents the fullness and completion of the work and power and judgment of God.

Consider the seven loaves (Mt. 15:34, 36; Mk. 8:5, 6), the seven basketfuls (Mt. 15:37; 16:10; Mk. 8:8, 20); seven times of forgiveness (Mt. 18:21, 22; Luke 17:4); the seven brothers all married in sequence to the same woman in the parable of Jesus (Mt. 22:25ff; Mk. 12:20, 22, 23; Luke 20:29, 31, 33); seven men of good report (perhaps deacons)—Acts 6:3.

A BOOK FULL OF SEVENS

Rev. 1:4, 11, 20—Seven Churches of Asia
Rev. 1:4—Seven Spirits of God—Rev. 1:4; 3:1
(Christ has the seven spirits that are seen as seven lamps burning before the throne.) Cf. **"Seven Eyes"** (Zech. 3:9) and **"seven lamps"** (Zech. 4:2). They are **"the eyes of the Lord that run to and fro upon the whole earth"** (Zech. 4:10).
Rev. 1:12—Seven Golden Candlesticks—Rev. 1:12, 20; 2:11

The seven golden candlesticks are the seven churches (Rev. 1:20)

Rev. 1:16—Seven Stars—Rev. 1:16, 20; 2:1
The seven stars are the angels (pastors) of the seven churches (1:20). The risen Christ holds the seven stars in His hand and walks in the midst of the seven golden candlesticks.

Rev. 1:20—Seven Angels or pastors of the seven churches

Rev. 3:1—The seven spirits of God

Rev. 4:5—The Seven lamps before the throne

Rev. 5:1—Seven Seals (that no man can open)—Rev. 5:1, 5; 6:1

Rev. 5:6—Seven Horns and Eyes (of the Lamb)—Rev. 5:6 (Which are the seven spirits of God sent forth into all the earth).

Rev. 8:2, 6—Seven Angels (that stand before God and receive seven trumpets to blow)

Rev. 10:3, 4—Seven Thunders

Rev. 11:13—Seven thousand persons killed in the great earthquake

Rev. 12:3—Seven heads and seven crowns upon the great red dragon

Rev. 13:1—Seven heads on the second beast that came up out of the sea

Rev. 15:1, 6, 8—Seven Angels holding bowls with seven plagues complete the wrath of God.

Rev. 15:1, 7; 16:1—Seven bowls of God's wrath given to the seven angels by one of the four living creatures.

Rev. 16:1—The seven bowls of God's wrath

Rev. 17:1—One of the seven angels with the seven bowls calls John to look upon the judgment of the great harlot.

Rev. 17:3, 7—The woman sits on the scarlet beast (the mystery beast) having seven heads

Rev. 17:9-10—The seven heads are seven mountains that are seven kings—Also Rev. 17:11

Rev. 17:11—The Enigma concerning the beast who is now the seventh

Rev. 21:9—One of the seven angels with the plagues reveals the bride of the Lamb.

- *All chapters in Revelation mention the number 7 except 7, 9, 14, 18, 19, 20, and 22.*

Chapter 5

THE GREATEST CORONATION

The Scroll That Cannot be Opened

Snapshot of Chapter 5

Who can open the book sealed with seven seals? Only God's Lamb, the Lion of the tribe of Judah, and the Root of David. He stands in the center of the throne in heaven surrounded by the four living creatures, the 24 elders, and the host of angels that cannot be numbered. He is worthy: to receive power and wealth and wisdom and strength and honor and glory and praise.

Text: Rev. 5:1-5

Rev.5:1 **And I saw in the right hand of the one seated on the throne a scroll with writing on the inside and back, and it was sealed with seven seals. ²And I saw a powerful angel proclaiming with a loud voice, Who is worthy to open the scroll, and to break its seals? ³And no one in heaven, nor on earth or under the earth, was able to open the scroll, nor to look inside. ⁴And I wept and wept, because no one was found worthy to open and to read the scroll or to look inside. ⁵And one of the elders said to me, 'Do not weep: behold, the Lion of the tribe of Judah, the Root of David, has prevailed to open the scroll, and to unlock** *(or break)* **the seven seals.'"** *(Easy KJV)*

Comments: John is witness to a tremendous problem in heaven. A scroll is observed in the hand of the occupant of the throne. While scrolls were normally only written on one side, this scroll is full **"with writing on both sides"** (v. 1). It is sealed seven times. Suddenly John sees a **"powerful** *(or mighty)* **angel proclaiming in a loud voice, 'Who is worthy to break the seals and open the scroll?'"** But there was no one in heaven, on earth, or under the earth with the ability to open the scroll. And John began to sob. **"I wept and wept"** (v.4). The undoubtedly awesome message of the scroll awaits one who is worthy to open it. John weeps because he knows the scroll will answer the questions about the end time and the things regarding Christ, the Lamb and God's final judgment on mankind.

It is announced: **"Behold, <u>the Lion of the tribe of Judah, the Root of David</u>, has prevailed."** (v. 5). See **"the root of Jesse"** (Isa. 11:10). Paul quotes Isaiah in Rom. 15:

Rom. 15:12 **And again, Isaiah said There shall be a root of Jesse, and he shall rise to reign over the Gentiles; in him shall the Gentiles trust."** (See also: Rev. 22:16).

Old Testament Connection

In Gen. 49:9, Jacob the Patriarch refers to Judah as a lion. Judah is in the line of Christ. The tribe of Judah is represented in the eternal kingdom by one of the elders. One of the twenty-four elders tells

John to stop weeping. But the elder also refers to Christ the Lamb of God triumphant as **"the root of David."** By the time we reach Chapter 6, the focus has changed from the One we would identify as God the Father to the Lamb that was slain, and He was seen standing in the center of the throne with the four living creatures surrounding.

The Lamb's New Song

Before us is one of the marvelous heavenly doxologies. This doxology is sung by the twenty-four elders and the four living creatures who accompany themselves with harps.

Text: Rev. 5:6-10
Rev. 5:6 **And I saw, there in the middle of the throne and the four creatures, and in the middle of the elders, stood a Lamb as it had been slain, and he had seven horns and seven eyes, which are the seven Spirits of God sent forth into all the earth. 7 And he came and took the scroll out of the right hand of the one that sat on the throne. 8 And when he had taken the book, the four creatures and the twenty-four elders fell down before the Lamb, and each of them had a harp, and a golden bowl full of incense, which are the prayers of the saints. 9 And they sang a new song, saying, You are worthy to take the scroll, and to open its seals for you were slain, and have redeemed us to God by your blood out of every tribe, and language, and people, and nation; 10 And you have made us kings and priests to serve our God: and we shall reign on the earth.** (Easy KJV)

- *Some translations have "slaughtered" rather than "slain."*

The Lamb's Unusual Appearance

He bears the marks of slaughter (v. 6). Lambs do not stand on two feet, but He is standing because He is alive forevermore. He is standing in the very center of the throne. And John sees the four living creatures and the elders forming a circle around him. Also, the Lamb has seven horns and seven eyes. We are told that the seven eyes represent the seven spirits of God sent out in the earth.

The Bowls of Prayers
Offered up as Incense

As we have said before, seven is a number of significance representing completeness in a purpose or act. Nothing is hidden and everything is open and obvious to the Lamb who sees all. Without hesitation, He takes the scroll from the right hand of the One seated on the throne. Immediately, the four creatures and the elders fall down before him. John observes that each has a harp presumably to provide music which follows their complete submission to the Lamb. They also hold golden bowls full of incense. We are told that the incense is the **"prayers of God's people."** And they begin to sing a song never sung before. It is the first **"worthy is the Lamb"** chorus (Rev. 5:4, 9, and 12).

The song is significant in several ways. First, it asserts the sacrifice of the Lamb who with his own blood **"has purchased for God persons from every tribe and language and people and nation."**

By His death He has fulfilled God's intention of world redemption. No nation or people are omitted. Wherever there are people, His gospel has been preached. What an amazing number of people is in mind here! More than that, these who have been redeemed have been **"...made us kings and priests unto our God: and we shall reign on the earth."** (5:10).

THE LAMB'S CORONATION ENTOURAGE

While the Lamb has been beside His Father since His ascension into heaven, He already occupies a place of prominence and significance. However in both the Old and New Testaments it is said that every knee in heaven and on earth will bow before Him. This occasion is the formal setting apart of God's gift to His Son.

Angels Without Number

Text: Rev. 5:11-13

Rev. 5:11 And I looked, and I heard the voice of many angels surrounding the throne and the creatures and the elders: and their number was *innumerable:* ten thousand times ten thousand, and thousands of thousands; [12] Saying with a loud voice, Worthy is the Lamb who was slain *(or slaughtered)* **to receive power, and riches, and wisdom, and strength, and honor, and glory, and blessing.** (Easy KJV)

[13] And I heard every creature in heaven, and on the earth, and under the earth, and in the sea, and all that are in them, saying,

Blessing, and honor, and glory, and power, to the One sitting on the throne, and to the Lamb forever and ever. (EKJV)

The Son appears with the Father on the throne (Rev. 3:21). But in this scene all eyes are trained on the worthy Lamb. The universal praise sounds somewhat like Psalm 150. The host of angels initiates the worship saying, **"Worthy is the Lamb, who was slain, to receive power and wealth and wisdom and strength and honor and glory and praise."** The angels of God are without number.

In Psalm 68 the writer says that **"the chariots of God are twenty thousand, even thousands of angels..."** (See Deut. 33:2. Compare Daniel 7:9-14 for a similar apocalyptic image of the judgment of God and the final authority of Christ; also Hebrews 12:22 for thousands of angels **"in joyful assembly;"** Jude 1:14-15; and here in Revelation 5:12-13 where John sees **"thousands upon thousands, and ten thousand times ten thousand angels surrounding the throne of God."**) The four living creatures and the elders worship and fall down before him.

Text: Rev. 5:14
Rev. 5:14 **And the four creatures said, Amen. And the twenty-four elders fell down and worshiped the One that lives forever and ever.**

The Heart of the Present Vision
Revelation 5
Before us is the coronation of the Lamb including the honor and praise of all creatures in heaven and in earth bringing Him glory and honor and praise.

THE CORONATION PROCLAMATION

It is so very easy to read right through this passage and get so totally caught up in the limitless sight of angels that we completely lose connection with the thrill and pageantry of the moment. We have just said that only the Lamb of God is in the focus here. He is surrounded by the four living creatures, then the twenty-four elders and now (5:11) the unlimited number of angels (ten-thousand times ten-thousand, and thousands of thousands) all surrounding the

Lamb for the brief but eternally powerful statements spoken by the angels contained in just two verses (Rev. 5:12-13).

More than that, **"all creatures in heaven and on earth and under the earth and on the sea, all that is in them"** are heard delivering praise to the Lamb. We have lost count, but the number comes to billions, perhaps, and is in the spirit of Psalm 150 which is an earthly foretelling of this heavenly scene.

The Coronation Proclamation is perfect by every measure of earth and heaven. It is only twenty-two words in English and yet it resounds to the ends of the universe. We are led to sense what John experienced. He had no time to record all of his impressions. Needless to say, we can fill in the blanks from what is said. The proclamation is voiced in unison by unlimited voices. It announces that the Lamb is the One and Only One with the right to the mysteries of the seals. Angels were chosen for this moment. Their presentation was perfect in every way.

> ➢ **It was perfect in the symmetry of the voices**. There were millions and yet they were in unison and unity in articulation and clarity.
> ➢ **They were perfect in service** rendering their mission at the highest and most glorious moment under God's authority. All were together and none assumed position.
> ➢ **They were perfect in their stance**. They formed endless circles around the central throne stretching to the outer sight limits of anyone in the middle.
> ➢ **They were perfect in subject** speaking the true praises of the One who died to redeem humanity and now stands alive in their midst.
> ➢ **They were perfect in splendor** rendering their immaculate appearance given them by the Father.
> ➢ **They were perfect in sweetness** speaking the words in the voices of heaven that the entire universe might hear the wonderful message of the coronation.
> No king and no kingdom could ever experience the slightest shadow of the glory that is provided to the King of kings and Lord of lords, our Lamb and Savior.

Christ is the Lamb

Revelation 5:6 The Lamb that looked as if it had been slain is standing in the center of the throne.

Revelation 5:8 The Lamb took the sealed scroll and the four living creatures and the twenty-four elders fell down before the **Lamb**.

Revelation 5:12 In a loud voice they were saying: "Worthy is the **Lamb**, who was slain, to receive power and wealth and wisdom and strength and honor and glory and praise!"

Revelation 5:13 Then I heard every creature in heaven and on earth and under the earth and on the sea, and all that is in them, saying: "To him who sits on the throne and to the **Lamb** praise and honor and glory and power, forever and ever!"

Revelation 6:1 I watched as the **Lamb** opened the first of the seven seals.

Revelation 6:3 When the **Lamb** opened the second seal, I heard the second living creature say, "Come!"

Revelation 6:5 When the **Lamb** opened the third seal, I heard the third living creature say, "Come!"

Revelation 6:7 When the **Lamb** opened the fourth seal, I heard the voice of the fourth living creature say, "Come!"

Revelation 6:16 They called to the mountains and the rocks, "Fall on us and hide us from the face of him who sits on the throne and from the wrath of the **Lamb**!

Revelation 7:9 After this I looked, and there before me was a great multitude that no one could count, from every nation, tribe, people and language, standing before the throne and before the **Lamb**.

Revelation 7:10 And they cried out in a loud voice: "Salvation belongs to our God, who sits on the throne, and to the **Lamb**."

Revelation 7:14 "These are they who have come out of the great tribulation; they have washed their robes and made them white in the blood of the **Lamb**.

Revelation 7:17 For the **Lamb** at the center of the throne will be their shepherd...

Revelation 12:11 They triumphed over him by the blood of the **Lamb** and by the word of their testimony...

Revelation 13:8 All inhabitants of the earth will worship the beast—all whose names have not been written in the **Lamb**'s book of life, the **Lamb** who was slain from the creation of the world.

Revelation 14:1 Then I looked, and there before me was the **Lamb**, standing on Mount Zion, and with him 144,000...

Revelation 14:4 They follow the **Lamb** wherever he goes. They were purchased from among mankind and offered as firstfruits to God and the **Lamb**.

Revelation 14:10 They will experience the torment of the Lake of Fire in the presence of the holy angels and of the **Lamb**.

Revelation 15:3 (They) sang the song of God's servant Moses and of the **Lamb**...

Revelation 17:14 They will wage war against the **Lamb**, but the **Lamb** will triumph over them because he is Lord of lords and King of kings...

Revelation 19:7 Let us rejoice and be glad and give him glory! For the wedding of the **Lamb** has come, and his bride has made herself ready.

Revelation 19:9 Then the angel said to me, "Write this: Blessed are those who are invited to the wedding supper of the **Lamb**!"

Revelation 21:9 "Come, I will show you the bride, the wife of the **Lamb.**"

Chapter 6

JUSTICE COMES IN THE END!

Snapshot of Chapter 6

Remember that only the Lamb that was slain can open the seals. In Chapter 6, the Lamb opens six of the scroll's seven seals. The term "Four Horses of the Apocalypse" comes from this chapter. Four horsemen or chariots appear twice in Zechariah (Chapters 1 and 6). These horsemen in Zechariah seem to represent the four winds. Their colors relate to the four directions of the wind.

When we come to Revelation, the four horsemen are not associated with chariots. Their colors relate to their tasks and their calling. Each of the horsemen is associated with the opening of one of the seven seals. One of the four living creatures presides over the vision of the opening of each of the first four seals.

Text: Rev. 6:1-2
^{Rev. 6:1} **I saw when the Lamb opened one of the seals, and I heard, the sound like thunder, and one of the four creatures saying, Come and see. ²And I saw, and behold a white horse: and he that sat on him had a bow; and a crown was given to him: and he went forth conquering, and to conquer.** (Easy KJV)

THE FIRST FOUR SEALS—THE FOUR HORSES AND THEIR RIDERS (6:1-8)

The seals, when opened, revealed the entire mystery of the end time as presented in John's Revelation. They explain the fulfillment of the completed plan of God for His creation.

The First Seal—the Rider on the White Horse (6:1-2)

The white horse is the symbol of world conquest. He stands for **CONQUEST.** He is given a crown and a bow. The crown is *stephanas* (στέφανος) in Greek, the garland wreath for victory in the athletic games, and used in Rev. 4:4, 10; 6:2; and 9:7; not *diadema (διάδημα)*, the crown of a king used three times in the NT: (Rev. 12:3; 13:1; 19:12). In the case of *diadema, the latter reference* is of Christ, while the first *diadema* is used of His enemies, and the second of the Antichrist triad. It reflects the events just before the close of the age. A world conqueror will appear on the scene. The crown indicates that he is a ruler. The **"bow"** indicates a great war.

The Second Seal—the Rider on the Red Horse (6:3-4)

Text: Rev. 6:3-4

Rev. 6:3 **And when he had opened the second seal, I heard the second creature say, Come and see. ⁴And another horse came out that was red: and power was given to the rider to take peace from the earth so that they should kill one another: and he was given a great sword.** (Easy KJV)

The red horse symbolizes the war of resistance of the conqueror. His color indicates his purpose—**BLOODSHED.** He receives a great sword. The rider does not kill—men under the influence of Satan kill. We are thinking of the most powerful nation in the world—a nation such as Russia, China, or North Korea. This power will never be satisfied until it has accomplished world conquest. Notice that the entire world is involved in a mighty war. There is no peace anywhere. He has power to remove peace from the earth. There has never been a war like this war. This is the war of world annihilation.

The Third Seal—the Rider on the Black Horse (6:5-6)
Text: 6:5
Rev. 6:5 **And when he had opened the third seal, I heard the third creature say, Come and see. And I looked, and there was a black horse; and he that sat on him had a pair of balances (scales) in his hand. ⁶ And I heard a voice in the middle of the four creatures say, A measure of wheat for a penny, and three measures of barley for a penny; and do not hurt the oil and the wine.** (Easy KJV)

The third living creature with a face like a man says, **"Come and see."** The black horse is the symbol of devastating world famine. This black horse represents **FAMINE.** His rider has a pair of balances or scales. The scales are for merchandizing and rationing. Many of you are too young to remember rationing during WW II. We are told about the enormous cost of food. A quart of wheat is the substance for a man for one day. A denarius is one day's pay. Barley was the most inferior of grains. But by eating this poor substitute, a family of three might survive. The oil and the wine suggest that there are still those who will insist upon luxuries while people are starving all around them. Bread is exorbitant but wine is plentiful. The poor folks are the ones who suffer first. A king of France once said of his starving people sarcastically: **"Let them eat cake."**

The Fourth Seal—the Rider on a Pale Horse (6:7-8)
Text: Rev. 6:7-8
Rev. 6:7 **And when he had opened the fourth seal, I heard the voice of the fourth creature say, Come and see. ⁸ And I looked, and I saw a pale horse: and the name of the rider was Death, and Hell followed close. And power was given to them over the fourth of the earth, to kill with sword, and with hunger, and with death, and with the animals of the earth.** (Easy KJV)

The pale horse is the symbol of **DEATH.** His color is **pale green** (GK). **Corpse-like.** Greek is *chlores* (χλωρός) from which we get chlorine and it denotes a yellowish green. The rider is **Death and Hades.** Death and the grave **travel together.** In other words, where one goes, the other is found. Power was given to them to kill one-fourth of the world with the sword and with starvation and death and wild animals of the earth. The Greek *thanatos* (θάνατος) is used here of **pestilence**, but fourteen other times in

Revelation it is use of of **death.** We are seeing a steep rise in **pestilence** in our world. There are new virus strains and deadly diseases where there is no known cure. The term **"beasts"** (wild animals) could mean those who run over the earth's inhabitants and brutalize them.

This passage is a parallel to Ezekiel 14:12-23.

Ezek.14:12 The word of the LORD came to me: 13 "Son of man, if a country sins against me by being unfaithful and I stretch out my hand against it to cut off its food supply and send famine upon it and kill its men and their animals, 14 even if these three men— Noah, Daniel and Job—were in it, they could save only themselves by their righteousness," declares the Sovereign LORD. (Easy KJV)

This final horror pictures a great plague of death that results in the decaying human bodies throughout the world. The bodies are the result of the previous plagues. When the plague comes there is nothing for people to do but die. **"Hades"** is the equivalent of **"Sheol"** in the Hebrew of the Old Testament. All of the horrors of verse 8 relate to Ezekiel 14. These are common expressions for the judgment of God upon the wicked throughout the prophets. They especially include the unrepentant Jewish people of the O.T. Take special note of Ezekiel 5:12, 16-17; 6:11-12.

The Fifth Seal—Souls under the Altar (6:9-11)
Text: Rev. 6:9-11
Rev. 6:9 And when he had opened the fifth seal, I saw under the altar the souls of those that were slain for the word of God, and for the testimony which they held: 10 And they cried with a loud voice, saying, How long, O Lord, holy and true, before you judge and avenge our blood on those that dwell on the earth? 11 And white robes were given to every one of them; and they were told that they should rest yet a little time, until their fellow servants and their brothers, who would be killed as they were, should also be fulfilled. (EKJV)

Those beneath the altar have been **"slaughtered."** The scripture does not say "they died." As Jesus was sacrificed, so these have been sacrificed by evil powers. They are martyrs slain because of the conditions in the world. The altar is the altar before the throne of God in heaven. The martyrs are under the care of God. This is another way of saying what Jesus said in Luke 23:43. Paradise is

the place in heaven where the spirits of the righteous dead go between their deaths and their resurrections. Jesus not only went to
Paradise, but He went to the realm of the fallen angels and proclaimed His victory over them (1 Peter 3:18ff).

**1 Pet. 3:18 For Christ died for sins once for all, the righteous for the
unrighteous, to bring you to God. He was put to death in the
body but made alive by the Spirit, ¹⁹ through whom he also went
and preached to the spirits in prison ²⁰ who disobeyed long ago
when God waited patiently in the days of Noah while the ark
was being built.** (Easy KJV)

He also **went to Hades.** Remember that He has the keys. He
preached the gospel to the dead (according to 1 Peter 4:6). Those
who died the martyr's death are under the altar (v. 9). Paul said
"...them also which sleep in Jesus will God bring with him"
(1 Thes. 4:14). When we leave our bodies, we will be in Paradise.
Nothing can harm them because they are underneath the altar
near the throne of God. They are given white robes and told to
rest until their fellows were killed also. White robes denote the
resurrection. In verse 11 they are told to wait until their number is
complete.

They pray **"How long...?"** (v. 10). This **sounds bloodthirsty.**
But, it is a cry for the kingdom to come and **for judgment to take
place.** Remember the entire universe is groaning for that day. This
means it is crying out for God's justice. Paul says that when we die
we will be clothed with immortality (1 Cor. 15:54). When
Christ returns we will receive a resurrection body that will be
clothed with immortality. To us to be clothed with immortality
means that we have been placed completely beyond the reach of
death.

> ## Heart of the Present Vision
> **We are shown the devastation and death coming upon the
> world through the wrath of God. We see upheaval and we
> see God's redemptive purpose.**

The Sixth Seal—the Great Day of God's Wrath (6:12-17)
Text: Rev. 6:12-14
^{Rev. 6:12} And I beheld when he had opened the sixth seal, and, there was a great earthquake; and the sun became black as sackcloth of hair, and the moon became as blood; ¹³ And the stars of heaven fell unto the earth, even as a fig tree casts her figs before they are ripe, when she is shaken by a mighty wind. ¹⁴ And the heaven departed *like* a scroll when it is rolled together; and every mountain and island were moved out of their places. (Note: See Rev. 20:11 where earth and heaven fled). (EKJV)

The Sixth Seal Results in Cosmic Upheaval (6:12-14). Mankind is devastated (6:15-17). This is a picture of God's judgment upon the wicked. They cry for the rocks and mountains to fall upon them.

Text: Rev. 6:15-17
^{Rev. 6:15} And the kings of the earth, and the great men, and the rich men, and the chief officers, and the mighty men, and every *slave*, and every free man, hid themselves in the dens and in the rocks of the mountains; ¹⁶ And *cried* to the mountains and rocks, Fall on us, and hide us from the face of him that sits on the throne, and from the wrath of the Lamb: ¹⁷ For the great day of his wrath has come; and who shall be able to stand? (Easy KJV)

We now have dozens of manuscripts that have the plural rather than the singular. Further it is in agreement with verse 16: **"hide us from the face of him who sits on the throne and from the wrath of the Lamb!"** The point is that this is the great day of final judgment. The prophets have this thought in a number of places.

The Prophecy of Joel for the Day of the Lord
Read Joel Chapters 2-3 and compare these verses to Revelation with special reference to Revelation 14, 16 and 19.

The Terrible and Fearful Day of the Lord – (Joel 2:1)
^{Joel 2:1} Blow the trumpet in Zion, and sound an alarm in my holy mountain: let all the inhabitants of the land tremble: for the day of the LORD *is coming, and it is* near at hand... (Easy KJV)

The Mighty Army Exceeding All Numbers – (Joel 2:2)

Joel 2:2 "...as the darkness spreads upon the mountains: so comes a great and mighty army; the like of which has never been seen, and will never be again even to all generations." (Easy KJV)

Nothing Escapes Their Advance – (Joel 2:3)

Joel 2:3 A fire devours before them; and behind them a flame burns. The land before them *is* as the garden of Eden, and behind them a desolate wilderness; yes, and nothing shall escape them. (Easy KJV)

They Appear Like Horses Galloping in a Cavalry (Joel 2:4-5)

Joel 2:4 Their appearance *is* like the appearance of horses; and they *leap and gallop* as horsemen. 5 Their noise is like the sound of chariots, and they leap to the tops of mountains. They are arrayed for battle like mighty soldiers, and the sound they make is like the sound of billowing flames devouring dry wheat stubble. (EKJV)

The Unstoppable Army Terrifies All Nations – (2:6-9)

Joel 2:6 As they approach the people will be in great fear: all shall melt in fear before them. 7 They will run like mighty men; they will scale the wall like men of war; and they march each one in step; and they shall not break their ranks: (Easy KJV)

The Heavenly Bodies Are Darkened – (2:10-11)

Joel 2:10 The earth will quake before them; the heavens will tremble: the sun and the moon will be dark, and the stars will cease shining: 11 And the LORD will give orders at the head of his army: for his troops are numberless: *those* that execute his commands are powerful; for the day of the LORD *is* great and terrible; and who can endure it? (Easy KJV)

Judgment in the Valley of Jehoshaphat – (3:12)

Joel 3:12 Let the *nations* be awakened, and let them come up to the valley of Jehoshaphat: for there I will sit to judge all the *surrounding nations*. (Easy KJV)

The Harvest and Trampling of the Winepress (Joel 3:13-14; Cp. Rev. 14)

Joel 3:13 *Swing* the sickle, for the harvest is ripe: come *and help*, for the winepress is full, the vats overflow; for their wickedness *is* great. 14 Multitudes, multitudes in the valley of decision: for the day of the LORD *is* near in the valley of decision. [15] The sun and the moon shall be darkened, and the stars shall *cease their* shining.

Isaiah 63
Who Treads the Winepress? (Cp. Rev. 14; 19)

Isa/ 63:1 Who *is* this coming from Edom, from Bozrah, with his garments stained crimson? *Who is this one* glorious in his apparel, *striding* in the greatness of his strength? *It is* I that speak in righteousness, mighty to save. [2] Why are your *garments* red like his that treads the winepress? [3] I have trodden the winepress alone; and *out of the nations there was* no one with me: for I will tread them in mine anger, and trample them in my fury; and their blood will be sprinkled upon my garments, and I will stain all my raiment. [4] For the day of vengeance *is* in my heart, and the year of my redeemed has come

[5] And I looked, and *there was* no one to help; and I was amazed that *there was* no one to uphold: therefore my own arm brought salvation to me; and my own wrath upheld me. [6] And I will tread down the nations in my anger, and make them drunk in my fury, and I will bring down their strength to the earth. (EKJV)

Also see: Zephaniah 1:14-18; Zechariah 14:3-19; Isaiah 34:8-10.

2 Pet. 3:11 *Seeing* then *that* all these things shall be dissolved, what manner *of persons* ought you to be? You should *live holy and godly lives,* [12] Looking forward in *anticipation* to the coming of the day of God, on which the heavens will be dissolved in *blazing* fire, and the elements shall melt with fervent heat? [13] Nevertheless we, according to his promise, look for new heavens and a new earth, in which righteousness dwells. (Easy KJV**)**

With the opening of the sixth seal we have the prophecy of the dramatic end of the world. Some even say it is the collapse of the universe.

ROLLING UP THE HEAVENS

> *Text: Rev. 6:12-14*
> Rev. 6:12 **And I beheld when he had opened the sixth seal, and, lo, there was a great earthquake; and the sun became black as sackcloth of hair, and the moon became like blood;** 13 **And the stars of heaven fell unto the earth, even as a fig tree casts her figs** *before they ripen,* **when she is shaken** *by* **a mighty wind.** 14 **And the heaven departed as a scroll when it is rolled together; and every mountain and island were moved out of their places.** (EKJV)

In verses 12-14 we are shown the end of the earth and the celestial order. Verse 12 may be connected to Joel's prophecy:
Joel 2:30 **And I will show wonders in the heavens and in the earth, blood, and fire, and pillars of smoke.** 31 **The sun will be turned into darkness, and the moon into blood, before the great and the** *awesome* **day of the LORD comes.** 32 **And in that day, everyone who calls on the name of the LORD shall be saved.** (Easy KJV)
The great earthquake is prophesied numerous times in scripture. The earthquake and the accompanying signs are the immediate prelude to the end. Simon Peter selected Joel's prophetic utterance as the text of his sermon in Acts 2:20. The earth and the heavenly stars collide and the earth is broken apart (vs. 13; 14b). Not one thing remains as it was up until this point. But even as these things begin to occur, it may not be too late to receive Christ. Peter chose this passage and emphasized the latter part: **"And everyone who calls on the name of the LORD will be saved..."** We should not gamble on a last minute reprieve. Obviously, the call is to fall before the Lord today in faith and surrender.

Where did John get this thought of God rolling up the heavens like a scroll? It comes from the everlasting strategy of God prophesied in scripture after scripture.

He Stretched Them Out and
He Will Roll Them Up Again
What is meant when it says in Rev. 6:14 that the heavens will be rolled up like a scroll? This is one of the clearest prophecies that we find from Psalms to Revelation. We are shown the beginning and the end of the created order—the creation and the consummation.

It is necessary to pay close attention to the meaning clearly laid out for us in the scriptures. Psalm 104 explains "the stretching out of the heavens."

> **Ps. 104:1** **Bless the LORD, O my soul. O LORD my God, You are very great; you are clothed with honor and majesty. ² Who covers *yourself* with light as *with* a garment: <u>who stretched out the heavens like a curtain</u>:** (EKJV)

Psalm 104 is the first passage that makes this most significant statement that is followed up in the prophets. Verse 2—It is God **"who stretched out the heavens like a curtain** (or **"tent"**-NIV)."** This precise language of the Psalm seems to place it in good company with Isaiah and Jeremiah. We can observe that God is even yet creating the universe as new stars come into being. The use of the word **"stretched"** is calculated to exactly explain that God did it with His own hand.

The Lord Created the Heavens and Stretched Them Out

Isa. 40:22—"It is he that sits upon the circle of the earth...that *stretches out the heavens as a curtain*, and <u>spreads them out as a tent</u> to dwell in..."

Isa. 42:5—The Lord...created the heavens and <u>stretched them out</u>..."

Isa. 44:24—"I am the Lord...that <u>stretched *out* the heavens</u> alone..."

Isa. 45:12—"I, even my hands, <u>have stretched out the heavens</u>..."

Isa. 51:13—"The Lord your Maker...has <u>stretched *out* the heavens</u>..."

Jer. 10:12—He "has <u>stretched out the heavens</u> by his discretion."

Jer. 51:15—It is the Lord "that has <u>stretched *out* the heavens</u>."

Zech. 12:1—It is "the Lord which <u>stretched *out* the heavens</u>..."

Psalm 8:3—"When I consider the heavens, <u>the work of your fingers</u>..."

> **Isa. 48:13—"my right hand hath <u>spanned the heavens</u>..."**
> **Isa. 45:18—"For thus says the Lord that <u>created the heavens</u>..."** Quotes from KJV

Just as I was researching this breakthrough thought that God **"stretches out the heavens"** an article appeared in **"The Atlantic,"** by Marina Koren (Oct. 4, 2016). The article has been widely reported by television and newspaper media. The summation of the article is that "For centuries, astronomers thought there might be just one [galaxy], our own. New research estimates there are 2 trillion galaxies in the observable region of the cosmos." The emphasis should be upon the word "observable." For several decades, the article states, astronomers believed "there are between 100 billion and 200 billion galaxies in the observable universe." She quotes further: "Astronomers at the University of Nottingham <u>now say "the number of galaxies in the observable universe is **2 trillion**</u>, or more than 10 times as many as previously thought." The concept of "the observable universe" may only be a thimble full of the actual. To me, the number is incomprehensible (I cannot wrap my mind around such numbers), yet entirely in keeping with the word of God. He made everything and He does nothing in a small way. The article also stated, "The light from distant galaxies takes billions of years to reach us; the most distant galaxy Hubble has ever imaged left 13.4 billion years ago..." [Note: Hubble is our telescope in space.]

While the scriptures are abundantly clear that God created the heavens and the earth and everything in both, it is not until we read Psalm 104:2 that we glean this new way of thinking about the creation of the heavens.

TAKING THE UNIVERSE APART

The biblical writers are saying God unfolded, rolled out, stretched out the heavens in their totality. But the reverse is also stated in scripture. God is going to fold up, roll up, incinerate, dissolve and bring it all to nothing. Is that all? Certainly not!

THE HEAVENS: ROLLED UP AND DISSOLVED

> Isa. 34:4—"And the host (stars) of heaven <u>shall be dissolved</u>, and the heavens <u>shall be rolled together as a scroll</u>..."
>
> Heb. 1:12—"And *like a robe you will* fold them up" (EKJV).
>
> Rev. 6:14—"And the heaven departed <u>as a scroll when it is rolled together</u>..."
>
> Ps. 102:26—"They (the earth and the heavens) <u>shall perish</u>...they shall *become* old like a garment; as vesture shall you change them..."
>
> 2 Pet. 3:12—"the heavens *shall* be on fire and <u>shall be dissolved</u>, and the elements shall be melted."
>
> Isa. 24:19—"...the earth <u>is clean (totally) dissolved</u>..."
>
> Matt. 24:29—"Immediately after the tribulation...<u>the stars shall fall from heaven</u>, and <u>the powers of heaven shall be shaken</u>...and they shall see the Son of man coming in the clouds of heaven with power and great glory."
>
> Isa. 13:13—"Therefore, <u>I will shake the heavens</u>..." (Cf. Hag. 2:6, 21; Ps. 46:3; Isa. 2:19, 21; 14:16; 24:18; Ezek. 38:20; Joel 3:16; Heb. 12:26.)
>
> Isa. 24:21—"In that day <u>I will punish the powers in the heavens above</u>..."

Observe how both the Old Testament and the New Testament describe the earth as being **"dissolved"** (KJV). Paul tied it together for believers: 2 Cor. 5:1—**"For we know that if our earthly home of this *tent* were dissolved, we have a building of God, a house not made with hands, eternal in the heavens."** So if the earth and heavens are to be dissolved, how can this be? God always plans ahead.

A New and Greater Creation

Isa. 65:17 For, behold, <u>I create new heavens and a new earth: and the former shall not be remembered, nor come into mind.</u> (KJV)

Isa. 66:22 For as <u>the new heavens and the new earth, which I will make</u>, shall remain before me, says the LORD, so shall your seed and your name remain. (KJV)

2 Pet. 3:13 Nevertheless we, according to his promise, look for <u>new heavens and a new earth, where righteousness dwells.</u> (KJV)

Rev. 21:1 And <u>I saw a new heaven and a new earth: for the first heaven and the first earth *had* passed away</u>; and there was no *longer any* sea. [2] And I, John, saw the holy city, New Jerusalem, coming down from God out of heaven, prepared as a bride adorned for her husband. [3] And I heard a great voice out of heaven saying, Behold, the tabernacle *(or tent)* of God *is* with men, and he will dwell with them, and they shall be his people, and God himself shall be with them, *and be* their God. (EKJV)

When God says: **"The tabernacle of God is with men,"** we understand that His **"tent"** is more than adequate for all who will come into it through the blood of Christ, the Lamb of God. In the new heaven we will have **a new name** (Rev. 2:17; 3:12); we will be **citizens of the New Jerusalem** (Rev. 3:12; 21:2); **a new song** will be sung through the ages (Rev. 5:9; 14:3); we will occupy **a new house not made with human hands**; and glory of glories—**"everything will be new"** (Rev. 21:5).

Everybody Will Cry Out:
"Fall on us"—Rev. 6:15-17

Text: Rev. 6:15-17

Rev. 6:15 And the kings of the earth, and the great men, and the rich men, and the chief captains, and the mighty men, and every *slave*, and every free man, hid themselves in the dens and in the rocks of the mountains; [16] And said to the mountains and rocks, Fall on us, and hide us from the face of him that sits on the throne, and from the wrath of the Lamb: [17] For the great day of his wrath has come; and who shall be able to <u>endure it</u>? (EKJV)

Old Testament Connection

Where is the origin of the scene of the ruling class, as well as the poor crying for the mountains and the rocks to **"fall on us and hide us…from the wrath of the Lamb?"**

John brings the historic prophecy into full focus. What men have sought for centuries will now be fulfilled. The wicked will face the wrath and judgment of Almighty God.

The Terror of Facing Messiah
(6:15)

Psalm 110 is a great messianic Psalm. It clearly lays out God's judgment to come through Christ, the Victorious Son of God.

Psalm 110:5 The Lord who is at your right hand will strike down kings on the day of his wrath. [6] He will judge the nations, and he

will pile up the dead bodies in the land; he will crush the rulers of the countries of the earth**. (Easy KJV)
(cf. 149:8-9; especially see Ezek. 32:1-16).
Isa. 24:19 **And it shall come to pass in that day,** *that* **the LORD will punish the powers of the host of the heavens on high, and the kings of the earth below.** (See vs. 17-23 for **"terror"**) (EKJV)

Hopeless and Helpless
(6:16)

When His wrath is revealed, there is no time to seek a place of shelter even if it might be available. The caves and rocks look inviting in a world of destruction. No one is able to face the fierceness of the wrath of God Almighty. These people never expected to face such a torrent of wrath. They felt that they lived above judgment and justice, and therefore they did not consider God or turn to Him in any way. They have no place to hide from the wrath of God.

Isa. 2:10 **Enter into the rock, and hide there in the dust,** *because of* **fear of the LORD, and for the glory of his majesty!** (EKJV)

Isa. 2:21 19 **And the people shall go into the holes of the rocks, and into the caves of the earth, out of fear of the LORD, and from the glory of his majesty, when he arises to violently shake the earth.**

Hos.10:8 b **...they shall say to the mountains, Cover us; and to the hills, Fall on us!"**

Jesus quoted Hosea 10:8 in Luke 23:30.
Luke 23:30 **"Then they will say to the mountains, "Fall on us!" and to the hills, "Cover us!"** [Hos. 10:8]

The Day No One Wants to Face
For the great day of their wrath has come,
and who can withstand it?" (6:17)

The great day of the Lord comes in Revelation. The day prophesied throughout the scriptures has finally come, and John is a witness to the final destruction of the universe. In the Scriptures we find mention of this **"great day"** in Zeph. 1:14; Jude 6; and in this location: Rev. 6:17; and in 16:14. Paul is also clear in Romans 2:

Rom. 2:5 As the result of your hardness and impenitent heart you are storing up wrath for yourself against the day when his wrath and righteous judgment is revealed.

The more we oppose God and reject His Son, the greater the amount of wrath we are storing up. When **"the day of God's wrath"** arrives, everyone will understand that His judgment is **"righteous."** Therefore, there can be no rebuttal. It has been prophesied for many centuries, and now His full wrath will be poured out upon the wicked and the rulers. In the following chapter, we find those who belong to God and therefore have no fear of His wrath. These will enjoy all of the benefits and blessings of a life of obedience and faith.

Chapter 7

THE NUMBERED AND THE INNUMERABLE
Sealed and Secure

> ### *Snapshot of Chapter 7*
> Chapter 7 introduces us to the 144,000 who have not been **"sealed."** We will see them again in Chapter 14 where they are sealed and are standing on the heavenly Mt. Zion with Christ the Lamb of God. Verse 4 looks forward to the scene in Chapter 14. We also see the great multitude from every nation and ethnic group standing before the Lamb at the throne of God. What a great vision!

Text: Rev. 7:1-8

144,000 Sealed

^{Rev. 7:1} **And after these things I saw four angels standing on the four corners of the earth, holding the four winds of the earth, that the wind should not blow on the earth, nor on the sea, nor on any tree.**

² **And I saw another angel ascending from the east, having the seal of the living God: and he cried with a loud voice to the four angels, to whom it was given to hurt the earth and the sea,** ³ **Saying, "*Do not hurt* the earth, neither the sea, nor the trees, till we have sealed the servants of our God in their foreheads."** ⁴ **And I heard the number of them which were sealed: and there were sealed a hundred and forty-four thousand of all the tribes of the children of Israel.** ⁵ **Of the tribe of Judah were sealed twelve thousand. Of the tribe of Reuben were sealed twelve thousand. Of the tribe of Gad were sealed twelve thousand.** ⁶ **Of the tribe of Aser were sealed twelve thousand. Of the tribe of Nephthalim were sealed twelve thousand. Of the tribe of Manasses were sealed twelve thousand.** ⁷ **Of the tribe of Simeon were sealed twelve thousand. Of the tribe of Levi were sealed twelve thousand. Of the tribe of Issachar were sealed twelve thousand.** ⁸ **Of the tribe of Zabulon were sealed twelve thousand. Of the tribe of Joseph were sealed twelve thousand. Of the tribe of Benjamin were sealed twelve thousand.** (Easy KJV; Note Names of the tribes are the KJV spelling).)

The List in Genesis 49 includes **Dan** while the list in Revelation 7 omits **Dan** and includes **Manasseh**.

Heart of the Present Vision

We see both Israel (the 144,000) and the Gentiles (people without number) who are the people of God. The angels are halted until a seal can be placed upon the saved. They will be in the hands of God no matter the dangers and consequences they may face.

Four Angels And the Winds of Destruction

In Chapter 7 four angels stand at the four corners of the earth, and they are holding back the wind so that it could not blow on the sea or the earth or the trees. A fifth angel comes from the east. He possesses **"the seal of the living God."** He tells the four angels to stop and wait. They are not to harm the land or the sea or the trees until "**we have sealed the servants of our God in their foreheads.**" John heard the number of those to be sealed: 144,000. The 144,000 that are **sealed** are the same as the 144,000 that are the **saved** in Rev. 14:1.

The lone angel (7:2) comes **"from the east"** consistent with Ezekiel 43:2. **"I saw the glory of the God of Israel coming from the east. His voice was like the roar of rushing waters, and the land was radiant with his glory."** (Easy KJV)

Next, we examine the meaning of a person being sealed.

What Does It Mean to Be Sealed?

First of all, God initiates and completes the sealing. This is not a "do it yourself" project. First, a believer is saved for the day of redemption. Redemption is when we are resurrected by God and given our eternal bodies. In the meantime, a believer is charged to live in a daily commitment of obedience to Christ in order not to **"grieve the Holy Spirit of God"** who lives within us.

Next, **"The Lord knows those who are his"** (2 Tim. 2:19). Again, he continues: **"Everyone who confesses the name of the Lord must turn away from wickedness."** When we discuss these 144,000 who are sealed as reported in Revelation 14, we will take note of their personal lives lived for the glory of God.

Next, when He sealed us, He has **"given the earnest of the Spirit in our hearts"** (2 Cor. 1:22). This means that He has given us assurance that we are saved and therefore sealed by the Holy Spirit. We may know that we belong to Him because the Holy Spirit gives us definite verification.

Finally, we **"were sealed with the Holy Spirit of promise..."** (Eph. 1:13). A seal is a promise that God will keep His word and redeem us because of the sacrifice of Jesus that we have accepted and followed. In all of these cases, we can know that we belong to God. This 144,000 out of the tribes of Israel will have been saved in accordance with God's own desire and promise for His chosen people. They have been brought in at the last, as it were; but finally they are saved.

In Chapter 14, not only are they sealed, but they are saved and they are with Christ, the Lamb of God. They are a kind of **"firstfruits"** to God (see our comments at Chapter 14). All that we have said is true. We are sealed by the Holy Spirit as saved and therefore belonging to God as we wait **"for the day of redemption"** for which we are sealed (Eph. 4:30). We are sealed because **"the Lord knows those who are his"** (2 Tim. 2:19).

How Can We Know That We are Saved and Sealed?

When we are saved, and therefore sealed, He gives us **"the earnest of the Spirit in our hearts"** to confirm this wonderful truth (2 Cor. 1:22). Yes, the scripture says we are **"sealed with the holy Spirit of promise..."** (Eph. 1:13) which provides us the guarantee of the abundant promises of God. We have assurance that He, who cannot lie, will keep His word and receive us to Himself on the glorious resurrection day.

But just one more thought must be added. Rev. 7:4 says: **Then I heard the number of those who were sealed: 144,000 from all the tribes of Israel.** We cannot leave this thought of sealing until we turn to the fulfillment in Revelation 14 where the 144,000 are gathered together rejoicing, playing their harps and praising with the Lamb of God in their midst on the heavenly Mt. Zion.

On their foreheads there are names: These are the **"144,000 who had his name and his Father's name written on their foreheads"** (Rev. 14:1). There it is as clear as day. The name of Christ their Redeemer and Savior, and the name of God their Father in heaven are written on the foreheads of each of the 144,000. It is plain for all to see that they are sealed in that they belong to the Savior and to His Father. The 144,000 obviously come out of Israel. Paul explains this in Romans.

Rom. 11:23 **And *if these also do not continue* in unbelief, *they* shall be grafted in: for God is able to graft them in again. ²⁴ For if *you were* cut out of the olive tree which is wild by nature, and *were* grafted, contrary to nature, into a good olive tree: how much more shall these, which *are* the natural branches, be grafted into their own olive tree?** (Easy KJV)

All Israel Will Be Saved

Rom. 11:25 **For** *brothers, I do not want you to be conceited so that you should* **be unaware of this mystery: a partial hardening** *has come* **upon Israel, until the** *full number* **of the Gentiles** *comes in.*

There is coming a day when those who are out of Israel will be saved and **"grafted in."** The Israelites from Paul's day until now "*continue* **in** (their) **unbelief"** (v. 23). Therefore he says: **"a partial hardening** *has come* **upon Israel, until the** *full number* **of the Gentiles** *comes in*" (v. 25, EKJV).

Those Sealed Are Protected in the Great Tribulation

The 144,000 stand on the threshold of the great tribulation, but the next group actually comes out of the tribulation. We understand from Rev. 7:3 that the wind that is being held back involves the beginning of the plagues of God's wrath upon the earth. These who are sealed are protected from the plagues sent upon the earth during the great tribulation. Notice in Rev. 9:3 that only those who did not have the seal of God on their foreheads are hurt by the locust creatures.

Rev. 9:3 **And locusts came down on the earth out of the smoke and were given power like that of scorpions of the earth. [4] They were told not to harm the grass of the earth or any plant or tree, <u>but only those people who did not have the seal of God on their foreheads</u>.**

In Rev. 16:2 the terrible festering sores only touched those that **"had the mark of the beast and upon those that worshiped his image."**

Rev. 16:2 **And the first** *(angel)* **went, and poured out his** *bowl* **upon the earth; and putrid and festering sores <u>broke out upon those that had the mark of the beast, and upon</u> *those that* <u>worshiped his image.</u>**

They might suffer the atrocities of the Antichrist, but none of the plagues of God's wrath fell upon them. These plagues will begin in Chapter 8, and more will be found in Chapter 16.

The Great Multitude in White Robes
A Multitude without Number

The members of the multitude without number are holding palm branches reminiscent of Jesus' triumphant entry into Jerusalem just before His death on the cross. They are praising God and are joined in praise by all of the angels of heaven, the four living creatures, and the 24 elders (vs. 9-11). We are told something of their identity:

Text: Rev. 7:9-10
Rev. 7:9 **After this I *looked*, and, lo, a great multitude, *that* no *one* could number, <u>of all nations, and *tribes*, and people, and tongues (or languages)</u>, stood before the throne, and before the Lamb, clothed with white robes, and palms** *(branches)* **in their hands;** [10] **And cried with a loud voice, saying, "Salvation to our God who *sits on* the throne, and unto the Lamb."** (Easy KJV)

Now here is the same list from Chapter 5:9 ...**for you were slain, and you have redeemed us to God by your blood <u>out of every tribe, and tongue</u>** (or language), **<u>and people, and nation.</u>** In addition, John is instructed to prophesy concerning these same four groups (Rev. 10:11). The composition of the two multitudes in Rev. 5:9 and 7:9 is the same except the order of the four composite groups is different. The question arises: is John talking about two different multitudes or the same multitude?

Are There Two Multitudes or One Mentioned Twice?

- Both multitudes are cleansed by the blood of the Lamb (5:9 and 7:14; also see 22:14).
- Both multitudes belong to Christ.
- Both multitudes are recognized as before the throne of God.
- Both multitudes are comprised of the earth's nations, tribes, languages and people groups.
- Both multitudes are mentioned in connection with the angels, the four living creatures and the 24 elders.
- Both multitudes are mentioned in regard to a wonderful heavenly anthem.
- Both multitudes are said to be of service to God.
- Both multitudes are seen before God following their death or rapture.

This Multitude Came Out of the Great Tribulation

Text: Rev. 7:11-17

[11] And all the angels stood *around* the throne, and *around* the elders and the four *creatures,* and fell before the throne on their faces, and worshiped God, [12] Saying, "Amen: Blessing, and glory, and wisdom, and thanksgiving, and *honor,* and power, and might, unto our God forever and ever. Amen."

[13] And one of the elders answered, saying to me, "*Who* are these *that* are *wearing* white robes? and *where did they come from*?" (EKJV)

It appears that the multitude from Rev. 5:8 is the same as the multitude in Rev. 7:14 who: "**_are the ones who came_ out of great tribulation.**"

There is Yet Another Mention in Revelation 13:7-8

Now what about the next group, that is definitely living during the great tribulation, and is identified by the KJV as **"the saints"** or in the NIV **as "God's holy people"**?

Who Are These Saints?

In the next passage in Rev. 13:7-8 we learn that there is a war against believers during the great tribulation. In the King James Version, these believers are called **"saints."** This is a perfectly good term for those who are saved and belong to Jesus, and it should not be confused with the same term used in Catholicism for special servants of God who are honored by the term. In the New Testament it always means ordinary Christians who live their lives daily in full faith in Christ. In the New Testament the ones called **"saints"** are always the saved—the believers in Christ.

The **"saints"** are alive in this passage in Rev. 13 and also in Rev. 14:12-13. Once again we are reminded of these innumerable believers that: **"have washed their robes, and made them white in the blood of the Lamb."** By this we understand that they are saved and bound for the new heaven of our God.

There is a War Against the Saints in the Tribulation

In Chapter 13 we are introduced to the beast that rises from the sea. He is the antichrist and he has come to help Satan in his diabolical attack upon the people of God. Now read the seventh verse of Chapter 13 below:

96

Rev. 13:7 And it *(the beast)* **was given** *the ability* **to make war with the saints, and to overcome them: and power was given him over all** *tribes,* **and** *languages,* **and nations.** (Easy KJV)

He is going to make war against the people of God. To say that he was given **"ability to make war with the saints, and to overcome them"** means that these believers are going to have to stand courageously for their faith just like believers did during the holocaust upon Jerusalem in 67-70 AD when Jews and believers were slaughtered by the Romans. What a disturbing thought. They will be persecuted by the antichrist. For details on the saints read the select section in my commentary in chapter 13 called **"The Saints."**

In the same sentence John says: **"and power was given him over all** *tribes,* **and** *languages* **and nations."**
Undoubtedly, the **"saints"** are among those just mentioned who make up the world's population during the great tribulation. In other words, the **"saints"** are subject to the control and persecution of the antichrist, but not the wrath of God. This is a scriptural truth that requires discussion.
⁸And all that dwell upon the earth shall worship him, whose names <u>are not written</u> in the book of life of the Lamb slain from the foundation of the world.

These people, who are identified as **"saints"** in the KJV, are going to be attacked by Satan's agent known to us as antichrist. We are told in verse 8 that the dwellers upon the earth are going to worship the beast, except those who are recorded **"in the book of life of the Lamb slain from the foundation of the world."**

Thus we have saints living among the total population of the earth during the great tribulation. Some people say that this is a special group of saints, but the scripture here does not tell us that. We could spend a lot of time discussing this. However, suffice it to say that there are some **"saints"** on the earth during the great tribulation that will experience attacks by Satan's beast, also known as the antichrist. And again we see a multitude of people from every nation, tongue (or language) and kindred (or tribe) on the earth.

(For more information on the multitudes on the earth, please see Rev. 10:11; 15:6-7). Note: for similar lists see Rev. 17:15 in regard to the great prostitute; also we see a **"great multitude"** in heaven shouting **"Hallelujah"** (19:1, 6). No doubt the **"great multitude"** in Chapter 14 on Mt. Zion with the Lamb is included in the great multitude in Chapter 19.

Now We Return to Chapter 7

In Revelation 7 the second or latter multitude is the multitude without number. While the first group—the 144,000—represents the saved from Israel, the second multitude represents the nations **"who have come out of the great tribulation"** (v. 14). In Chapter 6 we were shown the forecast of the Great Tribulation, and the ultimate end of creation as we know it. These who came out of the great tribulation did not experience the wrath of God, but only the persecution of the Antichrist (Rev. 9:4; 16:2, 10; 17:8; 18:4).

The Great Multitude Identified

John is mystified. He doesn't understand the identity of this enormous numberless mass of people. There are nationalities and racial groups that, to his personal knowledge, were never a part of the church of his day. Obviously, they are from a future age beyond his time. More than that, we face a mystery.

[13] And one of the elders answered, saying to me, "*Who* are these *that* are *wearing* white robes? and *where did they come from*?" [14] And I said to him, "Sir, *you know*." And he *replied*, "<u>They are the ones who came</u> out of great tribulation, and they have washed their robes, and made them white in the blood of the Lamb. (EKJV)

There are many different theories, but there is also a tremendous lack of scriptural evidence to verify these theories. One theory is that they were lost to Christ, but received Him as Savior during the tribulation. Again, there are many suggestions as to the evangelists that may have reached such a mass of people. The second thought, based on the enormous numbers, is that they represent the church, and the church entered the tribulation.

There are many interpretations of this theory. Some believe in a rapture (an old word used for the catching up or gathering up) of the church prior to the great tribulation. Others believe that the tribulation is seven years in length and the church is "raptured" or gathered up in the middle of the seven year period, etc. Still others believe that the church endures the great tribulation just as the New Testament Christians endured extensive and brutal persecution and tribulations on earth (Matt. 13:21; John 16:33; Acts 14:22; Rom. 5:3, 12:12; 2 Cor. 1:4; 7:4; Eph. 3:13; 1 Thes. 3:4; 2 Thes. 1:4, 6; Rev. 1:9; 2:9, 10 all in the KJV). Many of these suffered terrible deaths as martyrs for Christ.

The answers to all of these theories are complicated and require some delicate scriptural interpretation, often leaving one wanting more information. I have friends who have differing interpretations and we have learned not to be disagreeable. The bottom line is that while the Lord could have made the answer very clear, He did not, and all of the explanations are much more than we can treat in this book. The wonderful part is that no matter our answer, this enormous number of people are all saved and cleansed by the blood of Jesus, and for that we praise the Lord and give Him glory! That is the ultimate meaning of this part of Chapter 7. On the day when Christ returns, all of us who are raptured will find the answers in God's new heaven.

The salvation of this multitude involves a complete cleansing: **"they have washed their robes and made them white in the blood of the Lamb"** (v. 14; see 22:14). This is a way of saying that they came into faith, like we all do, through the sacrifice of Christ on the cross. He shed His blood that He might pay the terrible cost of our sin. Thereby, the statement arises that our robes have been made white in His blood. These who had no right to the white robes of purity are now so dressed by the grace and forgiveness received through Christ's blood.

Notice their Position: Before the Heavenly Throne
¹⁵ Therefore they *are* before the throne of God, and serve him day and night in his temple: and he that sits on the throne shall dwell among them. (Easy KJV)

Now they are before the throne of God and the Lamb and serve unceasingly (v. 15). They are forever freed from the want and terror of the Great Tribulation. There is no more suffering and there are no more tears (vs. 16-17; 21:1-6). Christ the Lamb is their Shepherd and He **"shall dwell among them"** eternally (v. 15). Chapter

99

7 gives blessed hope to those who face future suffering in the Great Tribulation, and also wonderful encouragement to the families of missionaries and Christians the world over who forfeited their lives in sacrificial faith in Christ.

THE WONDERFUL PROMISE

Rev. 7:16 **16 They shall not be hungry anymore, nor thirsty anymore; neither shall the sun *harm them*, nor any heat. 17 For the Lamb which is in the midst of the throne shall feed them, and shall lead them to fountains of living waters: and God shall wipe away all tears from their eyes."** (Easy KJV)

Chapter 8

THE SEVENTH SEAL AND THE SEVEN TRUMPETS

THE FIRST FOUR TRUMPETS

Snapshot of Chapter 8

Here we have mention of the seventh seal and the seven trumpets to be blown by the seven angels that stand before God. Each trumpet announces one of the plagues of the tribulation upon those who bear the name or mark of the beast. The altar is visible in hEaven.

Text—Rev. 8:1-2

Rev. 8:1 **And when he had opened the seventh seal, there was silence in heaven about half an hour. ² And I saw the seven angels that stood before God; and they were given seven trumpets.**

The Angels Are Ready to Sound Their Trumpets

We have been waiting with great anticipation for the opening of the seventh seal since Rev. 6:12. There is an interlude in Chapter 7 that heightens the suspense regarding the seventh trumpet. The trumpets are as the trumpets of a herald calling attention to something of great importance.

Remember the Lamb is the only one worthy and able to open the seven seals. Now the opening of the seals resumes (Rev. 8:1-9). The verse simply says: ^{Rev. 8:1} **When he opened the seventh seal, there was silence in heaven for about half an hour.** This word for **"half an hour"** *hemi horo* is only used here in the New Testament. Silence is said to be golden.

There are so many sounds for John from heaven such as angels, the elders, voices, etc. that we are amazed at this time of silence. In our world we seldom have times of silence and occasions to contemplate. The content of this passage is surprising.

JOHN MEETS ANOTHER ANGEL (8:3)
Text: Rev. 8:3
^{Rev. 8:3} **And another angel having a golden censer came and stood at the altar, and he was given a great amount of incense, that he should offer with the prayers of all saints upon the golden altar that was before the throne.** (Easy KJV)
He is going to offer up incense with the prayers of the saints on the golden altar in heaven. It is easy to miss something very important in this act.

Prayers that Payoff
This is the offering of the prayers of the **"saints"** (8:3 KJV; the NIV has **"all God's people;"** Cf. 11:15-19; especially v. 19 where the saints are rewarded as heaven opens once again). The KJV use of **"saints"** is preferred in our study of Revelation. The silence in heaven is solemn and impressive (8:1). Heaven has been a place of constant action and events until now.

The prayers of the saints are about to go up to God. The time is set aside as solemn because God is hearing the prayers of the saints on earth. The smoke of the incense of these prayers is received by God during this time when heaven is silent. Presumably these are the prayers of the saints of the period who are in great suffering and persecution. Christians are always being persecuted somewhere in the world, but this is a much more general persecution.

Text: Rev. 8:4
Rev. 8:4 **And the smoke of the incense,** *that came* **with the prayers of the saints, ascended up before God out of the angel's hand.** (EKJV)

We do have influence in heaven. Our prayers are important and they matter to God. Even in this time of the dispensing of God's wrath, there is a time when everything is halted for the prayers to be heard. What do the prayers of the saints consist of? They are pleading with God for judgment on the world that is assaulting and persecuting His church—His **ekklesia** *(in Greek)*.

The Angel Hurls Fire on the Earth (8:5)
Text—Rev. 8:5
Rev. 8:5 **And the angel took the censer, and filled it with fire** *from* **the altar, and** *hurled it* **to the earth: and there were voices, and thunders, and lightning, and an earthquake.** (Easy KJV)

REVELATION 8:5f.	REVELATION 11:19
Flashes of lightning	Flashes of lightning
Rumblings	Rumblings
Peals of thunder	Peals of thunder
An earthquake	An earthquake
Fire and hail	A great hailstorm

Compare the plagues in Egypt under Moses (Ex. 8:13-10:15; cf. Ps. 78:47-48; 105:32-33; 147:17). In Revelation 16 when the seventh bowl of God's wrath is poured out, massive hailstones fall upon the kingdoms of the wicked. God will certainly get the attention of those who have rejected Him. No one can ignore this awesome onslaught from heaven.

Rev. 16:21 **Huge hailstones** *fell* **on people** *from* **the sky, each weighing about a hundred pounds. And they cursed God on account of the plague of hail, because the plague was so terrible.** (Easy KJV)

In verses 1-2 we read of the seven trumpets given to the seven angels. This occurred when the seventh seal is broken. In the Old Testament the trumpet can be a call to battle. In the scriptures, the blast of the trumpet is the signal of a call to war. We also know that the trumpet blast will be heard at Christ's coming (Mt. 24:32f; 1

Thes. 4:16f; Rev. 11:15). We are reminded of the trumpet blast recorded in Exodus 19:16-20; 20:18 from the peak of Mt. Sinai when God delivered His commandments to Moses. Trumpets are meant to get our undivided attention. We have the words of Jesus and Paul regarding the trumpet blast, and the call of Michael, the archangel at His coming.

> Matt. 24:31 **And he will send his angels with a loud trumpet call, and they will gather his elect from the four winds, from one end of the heavens to the other.**

1 Thes. 4:16 **For the Lord himself will come down from heaven, with a loud command, with the voice of the archangel and with <u>the trumpet call of God</u>, and the dead in Christ will rise first. 17 After that, we who are still alive and are left will be caught up together with them in the clouds to meet the Lord in the air. And so we will be with the Lord forever. 18 Therefore encourage one another with these words.**

THE FIRST FOUR TRUMPETS ARE SOUNDED
The Trumpets Begin When
the Seventh Seal Is Broken

Text—Rev. 8:6
Rev. 8:6 **Then the seven angels who had the seven trumpets prepared to sound them.**

The seven angels all prepare to sound their trumpets (8:6). They are tuned and ready. These magnificent angels are fully ready to do the bidding of our God. What God commands they will certainly fully accomplish. The first four trumpets are sounded and then there is a brief interlude prior to the sounding of the last three.

Each of the first four relates to the plagues of Egypt. They are not the same, but they are reminiscent of the Egyptian plagues. The plague of the first trumpet destroys the grass. When the fire falls on earth, the saints have tangible evidence that their prayers have been heard. When the first angel sounds it says:

Text—Rev. 8:7
7 **The first angel sounded, and there followed hail and fire mingled with blood, and these were *hurled* upon the earth: and a third of the trees were burned up, and all green grass was burned up.**
(EKJV)

We noticed in the comments in verse 5 the hailstorm mentioned in Rev. 16. Hail destroys everything that it strikes—trees, agriculture, shelter, the food supply and much more. See hail and fire in the great Egyptian plague—cf. Ex. 9:24. (Compare 8:7 with 9:4 where the angels are told not to harm the grass—the source of animal food and thus human food).

This is not your dime-sized hail. The blood indicates the death of mankind (but not all). Fire is a totally destructive force that can easily far exceed the ability of men to control. And you notice **"it was hurled down on the earth."**

The First Trumpet marks the end of one-third of everything on earth. A third of the trees and the grass were burned up. As far-reaching and terrifying as is this punishment, it is only a light fore-taste to what is to follow. Trees and grass provide food for animals. Some trees provide food for mankind. As great and terrible as is this application of God's wrath, this is only the beginning. But there is a message for the saints who sent up their prayers. They share in the judgments to come—in requesting judgment.

The Second Trumpet marks the end of one-third of everything in the sea (8:8).

Text: Rev. 8:8-9
⁸ And the second angel sounded, and a great mountain burning with fire was cast into the sea: and a third of the sea became blood; ⁹ And a third portion of the living creatures in the sea died; and a third of the ships were destroyed. (EKJV)

It is volcanic in nature. There is great attention presently directed toward volcanic activity in our world. Geologists are concerned re-garding the possibility of what is known as a "super volcano." In the distant past, such volcanoes have destroyed life for thousands of miles by sending up a plume of volcanic ash that actually lowered the temperature in a large section of earth sufficient to prohibit a normal growing season for vegetables to feed the people. Such a volcano could easily throw a blazing mountain into the sea destroy-ing enormous ocean life. Just today great volumes of lava are flow-ing into the sea in Hawaii.

The Third Trumpet marks the end of one-third of everything in the rivers (8:10; cf. Exodus 7:20-25).

Text: Rev. 8:10-11
[10] **And the third angel sounded, and a great star fell from heaven burning like *a bright light*, and it fell on a third of the rivers, and on the fountains of waters;** [11] **And the name of the star is called Wormwood: and a third *portion* of the waters became *bitter*; and many people died from the waters, because they *became* bitter.** (EKJV)

The destruction that fell upon the oceans now falls upon the fresh-water streams and rivers. The bitterness makes it impossible to drink the water. Many millions of people would perish for lack of water. **"Wormword"** comes from the Exodus (pollution). Worm-wood has been called the fruit of idolatry (Deut. 29:16-18). In Revelation 8:11 **"Wormwood"** is the name of the star. In Isaiah Lucifer is referred to as a "morning star, son of the dawn" (Isa. 14:12 NIV, but see the KJV below).

[Isa. 14:12] **How art thou fallen from heaven, <u>O Lucifer, son of the morning</u>! *how* art thou cut down to the ground, which did weaken the nations!**

The Fourth Trumpet marks the end of one-third of all heavenly bodies.

Text: Rev. 8:12
[12] **And the fourth angel sounded, and a third of the sun was smitten, and the third of the moon, and a third of the stars; and a third of them was darkened, and in a third of the day the sun did not shine, and the night also.** (EKJV)

(Cf. Exodus 10:21ff.) There was darkness in Egypt but not in Go-shen. These judgments of God do not affect everybody. Only one-third of each of these elements is destroyed. These terrible events precede the end of planet earth, but are not the end in themselves.

Text—Rev. 8:13
[13] **And I watched, and I heard an angel flying through the midst of heaven, saying in a loud voice, Woe, woe, woe, to the inhabitants of the earth because *the other three angels are yet to sound their trumpets!*** (EKJV)

These four great destructions are a final warning! They are a prelude to the other three trumpet blasts. An eagle flies through midheaven (8:13); the KJV has **"angel"** but the Greek has **"eagle."**

Note: An eagle flying over the earth calls out a stern warning: **"Woe! Woe! Woe! To the inhabitants of the earth..."** **"Inhabitants (or dwellers**—KJV) **upon the earth"** (8:13) are those who do not heed the Word of God (cf. 14:6). Eagles have great sight and abilities to see beyond the eyes of humans. They can fly to great heights and soar down to capture their prey without warning. This passage is a reminder of Hosea 8:1. The eagle is warning of the final three trumpet blasts and the severity of the wrath to come during these blasts.

Hos. 8:1 *Put* the trumpet to thy mouth. *He shall come* as an eagle *over* the house of the LORD, because they have *broken my covenant, and rebelled* against my law. (EKJV)

Chapter 9

TERRORS FROM THE ABYSS

Snapshot of Chapter 9

This chapter is awesome because evil and horrible creatures rise and exit the abyss. Smoke billows out of the abyss like a gigantic furnace. **"They had as king over them the angel of the Abyss"** (9:11). His name is Apollyon. The fifth and sixth trumpets sound announcing the great punishments to come. The first and second of three woes is presented. The second **"woe"** prepares the earth for the battle of Armageddon in Chapter 19. Two hundred million enemy troops are preparing to cross the great river Euphrates (cf. chap. 16). Despite the awesome pronouncements of this chapter, the rest of mankind refused to repent.

The Sounding of the Fifth Trumpet—the Star

Text—Rev. 9:1-6

Rev. 9:1 **And the fifth angel sounded, and I saw a star fall from heaven to the earth: and he was given the key of the bottomless pit (or abyss). ²And he opened the bottomless pit; and smoke rose *from the pit like a great furnace*; and the sun and the air were darkened because of the smoke *from* the pit. ³And out of** the smoke locusts came upon the earth: and they were given power *like the* power of scorpions of the earth.

And they were commanded not to hurt the grass of the earth, nor any green thing, nor any tree; but only those men *that did not have* the seal of God in their foreheads. [5] And they *were not permitted to kill* them, but to torment them for five months: and their torment *was like* the torment of a scorpion, when *it stings* a man. [6] And in those days men *will* seek death, and *will* not find it; and shall desire to die, and death shall flee from them. (Easy KJV)

The Star Is Named "WORMWOOD"

John is shown the events when **"the fifth angel sounded"** (9:1). We must remember the three **"woes"** of the flying eagle in Chapter 8. He says, **"I saw a star fall from heaven to the earth."** The star is named **"Wormwood"** (Rev. 8:11). The star represents an angel with a very specific responsibility: **"and he was given the key of the bottomless pit (or abyss)."** The **"abyss"** is a bottomless pit. The pit represents the extremes of evil and the depravity of man. Under God there is no limit to the good that mankind can accomplish, and under Satan there is no limit to the evil that can be carried out. With the key the angel is enabled to open the bottomless pit (v. 2).

The bottomless pit is occupied by all manner of horrible and destructive evil. When **"the Abyss"** is opened, smoke billows from the abyss. John said: **"the smoke rose from the pit like a great furnace,"** and the smoke darkened the sun and the sky (v.2). This would be fearful enough, and this is added on top of the four other amazing, terrifying and dreadful events. The pit symbolizes man's depravity and Satan's diabolical evil designs.

Horrible Creatures like Locusts Emerge
from the Abyss

But this is not normal smoke. Look again: [3] **And out of the smoke locusts came upon the earth: and they were given power *like the* power of scorpions of the earth."** (v. 3). The locust-like creatures are sinister beyond normal thought. But they are limited in what they can do. They are given instructions, presumably by the angel with the key not to: **"hurt the grass of the earth, nor any green thing, nor any tree; but only those men** *that did not have* **the seal of God in their foreheads"** (v. 4). Those

109

who belong to Christ and have the seal of God on their foreheads are protected from these plagues. But those who have the mark of the beast (see chapter 13) will feel the full force of the plagues.

We are prepared for this in Rev. 7:2 where we are told **"another angel"** comes out of the east with the seal of the living God and cries: **"Do not harm the land or the sea or the trees until we put a seal on the foreheads of the servants of our God"** (7:3). The locust creatures **"*were not permitted to kill* them,"** (the people without the seal of God) **"but to torture them for five months"** (9:5). Their stings, like those of a scorpion, could be inflicted, but there were limits. Scorpion stings are almost unbearably painful. They inflicted terrible pain: **"their torment *was like* the torment of a scorpion, when *it stings* a man."** It would be so great that **"men *will* seek death, and *will* not find it; and shall desire to die, and death shall flee from them"** (9:5-6). We can only imagine this dreadful suffering.

The Terrible Sights and Sounds of the Locust Creatures

John's attention is focused again directly on the locust creatures. **And the shapes of the locusts were like horses prepared for battle"** (9:7).

Here we see the instruments of apocalyptic visions. They wear **"crowns like gold."** They have faces that **"were as the faces of men"** (9:7). Their hair is long **"like women's hair."** And they have sharp **"teeth"** like those of a lion 9:8). These hideous creatures are revealed to John. They had **"breastplates"** like iron. And then there was the sound: **"and the sound of their wings was *like* the sound of chariots of many horses running to battle."** (9:9; cp. Joel 2-3).

John observed their tails: ^{Rev. 9:10} **"they had tails like scorpions, and there were stingers on their tails, and they could hurt men for five months."**

Apollyon: The Destroyer

Out of the pit that covers man's evil also comes man's destruction. Some have likened these creatures to war planes with missiles, but we must be careful not to read into the text. **"They had a king over them; the angel of the bottomless pit"** (9:11). His name is given in Hebrew and in Greek. "**Abaddon**" is his name in Hebrew, and "**Apollyon**" is his name in Greek. It means "**destroyer.**"

Heart of the Present Vision

Before us is the attack of awesome and fearful creatures. We are reminded once again that we are in God's hands. Ultimately, God will bring us to glory.

THE END OF THE FIRST WOE AND THE BEGINNING OF THE SECOND WOE

This is just "**the first woe.**" But John is going to be shown something unprecedented.

Rev. 9:12 "**One woe is past; and two more woes** *are coming.*"

The Sounding of the Sixth Trumpet
Why Be Concerned About The River Euphrates?

Note: We must wait until Chapter 11:15 for the seventh trumpet.

Text: Rev. 9:13-15

Rev. 9:13 **And the sixth angel sounded** *his trumpet,* **and I heard a voice** *coming* **from the four horns of the golden altar which is before God,** [14] **Saying to the sixth angel that had the trumpet,** *Release* **the four angels that are bound** *at* **the great river Euphrates.** [15] **And the four angels were released that were prepared for** *the* **hour, and** *the* **day, and** *the* **month, and** *the* **year, to kill** *a third of mankind.* (EKJV)

In verse 13, the "**sixth angel sounded his trumpet.**" John heard one voice "*coming* **from the four horns of the golden altar which is before God**" (v. 13; cf. Ex. 27:2—Note the instructions regarding the original altar of Israel. That altar was overlaid with bronze—Ex. 38:2).

The voice that comes from the altar before God gives a command to the sixth angel of the trumpets: "**Release the four angels that are bound <u>at</u> the great river Euphrates**" (Rev. 9:14). The River Euphrates is the fourth river flowing out of the Garden of Eden (Gen. 2:14). God established it as the Eastern boundary of the land He allotted for Abraham (Gen. 15:18).

Moses told Israel to go next to the Euphrates (Deut. 1:7; 11:24). In Rev. 16:12 another sixth angel pours out his bowl upon the River Euphrates and it becomes dry so the great army from the east can cross.

The Four Angels Have Been Kept Ready for This Hour, Day and Month

---

We are not told why the four angels had been bound, but the language alerts us to the fact that this day had been in the plan of God for perhaps centuries or longer. The four angels **"were *released that* were prepared for *the* hour, and *the* day, and *the* month, and *the* year, to *kill* a third of *mankind*"** (v.15). You cannot be more specific. God has a time set and a schedule to follow. Nothing is left to chance. The timing is down to the hour. We grow tired in waiting for even short periods of time, but these angels had waited for an exceedingly long period of time. But they were assured that they were in the will and design of God. Would that we were even partially as obedient.

200 MILLION TROOPS CROSSING
THE RIVER

Text: Rev. 9:16
16 And I heard the number of the army of the horsemen and there were two hundred thousand thousand.

They are to let the waters go back so that an enormous army can cross the Euphrates River. This river was the extreme boundary of any land that could have constituted the land of Abraham, Isaac and Jacob. Across the river to the East were the Parthians, the Babylonians, the Medes and the Persians. God is going to bring a force that will bring judgment to the earth. This will be no ordinary army. It is composed of 200 million troops—an unimaginable-sized army. We can contemplate the millions in the nations of Asia and Europe that might compose this enormous army conscripted by evil national leaders.

The Power of the Fearful Horses

Text: Rev. 9:17-19

^{Rev. 9:17} **And I saw the horses in the vision, and *those* that sat on them, having breastplates *red like fire*, and of *blue* jacinth, and like *yellow sulfur*: and the heads of the horses were *like* the heads of lions; and out of their mouths came *fire* and smoke and *sulfur*. ¹⁸ By these three, *a third of mankind was killed*, by the fire, and by the smoke, and by the brimstone *(or sulfur)*, which issued out of their mouths. ¹⁹ For their power is in their mouth, and in their tails: for their tails were like serpents, and *they* had heads, by which *they were able to* hurt.** (Easy KJV)

In the Greek it is unclear who has the breastplates, but it is normally believed that they are on both the horses and the riders as verse 17 in the NIV states. Notice these unusual and fearful horses.

Observe verse 19 regarding the power of the horses: **"mouths, and their tails like snakes that had heads that could inflict injury.**" It is startling to us that the power of evil is under the command of God to accomplish his judgment just as He used Babylon to punish Israel in 586 B.C. A leader of the Old Plymouth Brethren Church is credited with saying in humor: "How wonderful! If it were not for the word of God we would never have known that such creatures existed."

Still There Was No Repentance

Text—Rev. 9:20-21

^{Rev. 9:20} **And the rest of *mankind that were not* killed by these plagues *did not repent* of the works of their hands, *but continued to* worship devils, and idols of gold, and silver, and brass, and stone, and wood: *that can* neither see, nor hear, nor walk: ²¹ Nor *did they* repent of their murders, nor of their *magic,* nor of their *sexual immorality*, nor of their thefts.** (Easy KJV)

After all this there still is no repentance of the numbers of mankind still remaining alive. They continued in their evil: worshiping demons and lifeless idols. There was no repentance: **"Nor did they repent of their murders, their magic acts, their sexual immorality or their thefts"** (v. 21; also v. 20; cf. Rev. 16:9, 11—**"refused to repent"**).

These persons are so hardened, obstinate, and filled with the Satan's lies that they absolutely refuse to repent of their sin and turn to God no matter the degree of His approaching wrath. God did not pardon His own chosen people Israel under the same circumstances. We should pay immediate attention.

SS
Select Section
THE NOISE AND SIZE OF THINGS IN HEAVEN

In Revelation Heaven Is Seldom Quiet, Numbers Are Endless and Figures Are Large

The angels often shout or speak in extremely loud voices. This is the case with an angel that asks: **"Who is worthy (5:2) to open the scroll and loose the (seven) seals"?** Or there is the announcement in the same chapter that the Lamb is worthy (5:12). There is the loud voice of the angel with **"the seal of the living God"** who cries out to halt the angels that are holding the winds back (7:2). There is the angel flying through the air (8:13) shouting **"woe, woe, woe"** to the earth. There is the angel who shouts **"Loose the four angels which are bound at the great river Euphrates."** Another angel appears (10:1ff.) who cries with a loud voice, as a lion roars.

The martyrs who are hidden under the altar in heaven (6:10) cry out **"How long, O Lord, holy and true"** until you judge the earth. There are great multitudes and naturally they raise their voices in great sound. Included we find the great multitude that cannot be counted standing before the throne of God (7:9), and the enormous multitude of the redeemed in heaven that raise a sound like **"the voice of many waters, and the voice of mighty thunders saying Alleluia: for the Lord God omnipotent reigns"** (19:6). There are **"great voices in heaven"** saying **"The kingdoms of this world have become the kingdoms of our Lord and His Christ"** (11:15).

We see gigantic or extremely large angels, persons and things. The KJV uses the word **"great"** to describe these. There is the **"mighty angel"** (10:1) who stands with **"his right foot on the sea, and**

114

his left foot on the earth," and a rainbow above his head. I have questioned people as to what they think of his size. Some say 100, or 150 feet tall or more. We are shown the heavenly woman **"clothed with the sun and the moon under her feet"** (12:2). There is the **"great dragon"**(12:9) who is identified as Satan. He is enormous! In the same chapter the woman is given the wings of a great eagle to fly away from the the dragon's wrath (12:14).

Other things are also very large or extensive. A great star falls from heaven (8:10). The tribulation (7:14 etc.) to come upon the world is **"great,"** as is the wrath of Satan (12:12). On earth John sees **"a great mountain burning with fire cast into the sea."** (8:8). Smoke rises from the bottomless pit **"like the smoke of a great furnace"** (8:2) and blocks out the sun. There is the **"great river Euphrates"** (9:14) where an army of 200 million will cross to fight the battle of Armageddon. And there is **"the great city"** where God's two faithful prophets will be slain (11:8). There is the **"great prostitute"** who in reality is a city doomed for everlasting destruction (Rev. 17-18).

Lightening and peals of thunder and voices are heard from the throne of God in heaven (4:5). There are more voices and peals of thunder and continuous lightening and an earthquake when the angel cast the censer filled with fire from the altar down upon the earth (8:5). The temple of God in heaven is opened and there is continuous lightening, peals of thunder, and an earthquake (11:18). In Rev. 16:18 there are voices and peals of thunder, and great flashes of lightening, and a **"mighty earthquake."** Hundred-pound hailstones fall upon the earth.

When the eternal city of God comes down from heaven, John sees the greatest high rise ever conceived (1500 miles in width and length and height). We continually sense the presence of endless numbers of saints and angels all serving God. There is the 144,000 (Rev. 7 and 14). There is a multitude of the saints standing on the sea of glass before the heavenly throne singing (Rev. 15). The great host of heaven follows Christ to the battle of Armageddon (Rev. 19). And with all of the shouts we should not forget that Paul reminds us that at the end of earth's existence at the second coming: **"the Lord himself shall descend from heaven with a shout"** (1 Thes. 4:16).

`

Chapter 10

A REALLY BIG ANGEL
WITH A TINY BOOK

Snapshot of Chapter 10

In this Chapter John sees an extra large angel with very bold and unusual characteristics. The angel offers John a very tiny scroll, and in keeping with God's instruction to Ezekiel in the Old Testament, he is told to eat the scroll. He is warned that it will be bitter or sour to his stomach, but sweet to his mouth. The message is bitter because it contains the ultimate wrath of God, but it is sweet because of the good news it contains of God's redemption. God's mystery of the ages will be revealed at last. He is told to preach it to all peoples, language, nation and kings.

We witnessed the scene in the previous chapter of 200 million troops coming as a mounted cavalry to destroy a great host of mankind. At an unexpected moment we are faced with an interlude just as was noted in Chapter 7. Also, John is back on earth after being summoned into heaven. Many commentators have noted that this is the renewing of his prophetic commission. There are enormous similarities here with Ezekiel 1 and 8.

Text: Rev. 10:1-4

Rev. 10:1 And I saw another mighty angel coming down from heaven, clothed with a cloud: and a rainbow was over his head, and his face was like the sun, and his feet *were like* pillars of fire: 2 And he had a little book open in his hand: and he *placed* his right foot on the sea, and his left foot on the earth, 3 And he gave a loud shout like a lion *roaring*: and *when he shouted*, the seven thunders *spoke*. 4 And when the seven thunders *had spoken*, I was about to write: and I heard a voice from heaven saying to me, "Seal up those things which the seven thunders said, and *do not write them.*" (EKJV)

FIRST, HE SEES THE MIGHTY ANGEL

A mighty angel appears—a majestic angel as in Daniel 10:4ff. This is the third mighty angel John has met.

Dan. 10:4 And in the twenty-fourth day of the first month, as I was by the side of the great river, which *is* Hiddekel *(the Tigris)*; 5 Then I looked up, and there was a man *in front of me* clothed in linen, with a *belt* of fine polished gold. 6 His body also *was* like beryl, and his face was like lightning, and his eyes *like burning torches*, and his arms and his *legs* like polished brass, and his voice like the *sound* of a multitude. (EKJV)

The Mighty Angel's Appearance
(Rev. 10:1-4)

Now we have another angel identified as **"another mighty angel"** (v. 1). We saw the first mighty angel in Rev. 5:2 crying in a loud voice, **"Who is worthy to break the seals and open the book?"** This angel is wrapped in a cloud. There is a rainbow above his head (see Ezek. 1:28; Rev. 4:3—the rainbow around the throne of God). The rainbow represents a promise and assurance of God's word to be fulfilled. God remembers His covenant between heaven and earth (Gen. 9:13-14, 16). **"His face was like the sun, and his feet *were like* pillars of fire"** (v. 1; Rev. 1:15-16). He is not to be confused with the risen Christ in Rev. 1, despite some similarities in appearance.

Could the Angel Be Gabriel?
(cf. Daniel 8:16; 9:20ff)

Gabriel is the angel of divine announcements as we see here in Daniel and in Luke 1:19, 26. It has been said that the name Gabriel is similar to the Hebrew **"gibbor"** meaning "mighty man." *(Gavri'el)* meaning "God is my strong man", is derived from גֶּבֶר *(gever)* **"strong man, hero."** The similarity between Gabriel as **"God is my strong or mighty man"** and **"a mighty angel"** has led some students of Revelation to believe that they are one and the same.

Dan. 8:15 While I, Daniel, was watching the vision and trying to understand it, there before me stood one who looked like a man. 16 And I heard a man's voice from the Ulai calling, "Gabriel, tell this man the meaning of the vision." Note: The vision is **of the end time** (v. 17).

Also, Gabriel appeared to Daniel (Dan. 9:20ff), assuring him that his prayers had been received instantly in heaven and answered immediately.

On closer inspection there is a little or tiny scroll in the angel's hand, and it was open or unrolled (v. 2). He is wrapped in a cloud with a large rainbow about his head, and his feet stretched from the sea to the land indicating the immensity of his size. And he gave a shout like the terrifying roar of a lion. Upon him shouting, the voice of the seven thunders spoke.

THE MYSTERIOUS UTTERANCE OF THE SEVEN THUNDERS

John heard the voice of the seven thunders, but he is commanded not to write the message. John is stopped in mid-action. He said: **"I was about to write: and I heard a voice from heaven saying to me, Seal up those things that the seven thunders said, and *do not write them*"** (v. 4). (EKJV)

The Mighty Angel's Oath

Text: Rev. 10:5-6
Rev. 10:5 And the angel that I *saw standing* on the sea and on the earth raised his right hand to heaven, 6 And he swore by him that lives forever and ever, who created heaven, and *everything in it,* and the earth, and everything in it, and the seas, and *everything in them, that there should be no more delay:* (EKJV)

We are very familiar with being called upon to swear an oath of truth in the court room. The angel **"raised his right hand to heaven, 6 And he swore by him that lives forever and ever, who created** heaven, and *everything in it,* and the earth, and everything in it, and the seas, and *everything in them* ..." (cf. 10:5-6). What was the oath? The oath was that **"Time shall be no more"** or **"There shall be no more delay."** There comes a time when God, who has patiently given mankind every opportunity, will wait no longer. The angel's oath is to affirm and assure all that his testimony is true. God will delay no longer!

The Seventh Angel Is About to Sound His Trumpet At Last (10:7)

Text: Rev. 10:7
Rev. 11:7 **But in the days of the voice of the seventh angel, when he** *begins* **to sound** *his trumpet,* **the mystery of God** *will be* **finished, as he** *has* **declared to his servants the prophets.** (EKJV)

The profound **"mystery of God** *will be* **finished."** He has revealed or announced the fact to **"his servants the prophets."** What is the mystery? It is that Israel will be saved, according to Paul. (See Chapter 7). God's plan for the end did not come together suddenly. It has been put forth in divine prophecy for many hundreds of years. We have cited these prophecies throughout this book. One of the chief reasons for God calling a prophet is to announce hundreds of years ahead of the time when God will enact an event. No one can say that God failed to give ample warning of His actions.

The Mystery of God Accomplished—Both Gentiles and Israel Will Be Saved

The primary scriptures on the mystery of God are printed here for the convenience of biblical students who desire to quickly see God's revelation to the prophets.

The prophets have long foretold these events of the mystery of God. The mystery is that the Gentiles are heirs together with Israel (Eph. 3:6). **"Christ in you, the hope of glory!"** (Col. 1:27). **"Christ in whom are hidden all the treasures of wisdom and knowledge..."** (Col. 2:2-3). God has been attempting to get Israel's attention for thousands of years. In Isaiah we are shown the teaching concerning the mystery.

119

Isa. 48:3-10

[3] I have declared the former things from the beginning; and they went forth out of my mouth, and I showed them; I did announce them suddenly, and they came to pass. [4] Because I knew that you are obstinate, and your neck is an iron sinew, and your brow *is* brass; [5] I have declared it to you from the *very* beginning; before it came to pass I *revealed it to* you lesT I defer mine anger *and you would say*, My idol has done these things, and my graven image, and my molten image, have commanded them. (EKJV)

Isa. 48:9 I will defer my anger for my name's sake, and for my praise I I will refrain *my anger* for you and I will not cut you off. *NOTE: The mystery concerning Israel.*

[10] Behold, I have refined you, but not with silver; I have chosen you when *you were* in the furnace of affliction.

Paul Explains This in Romans and Ephesians

Rom. 11:25 *Brothers,* I do not want you to be ignorant of this mystery, lest you should be wise in your own conceits; that *a partial* blindness has happened to Israel, until the fullness of the Gentiles have come in. [26] And so all Israel shall be saved: as it is written, The Deliverer, will come out of Zion, and will turn ungodliness away from Jacob: [27] For this is my covenant to them, when I shall take away their sins.

Rom. 16:25 Now to him *who* has power to establish you according to my gospel, and the preaching of Jesus Christ, <u>according to the revelation of the mystery</u>, which was kept secret since the world began, [26] But now is made manifest, and by the scriptures of the prophets, according to the commandment of the everlasting God, *has been* <u>made known to all nations</u> for the obedience of faith: — (EKJV; cf. Eph. 3:3, 6 9-10; Col. 1:26-27; 1 Tim. 3:1—**Christ...appeared in the flesh...was taken up to glory**").

Ephesians 1:7-10

[7] In whom we have redemption through his blood, the forgiveness of sins, according to the riches of his grace; [8] Wherein he has abounded toward us in all wisdom and *insight*; [9] Having made known to us the mystery of his will, according to his good pleasure which he purposed in himself: [10] That in the dispensation (or *plan*) of the fullness of times he might gather together, in Him, all things in Christ, both *that* are in heaven, and *that* are on earth: (EKJV)

Ephesians 3:2-6

[2] **If you have heard of the dispensation (or <u>commission</u>) of the grace of God which is given to me *for you*. [3] How he made known to me by revelation the mystery; (as I wrote *before* in *a* few words, [4] *So that*, when you read, you may understand my *own* knowledge *of* the mystery of Christ) [5] Which in other ages was not made known to the sons of men, as it is now revealed to his holy apostles and prophets by the Spirit; [6] That the Gentiles should be fellow heirs, and of the same body, and partakers of his promise in Christ *through* the gospel:** (EKJV

How could you make this any clearer? But read on in Colossians. It all happens at the end time when everything is placed under the Lordship of Christ. It may be difficult for us to comprehend because our eyes may not be fully opened, but Paul explains it in order that we can have **"complete understanding."**

Col. 1:25-27

[25] **Because I am made a minister, according to the dispensation (NIV = "commission") of God which is given to me for you, to ful-fill the word of God; [26] Even the mystery which has been hidden from ages *past* and from *many* generations, but now is *revealed plainly* to his saints: [27] To whom God would make known the rich-es of the glory of this mystery among the Gentiles; which is Christ in you, the hope of glory:** (EKJV)

Col. 2:2 My purpose is that their hearts might be comforted, being joined together in love, and that they might have the full riches of assured understanding, and have the knowledge of the mystery of God which is Christ; [3] In whom are hidden all the treasures of wisdom and knowledge.

The mystery means that God will unite the saved of all the nations and all the ages in Christ. Thus, the same Christ returns to complete the work of salvation among the Gentiles and the Jews, thereby ac-complishing the mystery of God. The mystery will be accomplished in the days of the proclamation of the seventh angel (10:7).

THE TINY BOOK (SCROLL)

Text: Rev. 10:8-11

Rev. 10:8 **Then the voice that I had heard *speaking* from heaven spoke to me once more: "Go, take the scroll that lies open in the**

hand of the angel who is standing on the sea and on the land."
[9] So I went to the angel and asked him to give me the little scroll.
He said to me, "Take it and eat it. It will turn your stomach sour,
but in your mouth it will be as sweet as honey. [10] I took the little
scroll from the angel's hand and ate it. It tasted as sweet as honey in my mouth, but when I had eaten it, my stomach turned
sour. [11]Then I was told, "You must prophesy again about many
peoples, nations, languages and kings. (EKJV)

John heard the voice from heaven once again. **"Go, take the
scroll that lies open in the hand of the angel who is standing on the sea and on the land"** (v. 8). John complied and when
he asked the angel if he might take the scroll, the angel said, **"Take
it and eat it. It will turn your stomach sour, but in your
mouth it will be as sweet as honey"** (10:9). It was just as the
angel stated. His stomach turned sour, but the message when he
proclaimed it was sweet as honey. We face what seems an endless
and even hopeless task.

It Is Bitter to Your Stom-
ach,
But Sweet to Your Mouth

at times, in preaching the gospel of Christ, but the message is
sweet when we deliver it according to God's design. John's new assignment: **"You must prophesy again about many people, nations, languages and kings."** (Cf. Rev. 7–the discussion of the
multitude without number is composed of these same four groups).
It is certainly not an easy task, or even one to be desired naturally,
but it is God's magnificent plan for His world and all who live in it.
But notice! It is sour in his stomach because of its contents. It contains the message of God's final wrath.

Old Testament Connection

Ezek. 2:9 **And when I looked, I saw a hand *stretched* out to me; with
a *scroll in it;* [10] And he *spread it out before me*; and it *was* written
on both sides with words of lamentations, and mourning, and
woe**. (EKJV)

Ezek. 3:1 **And he said to me, Son of man, eat *what you see before
you*, eat the scroll, and go speak to the house of Israel. [2] So I**

opened my mouth, and he caused me to eat that scroll. [3] **And he said to me, Son of man,** *eat the scroll,* **and fill** *your stomach* **with it. Then I ate** *it;* **and in my mouth it tasted sweet like honey.** (EKJV)

Jer. 15:16 **Your words were found, and I ate them; and Your word was the joy and rejoicing of my heart: for I am called by your name, O LORD God of hosts.**

REVELATION 11-14

Critical Issues and Questions in Revelation
(These are for your personal study and thought)

1. The measuring of **the holy temple**: where is this temple (11:1)?
2. The exclusion of **the outer court**: what is the meaning (11:2)?
3. The holy city is **to be trampled for 42 months** (11:2). What does prophecy tell us? (Luke 21:24; Isaiah 5:3-7; Isaiah 63:18; Daniel 8:9-14—especially in v. 13).
4. Who are the **two witnesses who appear, prophesy, are killed and resurrected**?
5. What is **the purpose of their prophecy** (11:6ff)?
6. What is the purpose and meaning of the **plagues** (11:6ff)?
7. What is the identity of the **"beast that comes from the Abyss"** (11:7)?
8. What is to be understood from **the resurrection and ascension of the two witnesses into heaven** (11:11-12)?
9. What is meant by the terms **42 months** (11:2), and **1260 days** (11:3)? Note the term 42 months in Rev. 13:5.
10. Is the meaning of the **1260 days** (11:3) and the **1260 days** (12:6) essentially the same?
11. How does the term **"time, times and half a time"** (12:14) relate to the above figures of time?
12. What is the identity of **the dragon with seven heads and ten horns?**
13. What is the identity of **the expectant heavenly "woman clothed with the sun, and the moon under her feet and a crown of twelve stars on her head"** (12:1f)?
14. Who is the woman's **male child**?
15. What is the understanding of the **"war in heaven"** (12:7)?

16. How are we to understand the **"war against the rest of her offspring"** (12:17)?
17. Who are these on earth **"who obey God's commandments and hold to the testimony of Jesus"** after the rapture or catching up when Christ returns (12:17)?
18. Who are the **saints** mentioned in Rev. 13:7, 10 and 14:12 since we assume that this scene occurs after the rapture? Consider Rev. 14:6.
19. What is the **mark of the beast** (13:16)?
20. What is the purpose of **the two harvests** (grain and grapes—Rev. 14:14-20)?

Chapter 11

THE ASSAULT AND EXECUTION OF THE TWO FAITHFUL WITNESSES

Snapshot of Chapter 11

John is introduced to God's two faithful messengers who resemble Moses and Elijah. They are the witnesses in the Great Tribulation, and will be killed but resurrected after three days. They remind us of passages in Zechariah, and we have a Select Section on this Old Testament character. Christ assumes His eternal role vss. 15-18). Finally, John sees the ark of the covenant in heaven to bring it all to a glorious close.

John reveals an approaching day of unprecedented persecution and suffering, but also a day of glory and power as God raises His two prophets to life after their slaughter.

The Measuring of the Temple and
The Trampling of the Holy City

Text: Rev. 11:1-2

Rev. 11:1 **I was given a reed like a measuring rod and was told, "Go and measure the temple of God and the altar, with its worshipers. ² But exclude the outer court; do not measure it, because it has**

been given to the Gentiles. They will trample on the holy city for 42 months. (Easy KJV)

John receives a **"measuring rod"** and is instructed **to "Go and measure the temple of God and the altar, with its worshipers"** (v. 1). There is an Old Testament connection for this. In Ezekiel 43:13-16 the prophet is provided with the measurements of the great altar. Regarding the trampling of the **"holy city,"** the Gentiles, or the nations, will have control and dominion of the outer court. This is the one occasion when the Gentiles are mentioned in Revelation (11:2). **"They will trample on the holy city..."** (v. 2; for further reference: Isa. 5:3-7; Isa. 63:18; Ezek. 26:10-12; Dan. 8:9-11; Luke 21:24).

We have Jesus' specific prophecy that **the Gentile will trod or trample down Jerusalem:** [Luke 21:24] **And they will fall *by* the edge of the sword, and shall be led away captive into all nations: and Jerusalem shall be trodden down *by* the Gentiles, until the times of the Gentiles is fulfilled.** (EKJV)

In other words, nothing will be sacred. This happened under the Babylonians (587-586 BC). It happened under the Romans in 70 AD. Today, the Islamic religion controls the temple mount where the temple once stood. The trampling down in history is continuous, but far from total domination since 1948. In the period mentioned here, all of Jerusalem will be overrun, and controlled by those who oppose God. In Revelation 11, the time frame of the desecration will be 42 months. Remember this time period. The period of 42 months equals three and one-half years.

These Two Prophecy Clothed in Sackcloth for 1260 Days

Text: Rev. 11:3
³ **And I will appoint my two witnesses, and they will prophesy for 1,260 days, clothed in sackcloth."**

At this time God is going **to "appoint my two witnesses, and they will prophesy for 1260 days, clothed in sackcloth"** (11:3). How does 1260 days relate to the 42 months spelled out in verse 2? The two periods are precisely the same. Both equal three and one-half years. Sackcloth is the garb of confession and repentance. They are clothed in sackcloth to illustrate the need for deep repentance on the part of the world.

Old Testament Connection

In Chapter 11, John's vision assumes that his readers have a strong familiarity with the Old Testament. This is true throughout the four visions of Revelation. For example, Zechariah is one of my favorite Old Testament books. It is among the books we call the Minor Prophets, not because they are unimportant, but because they are rather brief.

Two Apocalyptic Books: Zechariah and Revelation

Zechariah, like Revelation, is what we call an apocalyptic book. They both contain visions explained by an angel. In the scene connected to Zechariah, we find a single lampstand, but it has seven branches. It is the symbol of Israel today and is known as the Menorah. The next two scenes tell about God's two prophets. The things explained about these two remind us, first of Moses, who called down ten plagues upon Egypt; and Elijah, perhaps most famous among the original Old Testament prophets, who caused it not to rain on the earth (Rev. 11:6). I will attempt to connect these two prophets and the vision related to Zechariah in the following optional section. The "Exclusive Select Section" is for those who want a deeper understanding.

SS

Select Section

The Two Olive Trees

The Amazing Power of God's Redemption
In the Life of Zerubbabel

At the mention of the two olive trees in Revelation 11 any of John's readers with Jewish background would immediately remember Zerubbabel in the unfolding history of God's people. Why? First, you will miss the crucial meaning of the mention of two olive trees and the lampstands if you miss this miracle of God in Zerubbabel's life. **Who was he?** He was descended in the royal line from David. He was the son of Shealtiel, and more importantly, the grandson of Jehoiachin. Jehoiachin (a variant of his name is Koniah or Coniah; also Jeconiah in 1 Chron. 3:17) was not only counted among the wicked kings, as opposed to the righteous kings, in the line of David; but God placed a curse on him and his descendants through the prophet Jeremiah. He only served as a puppet king for three months and then was carried away to Babylon in the captivity. Eventually, he was released from prison and he was fed at the king's table, and provided a stipend as long as he lived, but the awful curse remained.

A Young Man Rose Like Cream to the Top of Milk

We fast forward to the end of the Babylonian captivity and the return to the holy land. A young man named Zerubbabel was quickly recognized as a very effective leader among the exiles who were permitted to return to the destroyed city of Jerusalem. He is mentioned frequently in the book of Ezra and also in Nehemiah. But for our purposes we must consider the books of the prophets Haggai and Zechariah. Homes had been built in Jerusalem by the returned exiles, but the temple was merely a pile of material on the ground.

Who will arise as a leader with the ability to muster the people to rebuild the temple? This young man named Zerubbabel was a chief candidate, but he knew, as did hundreds of others, that he was born under a curse. How could he become such a leader? First Haggai the prophet announced that God annulled the curse in regard to Zerubbabel. In Jeremiah 22 we find the horrible curse.

Jer. 22:24 **As I live, says the LORD, though Coniah the son of Jehoiakim king of Judah were the signet *ring* upon my right hand, yet would I *pull you off*; ²⁵ And I will give you into the hand of them that seek to kill you, and into the hand of those that you fear most, into the hand of Nebuchadrezzar king of Babylon, and into the hand of the Chaldeans.** (Easy KJV)

Jer. 22:30 **The LORD says, Write this man childless, a man who will not prosper in his lifetime: and none of his children will prosper, and none will sit upon the throne of David, and rule any more in Judah.**

The Curse Is Removed

This was the terrible curse on Zerubbabel's grandfather. How could there be any hope for him? But God had a plan. The prophet Haggai is sent to remove the curse from Zerubbabel. ^{Haggai 2:23} **In that day, says the LORD of hosts, I will take you, O Zerubbabel, my servant, the son of Shealtiel, says the LORD, and I will make you as my signet ring: for I have chosen you says the LORD of hosts.**

Thus, God removed the curse, but Zerubbabel faced an impossible assignment. God must encourage him in this assignment. That brings us to Zechariah.

The Mystery of the Two Olive Trees

Text: Rev. 11:4
^{Rev. 11:4} **These are the two olive trees, and the two lampstands standing before the God of the earth.**

In both Zechariah and Revelation we have the **"two olive trees"** (Zech. 4:3, 11; Rev. 11:4) plus the **"lampstand(s)"** (Zech. 4:11; Rev. 11:4). In Rev. 11:4 it is explained to John that the two witnesses in Revelation **"are two olive trees"** and two lampstands. This vision is quite different from what we find in Zechariah, because here the two prophets are said to be both two olive trees **AND** two lampstands. But in both books it states they stand **"before the Lord of the earth"** (NIV). So how are we to understand the two olive trees and the lampstands? The lampstands were first constructed as God commanded and instructed Moses in the days following the Exodus. Initially they were used in the tabernacle (a portable tent of worship), but when Solomon built the temple in Jerusalem they were brought into the new house of God.

The lampstands are in focus again in Zechariah 4 where Solomon's temple had been destroyed and Israel had returned to their land after seventy years of captivity. The Babylonians had leveled the city and left the temple in a pile of ruins. Nothing representing their faith in God was left, and now it must all be constructed once again. Enormous discouragement fell upon the entire fledging nation.

But under Zerubbabel the mountain of obstacles will become the level ground of success (Zech. 4:7). His hands will complete the temple and he will see the capstone placed on it (Zech. 4:8-9). "...**and you will know that the LORD of hosts has sent me to you.**" Obviously, they should not despise **"the day of small things"** such as the meager beginnings of the new temple (Zech. 4:10). Here we have a great encouragement of faith in God who never fails.

The future is also bleak in the account in Revelation. Great tribulation is going to fall upon the world prior to the end of creation, and the judgment of God. In both cases, no matter the difficulty, the prophets can be assured of completing their mission under the Spirit of **"the LORD of the whole earth."** It appears that this exact phrase is found only one additional time in scripture when Joshua told the priests who carried the **"ark of the covenant"** that the flow of water through the Jordan would cease the moment they placed their feet into the water (Joshua 3:13-14).

Zechariah Reveals God's Eternal Plan for Messiah and for the World

The angel explained to Zechariah that the two olive trees that furnished oil continually to the golden lampstand were intended to represent the word of God that shall never be extinguished, as we interpret the visions. God's light will never be extinguished. The scene is not about olive oil; it is about the mighty power of God to supply His messengers with the ability to deliver His word to the world. A lamp connected directly to an olive tree will never lack fuel, and the source of the oil for this lamp will never be exhausted. A prophet under the Spirit of the Lord will always deliver God's word despite obstacles, opposition, and contrary opinions. Zechariah is a book of Messianic prophecy certain to be fulfilled.

Satan Condemns Joshua, the High Priest

The opposition to God in that day was seen in the work of Satan, the adversary, who discouraged the ministry of Joshua, the High Priest (Zech. 3:1-7); and the construction of a new temple under Zerubbabel. Satan was correct in his charge that Joshua's garments were filthy rather than spotless. No doubt, there was no one yet capable of making the required robes and accessories. Joshua was wearing all that he had. And in what seems a miracle, the angel transformed Joshua's garments into beautiful and proper ones. Satan is always at war with God as we shall also see in Revelation 12.

Satan laid charges against Joshua, but initially not against Zerubbabel most likely because he felt that the curse would eliminate Zerubbabel. How wrong he was! God had matters well in hand. He can take a person the world discounts and do wonderful things beyond our belief and understanding.

Cyrus, the Persian king, had sent the exiles home under a temporary provincial governor. He was to construct the temple, but he lacked commitment to the work, and he only laid the foundation and stopped.

Ezra 5:16 **Then the same Sheshbazzar came and laid the foundation of the house of God in Jerusalem: and *from* that time until now it has been *under construction*, and *still* is not finished.** (EKJV)

Ezra 5:1 **Then the prophets, Haggai the prophet, and Zechariah the son of Iddo, prophesied unto the Jews that were in Judah and Jerusalem in the name of the God of Israel. ² Then Zerubbabel the son of Shealtiel *ascended to the task*, and Jeshua the son of Jozadak, and began to build the house of God which is in Jerusalem.** (EKJV)

But under Zerubbabel the temple will be completed. It would rest on the same spot until forty years after the death and resurrection of Christ, although there would be periods of destruction and sacrilege. The temple was where the people met God in worship. The people were encouraged because "**the prophets of God were with them**" (Zechariah and Joshua). But the future looks forward to one greater than the temple. Read on!

Prophesy: Christ Is the Branch and the Stone (Zech. 2:8-10)

Christ, "**the Branch**" (Zech. 3:8; cf. Is. 4:2; 11:1; Jer. 23:5; 33:15) "**will remove the sin of this land in a single day**" (Zech. 3:9). This chapter looks to the day of the Millennium (Rev. 20) when there will be a day of peace, comfort and prosperity (3:10). Christ is the (corner or foundation) **stone** (Zech. 3:10; Ps. 118:22; Is. 28:6; Mt. 21:4; Mk. 12:10; Acts 4:11; 1 Peter 2:6-8). The eternal gospel of our Savior Christ is forecast in these prophecies. As John views the new vision, he remembered the significance of Zerubbabel's place in God's plan. He understood how God was speaking through the vision in his day.

Zerubbabel Is in the Line of Christ in Both Mary and Joseph

The greater messages of the angel were very powerful to Zerubbabel, an ancestor of Christ (Matt. 1:12-13; Luke. 4:27). Zerubbabel is in the line of both Mary and Joseph. Zerubbabel was born under the curse God placed on his family (Jer. 22:24), but the Lord removed the curse for Zerubbabel the day that He chose him (Haggai 2:3). The life of Zerubbabel would result in the birth of Christ, the Savior of the world, and ultimately the church. He was a conduit of the line of David miraculously restored by God Himself.

The Lord Revealed that His Spirit Will Bring This About

Like many today, Zerubbabel had no clue what God would do through him. These are words of amazing hope and encouragement in God's astounding promise to His servant Zerubbabel. Zech. 4:6 **Then he answered and *said to* me, This is the word of the LORD to Zerubbabel: Not by might, nor by power, but by my Spirit, *says* the LORD of hosts.** (KJV)

The angel must explain the meaning to Zechariah, just as the angel must explain the vision before John's eyes. Remember that apocalyptic literature uses powerful symbols to express divine truth. The symbol is not the truth, but the symbol represents the truth. It is an example chosen by the Lord.

> Zech. 4:11 **Then I answered and said to him, What are these two olive trees on the right side of the lampstands and on the left side? 12 And I *asked another question*, What are these two olive branches that empty the golden oil out of themselves through the two golden pipes? 13 And he *replied*, Don't you know what these are? And I said, No, my lord. 14 Then he said, These are the two *who are* anointed *to* stand by the LORD of the whole earth**. (EKJV)

The vision of the two olive trees is similar in Zechariah 4 and Revelation 11. Both are meant to symbolize the word of God. In both cases, God's two servants are said to be **"olive trees"** directly supplying oil for God's lamps (Zech. 4:14). Just as the olive oil sends light out to the world through the lampstand(s), so the same is true through God's two prophets who serve as His messengers during the final days of planet earth (See Zech. 4:1-2). You see this clearly in the scriptures above..

Rev. 11:3 **"And I will appoint my two witnesses, and they will prophesy for 1,260 days, clothed in sackcloth."** [4] **These are the two olive trees, and the two *lampstands standing before the God of the earth.*** (EKJV)

Both Zerubbabel and the Two Prophets Were Appointed, Anointed or Chosen by God (Zech. 4:14; Rev. 11:3-4)

In summary, allow me to be redundant. The NIV translation expresses the same origin of purpose for the prophets in both Zechariah 4:3-14 and in Rev. 11:3. In Zech. 4:14 (NIV) we read "**These are the two who are anointed** to **serve the Lord of all the earth**." In Rev. 11:4 we have the same language regarding the two prophets who are similar to Moses and Elijah: "**they stand before the Lord of the earth**." To stand before the Lord in His service is a remarkable thought. This is not a coincidence nor is it a mistake. All true prophets serve under the God who is "**the Lord of all the earth**." The two passages reveal the fulfillment of divine prophecy, first in the days of the second temple and Zechariah when they faced overwhelming obstacles, and in Revelation in the days of John, and the terrible occurrences accompanying the end of the earth.

The Select Section on Zerubbabel Ends Here

The Two Prophets Are Shielded from Harm for Three and One-half Years

Text: Rev. 11:5
[5] **If anyone tries to harm them, fire comes from their mouths and devours their enemies. This is how anyone who wants to harm them must die.**
During the three and one-half years no harm will or can come to them. They are on a mission established by God that will not be in-

terrupted. Therefore, **"If anyone tries to harm them, fire comes from their mouths and devours them"** (v. 5). That is graphic and powerful. After a few have attempted to harm them the rest will be terrified of them. God has not left them defenseless.

Text: Rev. 11:6
^{Rev. 11:6} **They have power to shut up the heavens so that it will not rain during the time they are prophesying; and they have power to turn the waters into blood and to strike the earth with every kind of plague as often as they want.** (Easy KJV)

Old Testament Connection
They Are Like Elijah and Moses
Elijah was the prophet who shut up the heavens that it should not rain. The Lord will work through His two future prophets as He worked through these two ancient prophets. Moses was God's anointed who turned the waters of Egypt into blood, and who called down the plagues on Pharaoh and the people of Egypt. Also see the passages below where similar plagues are to be sent on the earth in the last days as seen through John's visions.

The Purpose of the Plagues in Egypt—Exodus 7:17ff; cf. Ex. 4:5
The Purpose of the Plagues: that you may **"know that I am the Lord."** The plagues were an affirmation of God's unlimited power.

The Result of the Plagues of Blood
All fish died. All water was contaminated. Blood is the **most repugnant** of all contamination. Repeatedly, God promised Israel's enemies blood to drink. It is as if to promise them death.

The Response to the Plagues
The point is that **Pharaoh ignored** even this act of God. Some years ago a great flood was experienced in Macon and other Georgia cities. It left 150,000 plus people without potable drinking water. We could ask: What did the citizens learn at that time? We are always experiencing terrifying and troubling events, but repentance is not long evident. We do not make the distinction **that God is warning us**. The magicians of Egypt counterfeited each plague. Pharaoh persisted in self-hardened unbelief and rejection. Israel also later rebelled against God. See Psalm 78:44 and Psalm 105:29.

The Second Angel's Trumpet

Rev. 8:8 **And the second angel sounded, and as it were a great mountain *ablaze* with fire was cast into the sea: and the third part of the sea became blood; ⁹ And the third part of the living creatures which were in the sea died; and the third part of the ships were destroyed.** (Easy KJV)

The Third Angel's Bowl (Rev. 16:4)
(Notice the similarity with Rev. 8:8)

Rev. 16:4 **The third angel poured out his bowl on the rivers and springs of water, and <u>they became blood</u>.**

The Two Witnesses Complete Their Mission

We are not compelled to see these two witnesses as Elijah and Moses, but at least they represent what God did in the days of these two. But this goes much further than God's two former notable prophets as we shall soon see. They will complete the mission God has sent them to accomplish, and then they will face death.

The Beast Who Kills Them (v. 7)
Is a Figure of Antichrist

Text: Rev. 11:7

Rev. 11:7 **And when they have finished their testimony, the beast that ascends out of the bottomless pit shall *wage* war against them, and shall overcome them, and kill them.**

> Matt. 24:15 **"So when you see standing in the holy place '<u>the abomination that causes desolation,' spoken of through the prophet Daniel</u>...let the reader understand—²¹ For then there will be great distress, unequaled from the beginning of the world until now—and never to be equaled again. ²² "<u>If those days had not been cut short, no one would survive</u>, but for the sake of the elect <u>those days will be shortened</u>. (See also Mk. 13:14)** Note: Keep the shortening of days in mind until we return to them.

Remember the Abyss from Chapter 9? We did not see the beast there; thus this is the first mention of him, but we see him come out of the Abyss in Rev. 17:8 to go to his final destruction (Rev. 19:20). This beast is the epitome of unrelenting evil. The two prophets do not die without a battle. He attacks them **"and** *(he will)* **overpower and kill them"** (11:7). The beast is the figure of the Antichrist who is so evident in Jewish and Christian belief. Jesus spoke of the **"abomination that causes desolation"**—the one who commits unmitigated sacrilege.

Christ speaks here of Daniel 7:8:
Dan 7:8 I considered the horns, and *just then*, **there came up another little horn, and three of the first horns** *were* **plucked up by the roots: and,** *I saw*, *that* **this horn had eyes like the eyes of man, and a mouth speaking** *boastful things*. (Easy KJV)

> **Dan. 7:20** **And of the ten horns that** *were* **on his head, and** *of* **the other that came up, and before whom three fell; even** *of* **the horn that had eyes, and a mouth that spoke very great things, who appeared** *stronger* **than** *the others.* [21] **I** *watched*, **and the same horn made war with the saints, and prevailed against them;** [22] **Until the Ancient of days came, and judgment was given** *in favor of* **the saints of the most High; and the time came that the saints possessed the kingdom.** (EKJV)

"The beast was given a mouth to utter proud words and blasphemies and to exercise his authority for forty-two months" (Rev. 13:5). This arrogant, boastful enemy of the people of God will meet his end. He will be thrown into the lake of fire (Rev. 19:20). **"... I continued looking until the beast was slain, and his body destroyed, and thrown into the burning flame"** (Dan. 7:11b; cf. Rev. 19:20). There is much more commentary when we get to Chapter 13.

> **Dan. 7:25** **And he** *will* **speak** *condemnation* **against the most High, and will** *tear down* **His saints, and** *attempt* **to change times and laws: and they shall be given into his hand for time, times and half a time.** (cf. Dan. 12:7). Again, remember *this period of time*. It is precisely the same as we find in Revelation.

The Death and Resurrection of the Two Prophets
Text: Rev. 11:8-10

⁸ And their dead bodies shall lie in the street of the great city, which spiritually is called Sodom and Egypt, where our Lord also was crucified. ⁹ And some of those from the people and *tribes and languages* and nations shall see their dead bodies for three and a half days, and shall not permit their dead bodies to be buried. ¹⁰ And some of *inhabitants* of the earth shall rejoice and celebrate, and shall send gifts to one another; because these two prophets had tormented those that live on the earth. (Easy KJV)

The city of the death of the two prophets is Jerusalem, but it is **"spiritually is called Sodom and Egypt"** (v. 8). We know that the city is Jerusalem because John writes that it is the city **"where our Lord also was crucified."** Their bodies will lie in the public square for **"three and a half days."** The entire world is not evil, but **"some from the people and tribal groups and languages and nations shall gawk over their dead bodies for three and a half days, and shall not permit their dead bodies to be buried."** (v. 9). The world will feel as they do at Christmas; they will have holidays, celebrations and the exchange of gifts because of the death of God's two prophets. Such is the unrelenting refusal to repent on the part of these who reject redemption through Christ.

The Two Prophets Come to Life After Three and a Half Days

Text: Rev. 11:11-12

Rev. 11:11 And after three and an half days the breath of life from God entered them, and they stood upon their feet; and great fear fell upon them that saw them. ¹² And they heard a loud voice from heaven saying to them, Come up here. And they ascended up to heaven in a cloud; and their enemies witnessed it.

They are resurrected not unlike the resurrection of Lazarus or even Christ. Everyone was satisfied that both Lazarus and Christ were permanently dead only to discover how wrong they were. God fully restored life in these two. And without further delay, the resurrected prophets are summoned up to heaven. **"Come up here,"** they are told. **"And they ascended up to heaven in a cloud; and their enemies witnessed it."** (v. 12). What a glorious moment of assurance John experienced in this vision.

Great Destruction Falls Upon the City
Text: Rev. 11:13
^{Rev. 11:13} **And the same hour there was a great earthquake, and a tenth of the city fell, and seven thousand people were killed by the earthquake: and the rest were afraid and glorified to the God of heaven.**

A great earthquake strikes the city. A tenth is a token. It is an example to the rest. If ten percent perished we could conclude that about 70,000 people occupied the city. Life and structures were destroyed in a tenth of the city. The example had the desired effect. **"The rest were afraid and glorified the God of heaven"** (v. 13). What will it require for people to repent when this actually takes place?

THE THIRD WOE
Text: Rev. 11:14
^{Rev. 11:14} **The second woe is past; and the third woe is coming quickly.**

A **"woe"** is a severe warning of the result of the wrong kind of life or activity. Two awesome **"woes"** are past and **"the third woe is coming..."** He wants us to be prepared for what is ahead. Get ready!

The Seventh Trumpet—the Rewarding of the Saints and the Wrath of God
The very thing that the scriptures have prophesied through all the years is commencing. **"Our Lord and his Messiah"** are assuming their everlasting reign (Rev. 11:13-18).

The Everlasting Kingdom of Christ Will Appear
Text: Rev. 11:15-18
^{Rev. 11:15} **And the seventh angel sounded; and there were *loud* voices in heaven, saying, <u>The kingdoms of this world have become the kingdoms of our Lord, and of his Christ; and he shall reign forever and ever.</u> ¹⁶ And the twenty-four elders, that sat on their thrones before God, fell on their faces, and worshiped God, ¹⁷ Saying, We give you thanks, O LORD God Almighty, who is, and was, and is to come; because you have taken your great power, and are now reigning. ¹⁸ And the nations were angry, and your**

wrath has come, and the time has arrived to judge the dead, and <u>reward your servants the prophets, and the saints</u>, and those that reverence your name, small and great; and to destroy those who destroy the earth.

Finally, Christ is Lord of all. He is in His eternally rightful place over all creation as Lord of lords, and King of kings. Once again the twenty-four elders we saw in Chapter 4 are speaking. They are expressing the everlasting purpose of God throughout history now being accomplished. God's mighty power is affirmed. The angry nations are called to judgment. The dead will hear their sentence. The saints will experience the glorious rewards of the saved. **"The time has arrived... to destroy those who destroy the earth."** (11:18; cf. Gen. 6:11-17). We should take note that God has assigned the stewardship of the earth to its inhabitants.

John Saw the Ark of the Covenant in Heaven (11:19)
Text: Rev. 11:19
¹⁹ **And the temple of God was opened in heaven, and the ark of his testament was visible in his temple: and there were lightning, and voices, and thundering, and an earthquake, and great hail.**

John is shown the ark of the covenant (or **"testament"** in the KJV) in heaven. A host of frightening heavenly signs are directed toward the earth in preparation for and warning of the final wrath of God. No one can say that God did not give them every opportunity. Both the rewards of the saints and the wrath of God upon the wicked are yet to be fully explained in Revelation. This will come in Revelation 19-22.

The ark of the covenant was settled in the Holy of holies in the earthly tabernacle and temple. We have been looking for the ark of the covenant as if it is something we need to find as a sort of consecrated element of worship today. John, in effect, said, "Don't look for the ark!" The ark was for that ancient day and time of the tabernacle and the temple, and John sees it in the last days of earth, permanently located in the eternal heavenly temple.

Compare Rev. 11:19 to Rev. 8:5. In Rev. 8:5 and 11:19 we see almost identical responses from heaven with the exception of the hail mentioned in Rev. 11:19 This is what we call a "theophany." The theophany signifies God's final wrath and judgment upon the earth and it should be taken very seriously. We are stewards of God's earth.

Summary

Many people believe, but they do not believe in Christ crucified, resurrected, and Savior. Many Christians are surprised to learn that Muslims believe: in the virgin birth of Christ, that Christ ascended into heaven, and that He is coming again to judge the dead. Those people say, "Well, they must be Christians!" But a lot of people believe these three things and they are not Christians. One BIG fact is missing. They leave out the fact that He died on a cross and God raised Him from the dead thereby to become the one and only Savior of the world.

In Revelation, Jesus will come after Moses and Elijah appear, but it is the Lamb of God we are looking for. Revelation 11 brings us to the Seventh Trumpet Blast, but it isn't what we were expecting. There is a solemn but joyful celebration in heaven because the reign of Christ has begun. Thus, the wrath of God is coming upon the wicked.

Chapter 12

WAR AGAINST THE HEAVENLY MOTHER AND HER CHILDREN
The Pregnant Woman, the Messiah, and the Monstrous Red Dragon

---

Snapshot of Chapter 12

The woman represents Israel, the people of God who fulfill the line of Christ the Messiah. Her other children represent the church—the redeemed in Christ. The red dragon is Satan, the evil one and the Devil. He is filled with confidence, but he becomes more violent with each failure to destroy the people of God. Satan is forced from heaven by war with Michael, the Archangel, who throws him down to earth. In this chapter we meet: the heavenly mother, the Great Red Serpent, Michael, and the children of the heavenly woman (the church, including those redeemed from Israel).

COMMENTARY ON REVELATION 12
The First Scene: The Heavenly Mother and Satan's Evil Strategy
The Birth of the Messiah (12:1-6)

Text: Rev. 12:1-2

Rev. 12:1 **And there appeared a great sign in heaven; a woman clothed with the sun, and the moon under her feet, and a crown of twelve stars on her head: ² And she was about to give birth and was in great pain.** (Easy KJV)

This amazing chapter is filled to the brim with astounding prophecies. The heavenly mother, the great red dragon, the war in heaven, Satan's pursuit of the people of God—the church, and the great tribulation all prepare us for the rise of Satan's two beasts in chapter 13.

The First Sign in Heaven—the Heavenly Woman's Dual Role

She represents the Israel of God—the line of the Messiah. (She is not Mary.) From Israel came the Messiah. We can see Satan's intent is to destroy the child of God. The dragon in front of the pregnant woman is a pretty awesome and fearful sight. The situation, by all appearances, is hopeless. But Satan cannot thwart God's plans.

She Is the Mother of the Church—God's People on Earth

The Great Red Dragon (12:3) is the visionary figure for Satan: the enemy of the woman and her child. Rev. 12:1 tells us that in the existence of the **"woman"** there is **"a great and wondrous sign...in heaven."** The Greek for sign is **semeion**. In the scriptures, a **"sign"** is something that points to a great truth or event.

Luke 11:30 **For <u>as Jonah was a sign unto the Ninevites, <u>so shall the Son of man also be to this generation</u>.** (Easy KJV)

THE WOMAN'S DESCRIPTION

- She is "a woman clothed with the sun" (12:1).
- "The moon *(is)* under her feet" (12:1).
- Obviously, she is enormous in size.
- "A crown of twelve stars on her head" (12:1) = the 12 tribes of Israel
- She is pregnant and will give birth to a male child (the Messiah).
- She is the heavenly mother, while in Rev. 17-18 we see the harlot woman.
- She appears in the heavenly Zion (Heb. 12:22) and represents the lasting glory of Israel, especially through the line of David, and then the Messiah.
- She is still in heaven until verse 9.
- She is to bring forth "a male child <u>who will rule all nations with a rod of iron</u>" (12:5).
- She is the mother of the messianic people (the people for whom Christ died).

She is clothed with the sun and the moon is under her feet. Her feet rise above the moon. She is glorious because her Lord is glorious. We have two important scriptures. The first is Genesis 37:9. Joseph, the Patriarch, had a dream. The dream goes like this:

Gen. 37:5 **And Joseph dreamed a dream, and he told his brothers: and they hated him *even* more. ⁶ And he said to them: I ask you to listen to the dream I had. ⁷ It is like this: We were binding sheaves in the field, and, lo, my sheaf stood upright; and, your sheaves stood round mine, and were obedient to my sheaf. ⁸ And his brothers said to him, Will you, indeed reign over us? or will you indeed have dominion over us? And they hated him all the more for his dreams, and for his words. ⁹ And he dreamed still another dream, and told his brothers, Listen, I have dreamed another dream; and, the sun and the moon and the eleven stars were obedient to me.** (EKJV)

Joseph's Dream: the Sun and the Moon Bow Down to Him

The celestial lights of our universe were paying homage to Joseph in this dream. Everything God made serves Him just as the desert serves Him (12:6). The sun and moon, so essential to life on this earth, gave unique recognition to Joseph as the one who would provide a place for Israel in Egypt to perpetuate a people for the name of our God. Again, this is Joseph's vision in a dream.

Israel's Place in God's Plan for Messiah

The heavenly mother with the moon beneath her feet and the sun surrounding her head illustrates the eternal place of Israel, God's chosen nation, together with the glory and brightness of His creation (the sun and the moon). The sun gives life and the moon gives light to humanity. God's creation depends upon them, just as all humanity depended upon Israel to serve God by providing a people from which the Messiah would come, did come, and did live among them in order to understand their lives, their heartaches, and needs, and to bring salvation to those willing to accept it, and Him. This glorious heavenly vision of the mother between the sun and moon reveals the great plan of God for His people Israel. The three stand together in their importance over this earth and humanity.

Israel's 400 Years in Egypt

These eleven brothers plus Joseph represent Israel. From them came the twelve tribes. Joseph is the forerunner of their salvation, and from their lineage, Christ, the Messiah, descended (Mt. 1:2). God sent him into Egypt to prepare a place where Israel could abide for 400 years. During this time they had no nation, no wealth, no king, no leaders, and no victories. They were slaves to the Gentiles—the Egyptians in this case. At the end of the 400 years, God raised up Moses to lead them out of Egypt to the Promised Land.

They Arrived With Nothing and Left With Wealth

When they arrived in Egypt they were few, but when they left they were millions in number. They came to Egypt out of a land of famine and starvation, but Joseph insured that there would be sufficient food for them all plus the Egyptians when famine came to Egypt. They came empty-handed, but they left with riches of gold and silver forced upon them by the families they had served. They left without a homeland but they arrived in Canaan, their new homeland. The new homeland provided them with structures, pastures, fields and cities already built by the previous pagan occupants. In every step, God had a plan.

David's Everlasting Line

Throughout the Bible we read of the twelve tribes and of the descendants from these twelve patriarchs. And in the great prophecy of God, David learns that he will have a descendant forever in the person of Messiah: Jesus Christ. Israel, as God ordained and planned, is the mother of Christianity. From her came Jesus as verified by His lineage published in Matthew and Luke. And all of this is testified to in Stephen's sermon in Acts 7:8-51. The entire history of Israel is the history of God's plan for Messiah.

Paul's Verification of the Significant Role of the Nation Israel and the Messiah

Rom. 9:4 ... *(Of)* the people of Israel. Theirs is the adoption to sonship; theirs the divine glory, the covenants, the receiving of the law, the temple worship and the promises. [5] <u>Theirs are the patriarchs, and from them is traced the human ancestry of the Messiah, who is God over all, forever praised!</u> Amen. (Easy KJV)

The moon will be established as a testimony that David's line will never end. **Ps. 89:37 It will be established forever like the moon, the faithful witness in the sky.**

Jesus said that the apostles will sit on twelve thrones judging the twelve tribes. **Matt. 19:28 Jesus said to them, "Truly I tell you, at the renewal of all things, when the Son of Man sits on his glorious throne, <u>you who have followed me will also sit on twelve thrones, judging the twelve tribes of Israel</u>.** (KJV)

Her child will **"rule all nations with a rod of iron"** (12:5; Rev. 2:27; 19:15; cf. Psalm 2:9; 110:2; **"Scepter":** Gen. 49:10; Ps.45:6; Heb.1:8). **Note: rod and scepter are the same**; cf. KJV and NIV for both).

The Second Sign *(semeion)*...in Heaven
The Great Red Dragon

Obviously by **"heaven"** John means the sky above just as he mentions the sun, moon, and stars in verse1; not the heaven of heavens where God dwells.

Text: Rev. 12:3-6

Rev. 12:3 **And another sign appeared in heaven: a great red dragon, having seven heads and ten horns, and seven crowns on his heads. [4] And his tail caught a third of the stars of heaven, and cast them to the earth: and the dragon stood before the woman that was about to give birth, to devour her child as soon as it was born. [5] And she gave birth to a son, who will rule all nations with an iron scepter: and her child was caught up to God, and *to* his throne. [6] And the woman fled into the wilderness, where she had a place prepared by God, where they would care for her there for 1260 days.** (Easy KJV)

The Heart of the Current Vision

> **John sees the continuing battle of Satan against God and all things holy. Satan wages war against the heavenly mother (Israel) and her Son (Jesus) and all of her other children (the saved throughout the ages until the end).**

Another Sign from Heaven—the Great Red Dragon

In Revelation 12:3—**"Then another sign appeared in heaven..."** What do we mean by **"sign?"** (Gk. *Semeion: καὶ ὤφθη ἄλλο σημεῖον ἐν τῷ οὐρανῷ*).

 A sign (or portent—NIV) represents a thing, event or occurrence. It is not the same as, but only points to, and illustrates the actual.

Thus a dragon, a fearful, fire-breathing creature, is a sign of the devil or Satan. Every nation, even today, understands the idea of a creature such as the dragon. The concept of this most terrible, earful and wickedly destructive of beasts is John's best image of the wicked, evil, unrelenting hatred for God and His people on the art of Satan. The size of the Pregnant Woman clothed with the sun and the great red dragon should not be lost. John saw two colossal figures. The latter figure plans to destroy the first.

He has seven heads. Seven in Hebrew thought represents the completeness of something. Normally seven reveals the complete-

146

ness of something that is desirable. But it can also express the completeness of evil as in this case. Seven heads suggests the completeness of diabolical wickedness, evil and total disobedience against God and His people. He is said to have **"ten horns"** and to wear **"seven crowns"** (12:3-4). The crowns represent rule, and the ten horns represent power and influence. The three extra horns represent greater power (perhaps the rule of additional Satan-led kings). Again, the seven crowns represent his rule over the kingdom of evil. Horns can represent righteous or evil power.

Ps. 75:10 (The God of Jacob) who says, "I will cut off the horns of all the wicked, but the horns of the righteous will be lifted up." (See Ps. 75:4-5.)

Something good can be said to be perfect or complete. Also something evil can be said to be complete in the same terminology. The seven heads demonstrate the absolute and total evil of the dragon that stands for Satan, or the Devil, or **"the evil one,"** etc. Jesus called him **"the prince of this world"** (John 12:31).

The seven heads also very likely indicate that, while Satan is certainly not omniscient, he is very busy in many, many places. He is the author of evil, the founder of discord, the initiator of all wars, the perpetuator of crime, greed, hatred, hostility, and all kinds of abuse. The seven crowns demonstrate how he infiltrates high earthly authority to carry out his desires. He controls kingdoms, dictators, national and international conspiracy, treachery, and world-wide destruction. He offered Jesus the control of the kingdoms of the world (Mt. 4:8-9).

Matt 4:8 Again, the devil took him to a very high mountain and showed him all the kingdoms of the world and their splendor. 9 "All this I will give you," he said, "if you will bow down and worship me."

Seven heads are a terrifying spectacle. They demonstrate his ability to reach in all directions and to be completely self-defensible. To meet such a creature, one knows immediately that his ability to kill and destroy is overwhelming.

THE DRAGON'S DESCRIPTION

- ➤ **He is a terrifying beast (12:3-4).**
- ➤ **He is an enormous red dragon (12:3).**
- ➤ **He has seven heads and seven crowns (12:3).**
- ➤ **He possesses ten horns (12:3).**
- ➤ **His tail is enormous in length (12:4).**
- ➤ **His tail swept a third of the stars (angels) out of the sky (12:4).**
- ➤ **This enormous red dragon stood right in front of the pregnant woman (12:4).**

He swept a third of the stars out of the sky. In Rev. 12:4 it says he caught a third of the stars of heaven with his tail and brought them down to earth. Scripture says **"he flung them down to earth"**. This indicates his haste in getting away from the throne of God. It is thought, by a number of biblical students, that these stars represent fallen angels that Satan induced to join him in his rebellion against God. At the sounding of the seventh trumpet, all authority in heaven and earth becomes the supreme and everlasting rule of Christ (cf. Rev. Chap. 11).

The number **"a third"** is generally reserved for the punishment of the wrath of God in Revelation (Rev. 8:7, 8, 9, 10, 11, 12; 9:15, 18; 12:4; etc.). The color red and fire are similar in Greek. His size alone was terrifying. In apocalyptic prophecy, this enormous size would point to his mastery of evil and his enormous hatred for God and His Son.

The great red dragon is the enemy of the woman (Israel) because the man child is the Christ. But **"her child was snatched (caught) up unto God and to his throne"** (12:5b). How long will He remain there? He is at the throne of God in heaven until the (parousia) Second Coming. He will come to raise the dead and judge the world (Ps. 96:13; 98:9; 110:6; Isa. 2:4; Mic. 4:3; Acts 10:42; **"he will judge the living and the dead:"** Acts 17:31; 2 Tim. 4:1; 1 Peter 4:5; Rev. 6:10; 20:4).

John mentions nothing of the life, ministry, death and resurrection of Christ because all of these events are certainly fully a part of the people of Christ already. He is answering the questions regarding the end of history, the end of the physical world, the end of the domination of evil (the battle of Armageddon), and the blessed fulfillment of all of God's promises to His faithful saints who are longing for the Savior's return in glory.

The Second Scene: Michael's Victory Over the Dragon (12:7-9)
War in Heaven (12:9; cf. Luke 10:18)

THE WAR IN HEAVEN

How unthinkable that war would break out in heaven. But rebellion can take place anywhere in heaven or on earth. Satan lusted for power. He was not satisfied to serve the Lord as an angel. He would not submit to the authority of God. He desired to be in charge of both heaven and earth. We know from Job that he had been occupied with spying out the earth to map a strategy for a takeover. God confronted him. God gave him the opportunity to explain himself, although He certainly knew Satan's desires and his evil propensity and potential.

Imagine this scene. Satan is fighting against God. But God doesn't lift a finger, so to speak. He taps Michael for this battle. Michael is mentioned three times in Daniel and once in Jude in addition to this passage. In the article on angels near the first of this book, Michael is identified as the "Military Angel." Michael came to Daniel's aid against the rulers of Persia (Dan. 10:13). He is mentioned again in verse 21. In Daniel 12:1 we see Michael again as he stands up for **"the children"** of Daniel's people—the Israelites. We assume that this means all of those who belong to the Lord through the blood of Christ. So Michael is the defender of God's people.

Michael and His Angels Overpowered Satan And Threw Him and His Angels Down to Earth

Text: Rev. 12:7-8

Rev.12:7 **And <u>there was war in heaven</u>. Michael and his angels fought against the dragon, and the dragon and his angels fought back. ⁸ But he was not strong enough, and they lost their place in heaven.**

Michael is also the subject in Jude 9 where he is called the archangel. He is a very powerful and important figure in the heavenly realm.

^{Jude 9} **Yet <u>Michael, the archangel, when contending with the devil,</u> and disputing about the body of Moses, did not dare bring a railing accusation against him, but said, The Lord rebuke you.**

Jesus Said He Saw Satan's Fall

^{Luke 10:18} **He replied, "<u>I saw Satan fall like lightning from heaven</u>. ¹⁹ I have given you authority to trample on snakes and scorpions and to overcome all the power of the enemy; nothing will harm you. ²⁰ However, do not rejoice that the spirits submit to you, but rejoice that your names are written in heaven."**

We have this striking passage regarding the devil and his angels. We hold this view of angels that they are rather perfect creatures. This passage describes angels in rebellion against our great God and His Christ. There was **"war in heaven"** (v. 7). The timing is crucial (cf. v. 6 and v. 13).

Text: Rev. 12:9
⁹ The great dragon was hurled down—that ancient serpent called the devil or Satan, who leads the whole world astray. He was hurled to the earth, and his angels with him.

In 12:9 we read **"he was hurled down to the earth."** It says he **"was hurled down"** twice in verse 9. In verse 12 we read **"the devil has gone down to you"** (cf. v. 13). The devil is defeated, but his time is not completed yet. He has a lot of helpers with the angels he brought with him.

The Third Scene: Song of Woe and Rejoicing (12:10-12)
Theme: Rejoicing in heaven because Satan is cast out. Woe to earth "because the devil has come down" (v. 12).

Text: Rev. 12:10-11
^{Rev. 12:10} **And I heard a loud voice in heaven *speaking*, Now has come salvation, and strength, and the kingdom of our God, and the power of his Christ: for the accuser of our brethren was *hurled* down *from heaven where* he accused them before our God day and night. ¹¹ And they overcame him by the blood of the**

Lamb, and by the word of their testimony; and *they were willing to give up their lives for His sake.* (Easy KJV)

It is the blood of the Lamb and the true testimony of the martyrs' witness that ultimately defeats the devil (12:11). We see that *"they were willing to give up their lives for His sake."*

Text: Rev. 12:12-13
[12] Therefore, rejoice *you heavens* and *you* that dwell in them. Woe to *those who live* on the earth and *the sea! Because the devil has come down to you with great wrath, because he knows that he only has* a short time. [13] And when the dragon saw that he *was hurled down to the* earth, he persecuted the *woman who gave birth to a son.* (Easy KJV)

Satan knows his time is short (12:12). Since his defeat has already been determined **"he is filled with fury."** The history of mankind is but a pulse beat in the life of the universe. It has been said a number of times that the light of the most distant star has yet to reach the earth.

The Fourth Scene: The Heavenly Woman and Her Other Children (12:13-17)

The Great Tribulation
SATAN'S FINAL GREAT ASSAULT

Text: Rev. 12:14-17
[14] And woman *was* given two wings *like those* of a great eagle, *in order* that she might fly into the wilderness, into her place, where she will be nourished for a time, and times, and half a time, from *the presence* of the serpent. [15] And the serpent *spewed a flood of water* out of his mouth *that it might overtake the woman and carry her away* in the flood. [16] And the earth *came to the aid* of the woman, and the earth opened its mouth, and swallowed up the flood that the dragon *spewed* out of his mouth. [17] And the dragon *was overcome with anger toward* the woman, and set out to make war *with the rest of her children*, that keep the commandments of God, and *hold* the testimony of Jesus Christ. (Easy KJV)

SATAN: THE GREAT RED DRAGON IS
THE FIRST OF THREE ANTAGONISTS

The first antagonist is the dragon who seeks to devour the child of the woman. (She represents the church—and her child is the Messiah–see vs. 10-11).

In Chapter 13 we shall see the other two antagonists against the work of Christ and His church. In addition to Satan we will see the beast from the sea, and the beast from the earth. We will observe the coming of the Antichrist. In the remainder of this paragraph is a summary of what we have learned about Satan who is shown as a great red dragon in Chapter 12. We see the dragon that is the second great heavenly sign. The dragon sweeps a third of the stars from the heavens. We have identified these stars as fallen angels. Satan pursues the heavenly woman who represents the people of God—Israel, that gave birth to the Messiah. From the Messiah comes the new people of God—the church. In a backward glance, John sees war in heaven with Michael, the archangel, waging war against the red dragon and throwing him down to the earth.

Text: Rev. 12:3-12 Read this text again above or from your Bible as a companion to this study.

The dragon is clearly identified in Rev. 12:9 as **"...that ancient serpent called the devil, or Satan who leads the whole world astray"** (cf. 12:3; Rev. 20:2, 10).

Issues Regarding the Dragon and the Beast

> ➢ Mankind **worshiped the dragon and the beast** (the Antichrist, cf. 13:3ff).
> ➢ Notice his time span is only **42 months**—Compare this to **"1260 days"** (Rev. 12:6); **"42 months"** (Rev. 11:2ff).
> ➢ He speaks **evil and blasphemous things for 42 months.**
> ➢ Of course, as previously said, **these three periods all equal 3 and ½ years and that is half of seven years.**

The Angels Choose Sides in Heaven

These angels have **chosen sides against spiritual truth**. They have become obedient to Satan. John refers to them as **"...his (Satan's) angels..."** (vs. 7, 9). You notice that Michael and the holy angels of God initiated the battle. There are occasions when one must oppose evil. There are times when we stand and fight for what we know to be right. The blood of the martyrs has covered the earth. Of all places, evil cannot coexist with the righteous Father. The divine records tell us that **"the dragon and his angels fought back"** (v. 7). Take note: **"an enormous red dragon"** (v. 3). This creature appears invincible.

The Devil Was Dismayed, Confused, and Overcome with Anger

Text: Rev. 12:13
Rev. 12:13 **When the dragon saw that he had been hurled to the earth, he pursued the woman who had given birth to the male child.**

John says, **"the dragon saw that he was hurled to the earth..."** (v. 13). It happened so rapidly he was unaware of his surroundings. If you lived back in the day in which I lived, you may have heard the term: **"I'll slap you into the middle of next week."** Well, that's what happened to Satan. **He is stunned!** **"When** *(he)* **saw..."**—that is **when he realized** where he was. We say, "He snapped out of it!"

"When he came to himself ..."

You know he was furious. He had been under the self-created delusion that he would be successful in his attack against the woman, her child, and her offspring. After that he adopted another tactic. **"He pursued the woman"**—the people of God. He is racing to catch up and destroy her. But God gave the woman wings. Satan could not catch her. She is not like a sparrow, but like **"a great eagle"** (v. 14). A sparrow flies, but an eagle soars. Just the moment Satan (like a cat) thinks he has the prey in his paws the woman soars into the heavens.

His Desire to Devour the Woman's Child

Therefore, we read: **"The dragon stood in front of the woman who was about to give birth, so that he might devour her child the moment it was born."** That is the war Satan waged and continues to wage against the people of God. He is winning some battles, especially in the church. He strives for mastery and domination. And remember his strategy—he transforms himself into whatever form he deems expedient in order to destroy the effectiveness of the church. So in all of Israel's history, Satan worked contrary to God's purpose. He put evil desires into the hearts of her kings. He placed temptations before her people—from the creation of the golden calf to the defilement of God's holy temple by vain and blasphemous worship.

The Dragon's Makes A Futile Attempt to Destroy the Woman's Child

The dragon pursued the woman, but she was given a place that was **"out of the serpent's reach"** (v. 14). **"...the place was prepared for her in the wilderness"** (v. 14). The sign of **"two wings of a great eagle"** (v. 14) illustrate how swiftly her flight was carried out. But Satan goes after her. Satan's next strategy is to flood the desert, but the desert is thirsty, and swallows the great river that **"spewed"** from the dragon's mouth (v. 15). Satan is prevented from persecuting the woman because God has provided her with shelter and protection so that Satan cannot destroy her. Israel went into the desert. The desert is the wilderness. She will be there **1,260 days.** Remember she goes into the desert (wilderness) for **1260 days** (or **three and one-half years,** or **42 months**—the times used in Rev. 11-13 are the same).

The Dragon Spews Water, Not Fire Into the Desert

This dragon does not spout fire but rather spews enormous volumes of water from his mouth. But as God forced back the waters of the Red Sea, God caused the river to be swallowed into the earth (v. 16). We read: **" And the dragon *was overcome with anger toward* the woman, and set out to make war *with the rest of her children*"** (v. 17). Her children are **"those who obey God's commandments and hold to the testimony of Jesus."**

Satan's Intentions against the Heavenly Woman's Other Children

Satan stands before the church today **waiting to "devour" her children. "He knows that his time is <u>short</u>"** (v. 12b). I want you to **notice something about Satan.** The Bible says that in this war in heaven **"he <u>was</u> not strong enough"** (12:8). What a great word of assurance we have! Satan struggles and he wages war and he keeps coming, but he lacks the strength to fight against Michael and his angels. God did not even step out to meet Satan. He did not acknowledge him. He just sent His powerful angels. And the divine record says: **"...they lost their place in heaven"** (v. 8). When it says **"they lost their place..."** it means **forever.**

Why Did God Create Angels and Give Them the Opportunity to Turn from Him?

The purpose of angels is identified in Hebrews 1:14—

Heb. 1:14 <u>are not all angels ministering spirits sent to serve</u> those who will inherit salvation?

1 Cor. 6:1-3 is striking. Paul says that we should not dispute with one another since it will be our assignment to **"judge the world."** Then he adds, **"Do you not know that we will judge angels?" The angels can sin just like we on earth can sin.**

1 Cor. 6:1 **If you have a matter against *another brother, how dare* you *go to court* before the unjust *judges,* and not before the saints? ² Don't you know that <u>the saints will judge the world?</u> and if the world will be judged by you, *are you* unworthy to judge the smallest matters? ³ *Don't you* know that <u>we shall judge angels</u>? how much more the things that pertain to this life?** (EKJV)

In Matthew 19:28 we are told that the **<u>disciples will sit on *twelve thrones* and judge the twelve tribes</u>.** (Easy KJV)

Select Section

SS

SATAN
His Strategy and His Plans of Attack

Satan Identified in Scripture

In Chapter 13 John will introduce us to the parody of Satan and his worldwide influence. Satan can suck you in before you can blink an eye and you will believe you are serving God. He is pictured as the GREAT Red Dragon. His name is **"Satan"** in the Old Testament (a Persian word). He is called **"the Devil"** (Greek) in the New Testament. In the account of Saul in the days of David Saul is said to have **"the evil spirit from the Lord."** Satan was created by the Lord, but he has fallen. (After the Babylonian exile Satan appears especially in Job and Zechariah). In the New Testament he is called **"Satan," "the Devil," "the Evil One,"** and **"the Dragon."** More than 40 terms in the Bible are used to describe him. Satan always has the appearance of success.

Satan's Attempt on David

Satan is first mentioned in Scripture in Psalm 109. The background is that an enemy has unfairly attacked David and he urges the Lord God to send Satan to **"stand at his right hand"** (Ps. 109:6) obviously to condemn him for judgment. In Zech. 3:1 Satan stands at the right hand of Joshua the high priest to condemn him. To stand at one's right hand meant to observe every action and deed. (See more commentary on Psalm 109 in my book *Psalms: Fresh Hope for Today*, Vol. 2).

Ps. 109:4 **For my love they are my adversaries: but I give myself to prayer. ⁵And they have rewarded me evil for good, and hatred for my love. ⁶Set a wicked man over him: and <u>let Satan stand at his right hand</u>. ⁷When he is judged, let him be condemned: and let his prayer be** *received as* **sin.** (Easy KJV)

David experienced the influence of Satan in his life when he fell into the trap and numbered Israel. It led to a terrible fall for David that brought tragic results. Take notice of his diabolically evil intentions: He deceived King David and all Israel with him to disobey God. It seemed so innocent. But his actions were gross disobedience to God.

1 Chron. 21:1 <u>**Satan rose up against Israel and incited David to take a census of Israel**</u>.

Satan's Desire for World Domination and Influence

In the temptation of Christ, Satan offered to give Him the kingdoms of the world without dying on a cross. He promised to give Him

"their authority and splendor..." He said, "for it has been given to me, and I can give it to anyone I desire."
Luke 4:5 And the devil, taking him up into an high mountain, showed unto him all the kingdoms of the world in a moment of time. 6 And the devil said to him, I will give you all this power, and their glory: for it has been given to me; and I can give it to anyone I desire." ((Easy KJV)

Was this a lie? He certainly had great influence in the kingdoms of the world. His influence is seen worldwide today. But Satan only gives momentary satisfaction. Then he brings us to our great downfall. That is his desire and intention from the beginning.

Satan Roams the Earth and Searches for Weakness in Its Inhabitants

Job 1:6 One day the angels came to present themselves before the LORD, and Satan also came with them. 7 <u>The LORD said to Satan, "Where have you come from?" Satan answered the LORD, "From roaming through the earth and going back and forth in it</u>."

Job 2:1 On another day the angels came to present themselves before the LORD, and Satan also came with them to present himself before him. 2 And <u>the LORD said to Satan, "Where have you come from?"</u>

Satan is mentioned in Job more than in any other biblical book. Ultimately there would be war in heaven. Satan set his heart on an irreversible course of action. He set out to defy God. He set out to destroy mankind—God's creation. He set out to defraud mankind of salvation and to destroy God's Son.

Jesus Suggested that Satan Possessed a Kingdom
(Matt. 12:26)

Matt. 12:26 <u>If Satan drives out Satan, he is divided</u> against himself. How then can his kingdom stand?
In 2 Corinthians, Paul calls Satan the **"god of this world"** (2 Cor. 4:4). Countless people worship him and this is even practiced in so-called "churches." He is defiant against God and all things related to Him.

Satan's Notorious Rebellion against God

The reason there was a battle is because Satan was leading a notorious rebellion against the very throne of God. We are made aware in Job that God had great difficulty with Satan. Satan had a rebellious spirit from the beginning. The angels appeared before the council of God one day and the book of Job says **"...and Satan was with them."** His response when God asked him where he had been was **"...roaming through the earth and going back and forth in it."** Satan, why weren't you in heaven with the other angels? What were you doing in the earth?

Satan in the Prophecy of Zechariah—Satan Is the Accuser of Believers

Zechariah in his vision sees Satan standing at the right hand of Joshua the High Priest to accuse him. (See additional commentary on Zechariah's prophecy in the special Select Section under Chapter 11). This is just how he attacked Job who was totally innocent of any charges he could bring against him.

Zech. 3:1 Then he showed me Joshua the high priest standing before the angel of the LORD, and Satan standing at his right side to accuse him. ² The LORD said to Satan, "The LORD rebuke you, Satan! The LORD, who has chosen Jerusalem, rebuke you! Is not this man *a burning stick* snatched from the fire?" (Easy KJV)

Satan Deceives and Destroys the Faith of Believers

Jesus said Satan snatches away the word of Almighty God the moment it is sown in the hearts of some people.

Mark 4:13 And he said to them, *Don't you understand* this parable? and how then *will you understand all the other* parables? ¹⁴ The sower sows the word. ¹⁵ And these are *the ones* by the way side, where the word is sown; but when they have heard, Satan comes immediately, and *takes* away the word that was sown in their hearts *(so they will not believe).* (Easy KJV)

Satan Brings Spiritual and Physical Bondage upon People

He holds people under spiritual and physical bondage. He kept a woman under domination **"for eighteen long years"** (NIV). Years of suffering are much longer than years of joy. That is why Jesus refers to them as **"long years."**

Luke 13:16 And should not this woman, *who is* a daughter of Abraham, whom Satan *has* bound, these eighteen years, *be set free* from this bondage. (Easy KJV)

He Found a Convenient Path into the Heart of Judas

Luke 22:3 Then <u>Satan entered Judas</u>, called Iscariot, one of the Twelve. ⁴ And Judas went to the chief priests and the officers of the temple guard and discussed with them how he might betray Jesus. (Easy KJV)

Satan took charge of Judas the moment he took the bread during the last supper of Christ with Christ fully aware of his intentions to betray him.

John 13:27 And after the sop Satan entered into him. Then Jesus said to him, *"What you do*, do quickly." (EKJV)

Jesus warned Peter what Satan intended to do to him. Jesus said, **"Satan has asked to sift you as wheat"** (Luke 22:31). Sifting is a winnowing process. The **"you"** is plural. Jesus is addressing all of the disciples. In regard to Simon Peter the literal Greek is: **"Satan has obtained you by asking."** Presumably, Satan had to secure permission. God sifts us and takes away the chaff, but Satan sifts us and leaves only the chaff. **"But, I have prayed for you"** (singular—addressed to Peter; Luke 22:32). Both Satan and Christ were asking for Peter. Satan was requesting that God allow him free access to Peter.

Satan Seeks to Fill the Hearts of Church Members

Believers must always be on their guard lest they be drawn into any of Satan's traps, especially to lie to enhance their influence in the body of Christ. It is not uncommon for people to seek positions of leadership under less than truthful statements. Such behavior removes us from our relationship with God.

Acts 5:3 But Peter said, Ananias, why has <u>Satan filled *your* heart to lie to the Holy *Spirit* and to keep back part of the *receipts for* the land</u>? (KJV)**Christians Can Lead People**

Away from Satan

Paul is sent to lead people away from the power of Satan. Therefore one does not, of necessity, remain under Satan's permanent domination. Through the gospel that we preach, the hearts of those under the influence of Satan can be transformed and turned toward a living faith in God through the power of Christ over their lives. God sent Paul to the Gentiles:

Acts 26:18 **"To open their eyes, and to turn them from darkness to light, and from the power of Satan to God, that they may receive forgiveness of sins, and inheritance among those *that* are sanctified *by their faith* that is in me."**

Satan Disguises Himself and Masquerades

Satan uses disguises, illusions and counterfeit measures to deceive the people of God. He can even appear as a glorious angel and cause believers to determine that he is from God.

2 Cor. 11:14 **...for <u>Satan himself masquerades as an angel of light</u>. ¹⁵ It is not surprising, then, if his servants masquerade as servants of righteousness.**

Satan's War against God's Servants

2 Cor. 12:7 **And lest I should be exalted above measure through the abundance of the revelations, <u>there was given me a thorn in the flesh, the messenger of Satan to *attack* me, lest I should be exalted above measure</u>. ⁸ For this thing <u>I begged the Lord *three times*, that it might *leave* me</u>.** (EKJV)

Paul accepted Satan's attack in his life through an infusion of suffering and pain. He saw the pain as a benefit that caused him to balance his life between the thrilling and amazing revelations of God and the painful disturbances that resulted in keeping him without conceit. Pain can open us to significant revelations because it removes our attitude toward self and pride and places us in a position where we must fully look to the Lord. Therefore Paul said in verse 6 of the same chapter above:

⁶ **"<u>For though I would desire to glory</u>, I shall not be a fool; for I will tell the truth: but *now I hold back*, lest *anyone might* think *more of me than what he sees me to be, or he hears concerning me.*"** (EKJV)

Those of us, who have physically suffered great pain and yet have found the glorious revelation and truth of God in the midst of suffering, can fully understand Paul's statement concerning his own suffering. Therefore, though Satan does attack believers, and according to Paul he brings suffering and pain in their lives, he has actually failed in his purpose because the experience of God's revelation can be heightened in such affliction. God takes our suffering and makes something positive and good so that we can see purpose in our suffering to the glory of God.

Satan's Thousand Years in Prison

There is one final imprisonment when the earth will be freed from Satan for 1000 years. A single angel binds him and throws him into his prison. After the thousand years he will be released briefly. Then his final doom will be sealed.

Rev. 20:2 **And he *grabbed hold* of the dragon, that old serpent, who is the Devil, and Satan, and bound him a thousand years, [3] And *threw* him into the bottomless pit, and shut him up, and set a seal upon him, *that he should no longer deceive the nations*, until the thousand years *had passed*: and *after that he will be set free for a brief time.*** (EKJV)

Satan's Punishment Is Assured by God

God has prepared special punishment for the devil and his wicked angels. He prepared eons ago for their final punishment. People who sin against God will share the **"eternal fire prepared for the devil and his angels."**

Matt. 25:41 **"Then he will say to those on his left, `Depart from me, you who are cursed, into the eternal fire prepared for the devil and his angels."**

Jesus Visualized Satan's Ultimate Demise

Luke 10:18 [18] **And he said to them, I *saw Satan fall from heaven like lightening.*** (EKJV)

Peter speaks of a special hell for the angels. He remarks that they have been isolated in **"gloomy dungeons to be held for judgment..."**

2 Pet. 2:4 **For if God did not spare angels when they sinned, but sent them to hell, putting them into gloomy dungeons to be held for judgment..."**

Jude affirms the same sentence. He adds that they are **"bound with everlasting chains."** These chains cannot be broken. God's prisons defy escape.

Jude 6 **And the angels who *did not keep their first position*, but left their own habitation, he has reserved in everlasting chains under darkness unto *the great day of judgment.*** (EKJV)

Satan's days are certainly numbered. His days are short.

The Select Section on Satan Concludes Here

SS
Select Section

THE GREAT TRIBULATION
IS COMING

Chapter 12 reveals the continual war of Satan against the church, and leads us to Chapter 13 where we see the development of Satan's final strategy for world domination, and the destruction of the church for which Christ died.

A Time of Trouble Unlike Anything
Ever Experienced on Earth (Dan. 12:1)

We read of this in the prophecy of Daniel. Observe the sequence: **"Michael shall stand up;"** he **"stands for the children of your people;"** and at the same time **"there will be a time of trouble, such as has never been seen since there was a nation;"** **"at that time your people will be delivered, everyone that will be found written in the book."** All of this is in just the first verse of Daniel Chapter 12.

For our purposes, we interpret this verse as follows: Michael, the prince, also known as the archangel is going to come to stand with the children of God. It says that he will **"stand for the children,"** generally meaning the people of someone. Here we interpret this to mean the people that belong to the Lord since they are the same ones **"written (or recorded) in the book,"** meaning the book of life (Rev. 20:11 ff.) That will be a period of trouble or distress or tribulation unlike anything ever known in history. This indicates a world-wide period of suffering and persecution that no one has ever seen or endured. But something else will happen. He states: **"your people shall be delivered"** meaning rescued, redeemed or set free in the spirit of the passage. But only those people **"found written in the book."**

The prophecy brings the worst news coupled with the best news. A time of trouble is coming so great that no one has ever seen such a time in all of history. No one can explain it. No one can tell you what it is like. No one has ever endured such a time. I think of the time when the Germans lined up 6,000 Jews in Poland—babies, children, women and men—and shot each and every one. It is a time unlike anything the world has ever seen. How could anyone possibly endure this? But then the news comes. An entire group of people here called **"children"** because they are loved and dear and precious to someone, will be delivered. More than that, their names are already written in a record referred to as **"the book."** We cannot understand at what point they will be delivered.

Those Days Will be Shortened
"And except those days shall be shortened, there would be no person spared." But listen, He continues **"but for the elect's sake those days will be shortened."** Who are the elect? Jesus uses this term to mean those who will be caught up to heaven by His angels at the time when He, our Savior, returns in the glory of God.
22 And except those days should be shortened, there *would be no persons spared;* but for the elect's sake those days will be shortened." (Easy KJV)

"Elect" means those who are special; those who have great importance and significance. Christ said: that **"false Christs"** will attempt to **"deceive the very elect"** (Matt. 24:24). He said: His angels are going **"to gather together his elect from the four winds"** (Matt. 24:31). Matthew, Mark and Luke quote Jesus in this regard. Paul talks of God's **"elect"** (Rom. 8:33; Col. 3:12). He speaks of **"the faith of God's elect"** (Titus 1:1). Peter is addressing believers in a number of places and refers to them as **"Elect according to God's foreknowledge..."** (1 Peter 1:2). The elect, therefore belong to God through faith in Christ. It is a wonderful title to be referred to as the **"elect."** Jesus obviously means the same thing as Daniel means when He refers to **"the children of your people"** (Dan. 12:1).

We have an Old Testament prophecy and the New Testament statements of Jesus in perfect agreement. I cannot overestimate the importance of understanding these two passages in our interpretation of the matter in hand in Revelation. Therefore, please read this material again until you are certain you have it clearly in mind.

How Can the Days Be Shortened?

The shortening of the days will have to be explained by something that God allows or permits. Jesus also quoted Daniel as follows and adds His interpretation.

Matt. 24:15 *"**Therefore when you** see <u>the abomination of desolation</u> standing in the holy place that <u>Daniel the prophet</u> spoke of, (**let the one who hears understand**)."* (Easy KJV)

The Abomination of Desolation

It is critical to our study to understand what is meant by the following phrase. The **"abomination of Desolation"** will stand in the holy place. Here, the **"holy place"** not only means the temple in Jerusalem, but what we often call **"the holy of holies,"** the innermost part of the temple only accessed by the high priest. Throughout scripture, an abomination is an act that opposes the holy nature of God or His worship (See Isa. 1:13; 66:17; Jer. 2:7; 32:35; Mal. 2:11; Luke 16:15; Rev. 21:27). Something is going to happen there. We know that **"desolation,"** as used in the Old Testament, means that something will no longer be used (See Isa. 51:19; 64:10-12; Jer. 44:22-23; Dan. 8:13-14; Luke 21:20-24). The temple and more precisely the holy place of the mercy seat, the ark of the covenant, and the ten Commandments among other things, will be left desolate. This normally means that it will never return to its former state.

An "abomination" means the person or thing that causes the desolation. This happened in 70 AD when the Romans slaughtered the Jewish people, including the **"elect,"** the people we would call Christians. They also destroyed the city of Jerusalem, and broke the temple down and left it in ruins, with nothing to indicate its former purpose. They desecrated the temple and removed every vestige and evidence of it having been the place of God. All of this took place following a three and one-half year war and siege and slaughter on the part of the Roman army (67-70 AD). Part of this took place during the days of Nero, a notorious enemy of Christianity, and one of the most evil persons to ever serve as an Emperor of Rome. The period was three and one-half years of tribulation.

In Matt: 24:29, Jesus is looking toward a different period of tribulation. He is looking toward what we call the great tribulation just prior to the resurrection of the righteous, or the elect, or as we say, the saved. At the conclusion of that great tribulation, Jesus will return to lead the forces of heaven in the destruction of the greatest army ever enlisted on earth in what the Bible calls the battle of Armageddon (Rev. 19).

The End of the Earth
This will be addressed in another Select Section following this one. Also, read Chapter 6 in this book for more details.

Mt. 24:29 **"Immediately after the tribulation of those days the sun will be darkened, and the moon will not give her light, and the stars will fall from heaven, and the powers of the heavens will be shaken."** (Easy KJV)

The end of the earth and the constellations will take place immediately following the great tribulation. The earth will be dissolved as explained in our Chapter 6, and the constellations will come crashing together as explained in Chapter 6 as well.

The Great Tribulation
The period of the Great Tribulation is the dragon's final war against the saints (Rev. 13:7-10). In order to conduct this war, he summons two hideous, evil and sinister figures, and gives them power to perform extraordinary evil acts against God's people called **"the saints"** in the King James Version of the Bible. Never let it be said that the devil is powerless. There are just limits to his power. Just as the attacks on Job were limited so this war is limited.

The Coming Great Disaster and Persecution of the Saints

Rev. 18:4 **And I heard another voice from heaven, saying, Come out of her, my people, so *that you do not partake* of her sins, and that *you do not suffer her* plagues.** (Easy KJV)

Like the great and disastrous doom of Sodom is the disaster to fall upon our world. Likewise the angel summons those who belong to God to abandon the city of destruction (Rev. 18:4). People are attracted and drawn to the evil city where the harlot woman dominates under Satan's power.

God's People Will Be Called to Come Out of Mystical Babylon

Those who do not come out by the blood of Jesus have no future hope of salvation. The end is near and with it, the destruction of this universe.

Daniel's Weeks of Years—How Do We Interpret Them?

Daniel 9:27—In the apocalyptic scripture written by Daniel, the prophet of the Lord, a week with seven days represents and is equivalent to seven years of actual time. This may seem strange to us, but once you understand this concept, then you are able to understand what is meant by **"weeks of years."** Weeks of years is the time frame for Daniel's prophecies used in the King James Bible. It is also footnoted in the New International Version. While it has been impossible to compute his time line precisely for all of Daniel's weeks of years, one of the weeks is the time of the tribulation. For that reason, the great tribulation is thought to be seven years (KJV).

The Two Halves of the Seven Years

Something happens in the middle of the seven years of tribulation. This leaves us with two half periods of time in regard to the great tribulation. **What happened <u>to the other half of the seven years</u>** when the year was divided? Those three and one-half years were already fulfilled? **Well, when were they fulfilled?** The first three and one-half years were fulfilled between the years 67-70 AD at the time of the Jerusalem tribulation and the destruction of Jerusalem by the Romans. This all followed the life, death and resurrection of Christ.

The temple was destroyed resulting in the end of **"the offerings and the sacrifices."** The sacrifice was cut off **in the middle** of the figurative week that represents seven years. That was a three and one-half year period of terrifying and terrible holocaust—a tribulation that no one had ever imagined. This is what Jesus referred to as **"cut short,"** and Daniel refers to as **"the middle of the week"** representing the seven years of tribulation (Dan. 9:27). By referring to the time period as the **"middle of the week,"** he indicates that three and one-half years have passed, and there are three and one-half years yet to come. In summation, the **"middle"** is 70 A.D. when the temple was destroyed and the offerings ceased.

To this date the offerings and the sacrifices have not been reinstituted because there is no temple, no holy of holies, and no altar. This same period (67-70 A.D) was also the time of the martyrdom of Peter and Paul in Rome, as well as the deaths of other disciples of Christ. John knew what Daniel and Jesus had taught.

Remember the two great prophets of Revelation 11? The time of their ministry totals three and one-half years. In Revelation, the great tribulation is always three and one half years in length (See Dan. 9:27 below). That is three and one-half years, just like we have in Revelation 11, 12 and 13. Let's follow scripture. By reading Daniel 12:7 we see the term **"a time, times, and an half."**

Dan. 9:27 **And he shall confirm the covenant with many for one week: and <u>in the middle of the week he will cause the sacrifice and the offering to cease</u>, and he will set up an abomination at the temple that will cause desolation, *up to the* consummation *(or end)*, that is determined *(for him)* will be poured upon him.** (Easy KJV)

Pay careful attention. The Gentiles will trample the court of the temple (see Rev. 11:1 ff). To this day, the Gentiles have had control of the temple mount and no temple can be constructed where the former temple stood. We are expecting a temple in the millennium age, but now there is no temple.

The time of **the great tribulation** is coming on the earth. In Revelation, the time of the two great prophets (Chap. 11 mentioned above) is three and one-half years. We are living in the age of the gospel and the Holy Spirit. This is the time between the death of Jesus coupled with the destruction of the temple, and at the end of this period—the approaching great tribulation and the coming of our Lord.

Daniel's Seven Years of Tribulation: When and Where?

Remember that the great tribulation in Daniel's prophecy is the second half of the seven years. There are seven years of tribulation clearly explained by Daniel, but with all of "the sevens" in Revelation, John never uses the number seven one time in regard to the tribulation.

To be sure, the tribulation, in sum, is seven years. But unless we clearly understand what Daniel said, and what Christ said, we may become confused. I subscribe to the concept of the divine inspiration of scripture. Our problem, then, is how do we interpret what has been recorded in Holy Scripture? God gives us eyes to see and scripture to understand. We should be very careful in interpreting scripture so as not to read into it something that is not there. We should read Revelation and Matthew together.

The Time Was Cut Short in 70 A.D.

The time was **"cut short"** in 70 A.D. Otherwise, see Matt. 24:22 below.

Matt. 24:22 And <u>except those days should be shortened, *no one would be spared*: but for the elect's sake those days shall be shortened</u>. (Easy KJV)

Jesus is talking about the tribulation in Matt. 24:21-22. He said **"those days should be shortened."** Remember that they were shortened by the first tribulation and the slaughter of thousands of Jews and Jewish Christians in Jerusalem in 70 A.D. He said unless this had happened, no one would have been spared. In other words there would have been no survivors. Therefore, we return to Revelation where we never find the number seven (as in a week of Daniel) in regard to the tribulation. Each scene in Revelation 11, 12, and

13 has the time period under consideration spelled out in different ways, always equal to three and one-half years.

EACH TIME PERIOD IS EXACTLY THREE AND ONE-HALF YEARS WE HAVE DAYS, MONTHS, YEARS

From Revelation 11, 12 and 13 in God's own word we learn the correct interpretation.

> ➤ Dan. 12:7 "It will be for <u>a time, times and half a time</u>."
> ➤ Rev. 11:2 They (the Gentiles) will trample on the holy city for <u>42 months</u>.
> ➤ Rev. 11:3 And I will appoint my two witnesses, and they will prophesy <u>for 1,260 days</u>...
> ➤ Rev. 12:14 The woman will "be taken care of for <u>a time, times and half a time</u>..."
> ➤ Rev. 13:5 The beast was given a mouth to utter...blasphemies and to exercise its authority for <u>forty-two months</u>.

TIME, TIMES AND HALF A TIME; FORTY-TWO MONTHS; AND 1260 DAYS
The Time of the Antichrist and the Tribulation
(All equal the same period of time which is three and one-half years.)

1. **Forty-two months**—the time of oppression of the holy city by the Gentiles (Rev. 11:2).
2. **A thousand, two hundred and three score days (1260)**—the length of the mission of God's two miraculous witnesses (Rev. 11:3).
3. **A time, times and half a time**—the time of the persecution of the heavenly woman (the people of God) in the wilderness (Rev. 12:14; also 12:6 = **1260 days**).
4. **Forty-two months**—the time during which the beast is allowed to exercise his authority (Rev. 13:5). **Also: Daniel 7:25; 12:7 ("...<u>him for a time, times and half a time</u>...")**

FROM THE DEATH OF CHRIST TO HIS RETURN AND THE GREAT TRIBULATION

---

33 AD
Death, Resurrection & Ascension of Christ
|
33-70 AD = Almost 40 Years
|
67-70 AD = 3 ½ Years
The Tribulation of Israel and Jerusalem
Destruction of the Temple - 70 AD
|

|

|
Age of the Holy Spirit
And the Gospel
From 70 AD to the Great Tribulation
|

|
The Great Tribulation = 3 ½ Years
Return of Christ in Glory
The End Time of Planet Earth
The Final Judgment
The New Jerusalem From Heaven

Jesus told us that the end will come immediately following the **"distress"** or tribulation of those days. **"Distress"** is the term Daniel used in Dan. 12:1.

> ²⁹ "Immediately <u>after the distress of those days</u> the sun will be darkened, and the moon will not give its light; the stars will fall from the sky, and the heavenly bodies will be shaken." (KJV)

³⁰ "<u>At that time</u> the sign of the Son of Man will appear in the sky, and all the nations of the earth will mourn. <u>They will see the Son of Man coming on the clouds of the sky, with power and great glory</u>. ³¹ And <u>he will send his angels with a loud trumpet call, and they will gather his elect from the four winds, from one end of the heavens to the other</u>." (KJV)

Clearly in Matt. 24:19-31 we are told that Christ and His angels are coming **"after the distress (the tribulation) of those days."**

Christ will come and **"at that time"** (i.e., **"after the distress"** (v. 29 above). When he comes there will be great mourning in all nations of those who have not believed. This will take place at the sight **"of the Son of Man coming on the clouds"** (v. 30). Notice: **"and he will send his angels with a loud trumpet call, and they will gather his elect from the four winds** (or four directions of the compass)**..."** It appears that God has a schedule already in place for the rapture. The trumpet call is for the rapture (cf. 1 Thessalonians 4:16 ff).

Jesus spoke of **"these days"** and **"those days."** When He spoke of **"these days"** He was speaking of the fall of Jerusalem under the Romans, an event in the lifetime of many of those who heard Him speak. This period of unparalleled persecution of the Jews, and destruction of the temple, and the environs (the area surrounding Jerusalem) was endured for **exactly three and one-half years**. The time **between the days of Christ in "these days" and the Great Tribulation "in those days"** is the age of the gospel. The days prior to the great tribulation are in order for believers to proclaim the name of Jesus to the ends of the earth. It is often called **"the age of the Holy Spirit."**

When the last three and one-half years are fulfilled, God will have preserved Israel in the desert (12:6). It is where Moses gathered the people when he took them out of Egypt. God will preserve them just as He preserved their ancestors when they fled from Egypt at the time of the Exodus. Moses took them out of Egypt when the blood of the Lamb was placed on the doorposts.

Now We Focus on the Two Great Prophets
To be perfectly clear: the time of the two prophets who are similar to Moses and Elijah is three and one-half years and then they are killed under the authority of the Antichrist (Rev. 11). The time of the heavenly woman's exile to the desert is three and one-half years (Rev. 12). The time of the antichrist (the first beast of Rev. 13) is three and one-half years. At the end of the three and one-half years we see Christ, the Lamb of God, standing in the midst of the sealed 144,000 from Chapter 7, and they are on the heavenly Mt. Zion (Rev. 14). Also in Chapter 14 we see the epitaph of the saints, the harvest of the righteous, the harvest of the wicked, and

the grapes of God's wrath trampled until "the blood" runs out for 200 miles up to the bridle of a horse. The three and one-half years is never mentioned after Rev. 13.

Chapters 15-16 spell out the plagues that God will have sent upon the earth. Rev. 17 and 18 spell the end of the harlot woman representing the evil world city under the domination of the antichrist. Rev. 19 brings us to the great battle of Armageddon that ends in an instant when Christ appears on a white horse symbolic of victory. In the same chapter, the two beasts are captured and thrown into the lake of fire. Of course the first beast is the antichrist, and the second beast is his helper who carries out his atrocious persecutions against believers.

Many books divide a seven year tribulation into two halves: the first half is said to be the Antichrist's false lie to the people that he is bringing peace upon the earth. The second half is the great tribulation. There is no lack of ideas, theories, and teachings published. People will disagree about this. They have written hundreds of books. They have produced intricate charts; and people follow these charts. We should not be disagreeable when others hold different understandings. But we must rely on the Holy Scripture first and foremost.

Select Session on the Great Tribulation Ends Here

SS
SELECT SECTION

THE LAST DAYS OF PLANET EARTH
THE TIME OF DISTRESS

Dan. 12:1 **"At that time Michael, the great prince who protects your people, will arise. <u>There will be a time of distress such as has not happened from the beginning of nations until then</u>."**

We recognize this **"distress"** as the great tribulation on the earth. Jesus gave us twenty-one statements for recognizing the signs of the end and preparing for the tribulation. At the same time we are looking for His marvelous return in all the glory and splendor of heaven. While it is tempting to devote several chapters to these issues, we must refrain in light of the primary subject at hand. However, Revelation is a guide to understanding these signs, the great tribulation, the final battle with the evil forces of earth, the judgment of mankind, and the coming of the new heaven and the new earth. The new heaven and earth is not to be confused with an earth of elements, water, soil, seas, etc., that is a physical earth as we know it.

Before Jesus begins His statement He gives a serious warning regarding falling into the deception of false religion. False christs are anything but real and genuine guides toward faith in God. It seems that people, throughout history, have delighted in dishing up teachings that defile true faith in God. This is the religion of Satan who will do anything to redirect us away from saving faith in Christ who died for our sins and rose again.

Jesus, the End Time and His Return in Glory

Luke 21:8 **And he said, <u>Pay attention</u> that you are not deceived: for many will come in** (or under the pretense of) **my name, saying, I am** *Christ;* **and the time is near:** *do* **not** *follow* **them. 9 But when you hear of wars and commotions,** *don't* **be terrified: for these things must first take place; but the end** *will not follow immediately*.
10 **Then he said to them, Nation shall rise against nation, and kingdom against kingdom: 11 And great earthquakes shall occur in** *various* **places, and famines, and** *plagues* **and fearful sights, and there will be great signs from heaven.**

12 **But before all these, they will** *take you in their* **hands by force, and persecute** *you,* **delivering** *you* **up to the synagogues, and to prisons, being brought before kings and rulers for my name's sake. 13 And it shall** *come your turn to give a testimony. 14 Decide therefore in* **your hearts, not to meditate before what you shall answer: 15 For I will give you** *words* **to speak, and wisdom, which all your adversaries shall not be able to** *rebuff* **nor resist. 16 And you will be betrayed both by parents, and brothers, and relatives, and friends; and they shall cause** *some* **of you to be put to death.**

173

17 And you will be hated by all *people* for my name's sake. **18** But not a hair of your head will perish. **19** By your *endurance* you will gain *the salvation* of your soul. (Easy KJV)

Seven Signs of the End of Planet Earth

1. The rise of false religion (Luke 21:8)
2. Wars, Insurrections and Commotions (21:9)
3. Conflict between nations and rulers (21:10)
4. Widespread Earthquakes in many places (21:11)
5. Famines and Pestilence and Death (21:11)
6. Fearful and Astonishing Signs in the heavens (21:11)
7. Unrelenting Persecution of Believers (21:12)

We are seeing many of these signs already, but the news media does not report them. By careful searching you can find out what is going on in the world. One of the great signs is the rise of Islam and its bent upon destroying all Christians. This is certainly not the great tribulation, but Christians are experiencing a tribulation that is great to them, but just not universal yet.

Earthquakes on the earth are a daily occurrence. It is reported on the big island in Hawaii that during the eruption of a volcano that there were as many as 500 earthquakes per day. On Jan. 12, 2010 an earthquake in Haiti killed as many as 330,000 people. All of the signs above are happening in our world today. They do not mark the end but they are signs of a much larger and unprecedented devastation to come at the end of our earth.

Seven Truths for a Believers in Times of Persecution and Tribulation

1. You will be arrested and persecuted (21:12)
2. They will call on you for a testimony (21:13)
3. Prepare your heart, not your answer (21:14)
4. Christ will give you wisdom to answer (21:15)
5. You will be betrayed by those closest to you (21:16)
6. You will be hatred because you belong to Christ (21:17)
7. Your endurance will result in your salvation (21:19)

These seven truths all applied to the Jerusalem tribulation in 67-70 A.D. But, they will also apply to the great world-wide tribulation that is certainly coming upon the world in the last days.

Luke 21:25 **And there will be signs in the sun, and in the moon, and in the stars; and distress of nations upon the earth, with perplexity; the sea and the waves roaring;** [26] **Men's hearts failing them** *due to* **fear, and** *because* **they are looking** *toward those* **things that are** *coming* **on the earth: for the powers of heaven will be shaken.** [27] **And then they will see the Son of man coming in a cloud with power and great glory.** [28] **And when these things begin** *to take place,* **lift up your heads and** *start looking up,* **because your redemption** *is very close.* (Easy KJV)

Seven Signs of the Coming of Christ

1. **Signs in the sun and the moon and the stars (21:25)**
2. **On the earth: Distress between nations (21:25)**
3. **Perplexity in life (21:25)**
4. **Convulsions of the Seas (21:25)**
5. **The hearts of mankind failing in the face of fearful upheavals in the universe (21:26)**
6. **The shaking of the heavens (21:26)**
7. **Then you shall see the Son of man coming in a cloud with power and awesome splendor (21:17)**

These signs above will occur in a relative brief moment of time. They mark the imminent return of Christ. Of course, the seventh sign is the actual return of the Lord visibly and in wondrous glory.

You will note that Jesus warned of distress in Luke 21:25, but also what the KJV calls **"perplexity"** or confusion. Many translations relate this perplexity to the roaring of the seas. I take this roaring to be unprecedented hurricanes. We are already seeing evidence of the development of greater and more powerful storms. But we are also seeing the rise of tsunamis as earthquakes increase. It is probable that Jesus had all of this in mind in Luke 21:25.

The Japanese tsunami was a truly disastrous event resulting in almost 16,000 deaths, and the Indian Ocean tsunami in 2004 killed approximately 230,000 people. Tsunamis will become larger and more deadly. Tsunamis are caused by volcanoes, underwater earthquakes and other events, and produce a series of waves as high as 100 feet surging onto coastal areas resulting in great loss of life and property. Low coastal areas will be completely destroyed. No wonder minds are confused and filled with complexity.

However, in my view, this perplexity certainly is highly influenced by the oceanic upheavals, but also by the **"distress among nations"** mentioned just prior to the perplexity issue. You will also note that there will be a great rise in heart failure **"due to fear"** (v. 26) as people come to the realization of what is ahead and conclude that they are bereft of hope in a world headed for destruction. Having omitted God and all thing spiritual from their lives, they are adrift in a world that is disintegrating, and have no lifeboat to God's new world. Christ is coming, and this is certainly a time for readiness and preparation.

How to Gain Greater Insight

Compare these 21 thoughts with the associated scripture verses. Keep them in mind as you study Chapters 13 and 14. Mark 13:24 (below) plainly tells us, in Jesus' words, He will return **after the tribulation**.

After completing Chapter 14, return and read the 21 thoughts from Christ and these scripture passages once again. In explaining Revelation, our intent is that you become familiar with the prophecies of both the Old Testament and the New Testament, and especially the explanation of Christ regarding them.

Jesus' Prophecy of the End Time
(See also Matt. 24:29-31)

Mark 13:24 **"But in those days, *after that tribulation*, the sun will be darkened, and the moon will not give her light, [5] And the stars of heaven will fall, and the powers that are in heaven will be shaken. [26] At that time men will see the Son of Man coming in clouds with great power and glory. [27] And he will send his angels and gather his elect from the four winds, from the ends of the earth."** (Easy KJV)

Matthew adds: **"And he will send his angels with a loud trumpet call and they will gather his elect..." (Cf. Matt. 24:31).**
Also: Mark 13:19; Daniel 12:1.

The Great Multitude
(Compare to Revelation 7)

^{Dan. 12:2} <u>Multitudes who sleep in the dust of the earth will awake:</u> <u>some to everlasting life, others to shame and everlasting con-</u> <u>tempt</u>. (See Daniel 12:1-4).

Daniel affirms the book of life as found in Revelation. Names of those who belong to God are recorded. What about the multitudes that have denied Christ and worked against all things spiritual? The ones who will shine in eternity are **"those who lead many to righteousness."** The call to evangelism and the winning of the lost is a profound thought in Daniel 12.

Sealed to the Time of the End

The man above the waters dressed in white linen (Dan. 12:6) is without doubt an angel. We cannot miss the similarity of this figure (Rev. 10:5) and the angels in heaven. In both cases, the angel raises his right hand toward heaven and swears an oath of the validity of what he says.

^{Dan. 12:5} **Then I Daniel looked, and there stood** *two other men*, **one on this side of the bank of the river, and the other** *on the opposite* **side of the river. ⁶ And one said to the man** *dressed* **in linen, that was upon the waters of the river, How long will it be to the end of these wonders? ⁷ And I heard the man** *dressed* **in linen, who was on the waters of the river, who held up his right hand and his left hand to heaven, and** *swore* **by him that lives forever <u>that it will</u> <u>be for a time, times, and a half; and when he will have</u> *completed* <u>scattering the power of the holy people, all these things will be</u> <u>concluded.</u> ⁸ And I heard, but** *I did not understand*: **then I said, O my Lord, what shall be the end of these things? ⁹ And he said, Go your way, Daniel: for <u>the words are closed up and sealed till the</u> <u>time of the end.</u>** (Easy KJV) Note: the statement concerning sealing the book unto the end also is found in verse 4.

He heard the angel explain the purification of believers (we know this purification through the blood of Christ); and the continuation of the wicked in their wickedness. It requires spiritual wisdom to understand.

^{Dan. 12:10} **Many will be purified, and made white, and tried; but the wicked will do wickedly: and none of the wicked will understand; but the wise will understand.** (Easy KJV)

Select Session on The End of Planet Earth Concludes Here

SS
Select Section

"The Restrainer"
FIRST MYSTERY—WHO IS THE RESTRAINER?

Who or what restrains the time of the end? Some translations use the term **"he that restrains"** or **"what restrains."** Some writers suggest that the Holy Spirit restrains. They seem to say, "If only the Holy Spirit would get out of the way this will happen." Certainly that is not the case. That is not the type of ministry that the Holy Spirit has at all. The meaning of the war between Michael and the dragon **is that there is a power that restrains the antichrist.** The term is found in 2 Thes. 2:6. The Greek is: $\kappa\alpha\tau\ \acute{\epsilon}\chi o\nu$ meaning **"he that holds back" or** restrains. I believe that the best translation of this verse is in the American Standard Version below. Verse 6 continues in the Greek: $\tau\tilde{\omega}\ \acute{\epsilon}\alpha\upsilon\tau o\tilde{\upsilon}\ \kappa\alpha\iota\rho\tilde{\omega}$ translated: **"until his proper time."**

2 Thes. 2:5 *Do you not remember,* **that when I was yet with *you*, I told you these things?** [6] **And now _you_ know he that restrains, to the end that he may be revealed in his own season.** (ASV)

[6] **And you know what is now restraining him, so that he may be revealed when his time comes.** (NRSV)

[6] **And now you know what is holding him back, so that he may be revealed at the proper time.** (NIV)

[6] **And you know what currently restrains him, so that he will be revealed in his time.** (HCSB

The First Mention of Michael

The book of Daniel (Chapters 10:13-21; and 12:1-3) **tells you who restrains the antichrist.** Michael is identified as **"one of the chief princes"** (Dan. 10:13); and also as **"your prince"** (Dan. 19:21). In Daniel 12:1 he refers to Michael as **"the great prince."**

179

Michael is the **"archangel"** as we note in Jude 1:9, therefore the term **"prince"** informs us of his high position before the throne of God. It is a wonderful thought that the archangel stands between God's people and Satan.

Daniel 10:13-21

We know Michael is the archangel, but also he is the military angel who guards Israel, the people of God, and defends believers today. He commands the army of heaven. It is Michael who fought Satan's forces and threw them from heaven (Rev. 12). It is Michael that holds a unique responsibility under God in the continuing battle against Satan.

Satan will not cause the world to end. Only when God permits can he bring in the great tribulation that is the prelude to the end. Michael has always been the one to stand between Satan and his final objective. Satan is restrained until God says the time has come for Me to judge Satan and permit the release of my wrath against Satan. This includes all the forces of wickedness and evil on the day of the battle of Armageddon.

The "time of distress"
Daniel 12:1
Clearly Refers to the Great Tribulation
and the End Time

In the two passages below from Daniel Chapters 10 and 12 we see the position assigned to Michael in relation to God's people and the end time. The 12th chapter sounds like the New Testament gospel. It calls for people to turn. It relates the fact of the names recorded in what we call the book of life. It clearly teaches that in the proper moment when God permits the trumpet to sound there will be a resurrection day.

Dan. 12:1 "**At that time Michael, the great prince who protects your people, will arise. There will be a time of distress such as has not happened from the beginning of nations until then. But at that time your people—everyone whose name is found written in the book—will be delivered.** ² Multitudes who sleep in the dust of the earth will awake: some to everlasting life, others to shame and everlasting contempt. [3] Those that are wise will shine like the brightness of the heavens, and those who lead many to righteousness, like the stars forever and ever. (EKJV)

The Good News in Daniel 12:1-3
The Great Resurrection Day
See 1 Cor. 15:52; 1 Thes. 4

Everything below coincides with the end of the great tribulation and the arrival of the Day of the Lord.

- ✓ **The resurrection of those who have died (12:1)**
- ✓ **Michael is clearly the protector of the people of God (12:1)**
- ✓ **He will arise in the "time of distress" (the great tribulation – 12:1)**
- ✓ **"Multitudes who sleep in the dust of the earth will awake" (12:2;** also 1 Cor. 15:52; Matt. 24:31 – **"the last trump")**
- ✓ **The two passages above are in agreement and it seems logical that Michael, the archangel, will be the one to blow the trumpet – see 1 Thes. 4:16 where the voice of the archangel (Michael) is heard and the trumpet sounds.**
- ✓ **Two outcomes – "some to everlasting life, others to shame and everlasting contempt" (12:2)**
- ✓ **The wise ones that will shine: "those who lead many to righteousness,** *(will shine)* **like the stars forever and ever."**

Dan. 10:13 **But the prince of the kingdom of Persia withstood me twenty-one days: but,** *behold,* Michael, one of the chief princes, came to help me; **and I remained there with the kings of Persia.** [14] **Now I** *have* **come to make** *you* **understand** what shall *happen to your people* **in the latter days:** *because the vision is for a distant* *future*. [15] And when he had spoken to me in this manner, I *turned* my face toward the ground, and I became *speechless*. [16] And, behold, <u>one like the *appearance* of the sons of men touched my lips</u>: then I opened my mouth, and *spoke*, and said to *the one* that stood *in front of* me, O my lord, I am *overwhelmed with* sorrows, by the vision and *all my* strength *is gone*. (Easy KJV)

[17] For how can I, your servant, talk with you my lord? for as for me, my strength is gone, and I am breathless. [18] <u>Then *the one with* the appearance of a man came again and touched me, and he strengthened me</u>, [19] And said, O man greatly beloved, *do not be afraid: and be at peace*, be *strong and have courage*. And when he had spoken to me, I was strengthened, and I said, speak my lord for you have given me strength. [20] Then he said: Do y*ou know why I came to you? and* now I will return to fight with the prince of Persia: and *when I leave* here, behold, the prince of Greece shall come. [21] But *I will show you what* is written in the scripture of truth: and <u>there is *no one that stands beside me in the battle except* Michael your prince</u>. (Easy KJV)

Notice that verse 14 refers to **"what shall happen to your people in the latter days,"** and **"the vision is for a distant future."** This all fits very well with the references Jesus made to Daniel's prophecy.

Michael Cast Satan and His Angels Out into the Earth (Rev. 12:9)

There are two chapters in Revelation that reflect the work of Michael (Revelation 12 and 20). Satan no longer has any place or power in heaven. There are saints on the earth at this time as testified to in at least four verses in Chapters 11-14 (Rev. 11:18; 13:7, 10; 14:12; also refer to 2 Thes. 2:5-10).**ichael Confronts Satan**

Michael would not dare overstep his bounds to speak judgment against anyone. That is left up to the plan of God. Yet Michael is commanded by God to expel Satan and his angels.

[Jude 9] **Yet Michael the archangel, when contending with the devil, and disputing about the body of Moses, did not dare bring a railing accusation against him, but said, The Lord rebuke you.**

[Rev. 12:7] **And there was war in heaven: Michael and his angels fought against the dragon; and the dragon fought and his angels,** [8] **And *the devil's strength was insufficient*; neither was their place found any more in heaven.** (Easy KJV)

Michael's Victory in Prophecy

In Summary: Michael's victory is prophesied in the ancient book of Daniel. We know how this great battle ends. Christ has returned to rule and reign on His eternal throne. God has assigned Michael as the protector of His people. He is also the one who has power over Satan as just stated. As indicated above, he has consistently confronted, opposed, and defeated Satan. From scripture we learn that Michael is the restrainer, and we could expect God to work through him in additional ways as we await the return of Christ.

This Concludes the Special Section on the Restrainer

Chapter 13

THE DRAGON'S CO-CONSPIRATORS

Snapshot of Chapter 13

John sees two beasts: one rises from the sea (he is the antichrist) and one rises from earth (the assistant and supporter of the antichrist). Here we refer to them as **co-conspirators**. The beast from the sea mimics Satan, and the second beast mimics Christ. He is the lamb of Satan as opposed to Christ who is the Lamb of God. The antichrist wages war against the saints for 42 months until he meets his end. His name is not revealed, but the code for his name is 666 which stands for evil raised to the highest level as compared to 777 standing for good raised to the highest level.

In Chapter 13 we see the stark contrast of the dragon, the beast from the sea and the beast from the earth in view of the magnificent and dramatic scene in Chapter 14 of the Lamb of God standing on Mount Zion with the 144,000 who had His name and His Father's name written on their foreheads.

They may have been martyred but they took their stand, and they received their everlasting reward. They stand in marked contrast to those of the earth who have the number of the beast on their foreheads. We will also see the devil's lamb compared to the Lamb of God.

We should remember that in John's apocalyptic vision we are shown caricatures of people and their place in these events. Therefore, a dragon is actually Satan and a beast is actually an evil world leader who will come at the end time.

THE SECOND MYSTERY:
THE MONSTROUS BEAST FROM THE SEA
Satan Welcomes the Second Antagonist from the Sea
(Revelation 13:1-6 is primary; 11:7-9; 13:1-18; 14:9, 11; etc.)

Text: Rev. 13:1-4

Rev. 13:1 **And I stood on the sea** *shore*, **and saw a beast rise out of the sea, having seven heads and ten horns, and ten crowns upon his horns, and on his heads the name of blasphemy.**
[2] **And the beast I saw was** *something like* **a leopard, and his feet** *were like* **the feet of a bear, and his mouth** *was like* **the mouth of a lion: and the dragon gave him his power, and his** *rule*, **and great authority.**

[3] **And I saw one of his heads appeared to have been** *wounded that would result in death*; **and his deadly wound was healed: and all the world wondered at the beast.**
[4] **And they worshipped the dragon that gave the beast his power: and they also worshiped the beast, and they said who is like the beast? Who is able to make war with him?** (EKJV)

Remember that we are in the interlude between the sounding of the seven trumpets and the pouring out of the seven bowls of God's wrath (Rev. 11:15; 16:1). Satan is the first antagonist. The Antichrist (here he is the beast from the sea) is the second antagonist.

The First Beast Comes Out of the Sea

The **"beast coming out of the sea"** (13:1) had seven heads, ten horns, and ten crowns. On each head was **"a blasphemous name."** We see the beast again in Rev. 17:3 with seven heads and ten horns and blasphemous names all over. In Chapter 17 the woman is sitting on the beast. The ten horns represent ten evil kings that appear at the end time (17:12). Daniel saw a beast with ten horns (Dan. 7:7).

John 12:31 **"Now is the time for judgment on this world; now the prince of this world will be driven out."**

This figure is the **ten-horned and seven-headed beast from the sea** (Rev. 13:1). This great beast is Satan incarnate. His name is **"blasphemy."** The dragon stands on the shore of the sea to welcome the first beast who has a terrifying appearance in John's vision. His names and his being are blasphemous to God and the Lamb.

The first beast (the Antichrist) has special powers **"...and great authority"** (13:2b NIV). He has been called **"the embodiment of Satanic evil"**—G. E. Ladd, *Commentary on the Revelation of John,* William B. Eerdmans Publishing Co., Grand Rapids, © 1972, p. 178.

His is a specific time—**"He exercised his authority for forty-two months"** (13:5). Satan is receiving an assistant who will bring great harm to the people of God. Satan cannot accomplish anything without a human agent. He must enlist and control his agents to attempt to demolish the work of God and the church.

There are Horns on the Red Dragon and the Beast

The kinship between the beast and the dragon is that **both have ten horns and seven heads**. Horns represent power and authority. There are many other ways to describe the Antichrist. Antichrist is a Satan-filled man. He will be a world ruler like Nero. Just as Satan worked in Nero from A.D. 64-68, he is going to work in Antichrist for three and one-half years. Revelation was written just after Nero committed suicide. We remember Nero as a notoriously evil man who delighted in murder, fear and terror. Antichrist will be like Nero.

Many were anointed King like Saul and David, but only Messiah was **"the Anointed"** of God. There have been many antichrists in history, but in the end the one identified as **"the Antichrist"** will come. He is a world ruler—**"The dragon had given the beast his power and his honor..."** (13:2b).

Characteristics of the Beast from the Sea

> ➤ **He rises from the sea (v. 1); He resembles the dragon (v. 1),** the second figure is the **ten-horned and seven-headed beast from the sea (v. 1)**. This great beast is Satan incarnate. His name is **"blasphemy."** In addition, there are no fewer than **a dozen further references in Revelation to the beast** (11:7, 14:9, 11; 15:2, 16:2, 10, 13; 19:19-20, 20:4, 10).
>
> ➤ **He has composite animal features (v. 2).**
>
> ➤ **He is dragon-empowered (v. 2).**
>
> ➤ **He has one head wounded to death but healed (vs. 3-4, 12).**
>
> ➤ **He blasphemes God and God's people for forty-two months (vs. 5-6).**
>
> ➤ **He makes war against the saints and kills them (vs. 7a, 15).**
>
> ➤ **He gives to those who follow him his "mark" (either his name or his number).**
>
> ➤ Mankind **worshiped the dragon and the beast** (the Antichrist, cf. 13:3ff).
>
> ➤ Notice his time span is only **42 months.**
>
> ➤ Compare this to 12:6—**"1260 days"** of the woman's exile.
>
> ➤ Also compare Rev. 11:2ff where it states that the outer court of God's temple has been given to the Gentiles for **42 months.**
>
> ➤ He speaks **evil and blasphemous things for 42 months.**
>
> ➤ Of course, as we have previously said, **these three periods all equal 3 and ½ years, and that is half of seven years.**
>
> ➤ He represents **an evil political power.**
>
> ➤ The one that calls himself God is **blasphemous.**
>
> ➤ As he comes up out of the sea, the **horns break the water first.**
>
> ➤ He has **attributes of a leopard, feet like a bear, and a mouth like a lion (v. 2).**
>
> ➤ The Dragon (Satan) gave him **his power, and seat, and authority (v. 2).**

Antichrist Is a Satan-Filled Man

Satan dwells in Antichrist just like God dwells in Jesus. The glory of God dwelt in the Tabernacle in the wilderness, in the Temple in Jerusalem, and in Jesus of Nazareth, Son of God. The glory of God dwelt in Jesus as it never dwelt in the tabernacle.

His Blasphemous Mouth

Text: Rev. 13:5-10

Rev. 13:5 And *the beast was given a mouth* that spoke outlandish things and blasphemies; and power was given to him to continue forty-two months. [6] And he opened his mouth *and spoke* blasphemy against God: his name, and his tabernacle, and *all* that *are* in heaven. [7] And *he was given the ability* to *wage* war with the saints, and to overcome them: and power was given him over all *tribes*, and *languages*, and nations. [8] And all *inhabitants* of the earth shall worship him, whose names are not written in the book of life of the Lamb slain from the foundation of the world. [9] *Anyone who has ears let him hear.* [10] He that is to go into captivity into captivity he will go: he that is to be killed with the sword, with the sword will be killed. Here is the patience and the faith of the saints. (EKJV)

Verse 5 – The beast **"spoke outlandish things and blasphemies"** during the period of forty-two months (or three and one-half years). When he opened his mouth, all kinds of blasphemies poured out against God, his people and heaven. It was natural for him to attack the people of God on earth. They have been Satan's target all along.

His War Against the Saints

These verses are crucial, and mark a vital point for interpreting an important portion of Revelation. Not only are the saints alive during the terrible workings of the antichrist, but they are persecuted for their faith in Christ, and their refusal to worship the beast. See Revelation, Chapter 7 for additional details. The beast will wage war against the saints who certainly are alive during his time on earth. In keeping with Daniel's specific prophecy, he will **"overcome them."**

There are two obvious groups: the saints who have their names recorded in the book of life (v. 8); and the population of the world who worship the beast. John says: **"Anyone who has ears let him hear"** (v. 9). In other words: "Pay attention, because this is how it will be under the reign of the antichrist." Much additional information follows in the Select Sections on the Antichrist, and on the Saints.

We see the saints alive through Chapter 14, verse 12. In addition, he will exercise power over all other peoples in the world (13:7-8). A special note: the saints do not suffer the plagues of the wrath of God. They are exempted while the kingdoms of the world, dominated by the antichrist, receive the full force of God's wrath. In chapter 7 we see an innumerable host of people who came out of the great tribulation. These believers in Christ did not experience the wrath of God, but only the persecution of the Antichrist (Rev. 9:4; 16:2, 10; 17:8; 18:4).

SS
Select Section

THE ANTICHRIST IN PROPHECY
THE ANTICHRIST—WHO IS HE?
Revelation 13

Remember: **We are in the interlude** between the sounding of the seven trumpets and the pouring out of the seven bowls of God's wrath (Rev. 11:15; 16:1).

How to Describe the Antichrist?
Antichrist: A Satan-filled Man (13:5-8)
First: He Will Be a Secular Ruler
Over the Entire World

"The dragon had given the beast his power and his throne..."(13:2b). Many fall into Satan's trap that Jesus adamantly refused.

Luke 4:5 **And the devil took him up into a high mountain, and showed him all the kingdoms of the world in a moment of time.**
6 **And the devil said, I will give you all this power, and the glory** *of these: for it has been given to me; and* **I** *will give it* *to whoev-*

er I desire. [7] **Therefore, if you will worship me, all this will be yours.** (EKJV)

His Special Powers—"...and great authority" (13:2b-NIV). He uses his authority to oppose God, His people and everything that is holy. He holds the key to life and death for believers. He strikes back at everything holy.

His Specific Time—"He exercises his authority for forty-two months" (13:5). He is only permitted to assault the saints for a limited time.

His Strife with the Saints—(Rev.13:7). It is said of the beast (monster) from the sea:

Rev. 13:7 **And** *he was given the ability* **to** *wage* **war with the saints, and to overcome them: and power was given him over all** *tribes,* **and languages, and nations.** (EKJV)

He is Determined to Destroy the Saints

The war against the saints is described in following chapters of Revelation. Regarding the beast from the earth and his attack upon the saints it is said:

Rev. 13:10 **He that is to go into captivity into captivity he will go: he that is to be killed with the sword, with the sword will be killed. Here is the patience and the faith of the saints.**

"This calls for patient endurance and faithfulness on the part of the saints." (KJV-Rev. 13:10; also 14:12) —See commentary at that point in Chapter 14.

If there are no saints on the earth—what could this possibly mean? If these people are a number of redeemed Jews, we are confused because this is never expressed in Revelation or elsewhere. Up to 150 years ago, no one ever raised this question. This arose with the publishing of the Scofield Reference Bible over one hundred years ago. There is nothing written about this prior to that publishing. If saints are not on the earth, why would we ever be concerned about the mark of the beast? What possible consequence could it have for believers? Therefore we need to reconsider all the books written and influenced by a Bible with those footnotes. There is great confusion regarding these issues, but such confusion is unnecessary. Inspired scripture is the most perfect commentary on other scripture. In reading God's word, His Spirit guides our interpretation.

THE PERSON AND WORK OF THE ANTICHRIST
The Battle against the Devil and the Antichrist

1 John 3:8, 10 explains the problem of the devil.

1 John 3:8 **He who does what is sinful is of the devil, because the devil has been sinning from the beginning.** The reason the Son of God appeared was to destroy the devil's work. **[10] This is how we know who the children of God are and who the children of the devil are: Anyone who does not do what is right is not a child of God; nor is anyone who does not love his brother.**

There has never been a single day that the devil was not engrossed in awesome sin and evil.

Antichrist	Believers
Unspiritual	**Spiritual**
Temporary	**Permanent**
Superficial	**Genuine**
Deceivers	**Faithful**
Children of the Devil	**Children of God**

Test for the Spirit of Antichrist (1 John 4:1-6)

The test for the spirit of antichrist is presented in the verses below. You can tell who is genuine in their experience with Christ and who is false. The bottom line is those who have the spirit of antichrist are of the world, and those who pass the test of Christ are not of the world. The two can never be successfully joined together.

1 John 4:1 **Beloved, do not believe every spirit, but try the spirits to discern if they are from God: because many false prophets have gone out into the world. [2] Hereby you know the Spirit of God: Every spirit that confesses that Jesus Christ is come in the flesh is of God: [3] And every spirit that does not confess that Jesus Christ is come in the flesh is not of God: and this is that *spirit* of antichrist, whereof you have heard that it should come; and even now already is it in the world. [4] You are of God, little children, and have overcome them: because greater is he that is in you, than he that is in the world. [5] They are of the world: therefore they speak the words of the world, and the world *listens to* them. [6] We are from God. Whoever knows God *listens to* us, and whoever is not from God *does not listen to* us. From this we know the spirit of truth and the spirit of error**. (EKJV)

The Great Sin (1 John 5:16) is the sin that leads to death. John expresses grave concern for those who are committing, or are on the verge of committing the great sin.

^{1 John 5:16} If *anyone sees* his brother *commit* a sin which is not a *mortal* sin, he shall ask, and *God will* give life to *those* that do not *commit a mortal* sin. There is *a mortal* sin: I do not say that he *should* pray for it.

Predictions of Christ Concerning the Antichrist Figure
The Little Apocalypse—Matthew 24:23-25; Mark 13:21-23

These passages, somewhat like Revelation, are also apocalyptic. These are the words of Christ and it behooves us to note and pay attention to them.

^{Matt. 24:23} Then if any man *says* to you, *Look,* here is Christ, or there; *do not* believe it. ²⁴ For false Christs shall arise, and false prophets, and shall show great signs and wonders; so that, if it were possible, *they would* deceive the very elect. ²⁵ *But listen,* I have told you before. (Note: "false christs"—Greek = *pseudochristoi*).

Daniel's Prophecy of the Antichrist Figure and the End Time
DANIEL, THE GOSPELS, 2 THESSALONIANS AND REVELATION

THE FOURTH BEAST OF DANIEL HAVING TEN HORNS

Remember we are dealing with symbols. The image of a beast is meant to indicate his enormous evil, danger, and harm just as a beast could destroy whole communities. Therefore we are meant to see the extent of the evil inflicted by Antichrist. Daniel was an Old Testament prophet who was permitted to see the end time when the Antichrist is to come. There are definite similarities in Daniel and in Revelation. Read the following words of Daniel's prophecy in light of Revelation.

The Prophecy from Daniel
The Fourth Beast—He Wages War against
the Saints of God

You will notice that the antichrist not only wages war against the saints, but the saints are defeated (Dan. 7:21). The Ancient of Days (God) comes and **"pronounces judgment in favor of the saints of the Most High"** (Dan. 7:22). It is at that time that **"they possessed the kingdom."** Dan. 7:23 explains the onslaught of the savage antichrist (hence his designation as a beast) and how he **"will devour the whole earth, trampling it down and crushing it."** Daniel, as in the Revelation of John, is allowed to see in a vision the vast war and suffering of this period: **"I watched..."** (v. 21). The following is inspired scripture: **"The saints will be handed over to him (the antichrist) for a time, times, and half a time"** (v. 25 printed below). We need to see and understand that both Daniel and John agree on the three and one half years of the tribulation. Check out these scriptures for yourself.

Key Prophecies from Daniel 7 and 8
Daniel 7:19-27

Dan. 7:19 **Then I *desired to* know the truth *concerning* the fourth beast, which was *different* from all the others, exceedingly dreadful, whose teeth were of iron, and his claws of brass; who devoured, broke in pieces, and *trampled the rest* with his feet;** **20 And also of the ten horns that were *on* his head, and of the other *horn* which came up, and before whom three fell; even of that horn that had eyes, and a mouth that spoke very great things, who looked greater than his associates.**

21 *While I looked* the same horn made war with the saints, and *overcame* them; *(See Rev. 13:7)* **22 Until the Ancient of days came, and judgment was given to the saints of the most High; and the time came that the saints possessed the kingdom. 23 Thus he said, The fourth beast shall be the fourth kingdom upon earth, which shall be different from all kingdoms, and shall devour the whole earth, and shall tread it down, and break it in pieces.**

24 And the ten horns out of this kingdom are ten kings that shall arise: and another shall rise after them; and he shall be *different* from the first, and he shall subdue three kings.

[25] And he shall speak *strong* words against the most High, and shall wear *down* the saints of the most High, and *decide* to change times and laws: *(See Rev. 13:6)* and they shall be given into his hand until a time and times and a *half* time. (See note below.)

[26] But *there shall* be a judgment *rendered*, and they shall take away his dominion, to consume and to destroy it unto the end. [27] And the kingdom and dominion, and the greatness of the kingdom under the whole heaven, shall be given to the people of the saints of the most High, whose kingdom is an everlasting kingdom, and all dominions shall serve and obey him. (EKJV)

As we read Daniel 7 and 8 we note distinct prophesies that we find fulfilled in Revelation. Now we move to Daniel 8.

His Devastating and Destructive Plans
Daniel 7:23-25

[23] And in the latter period of their kingdom, when the *wicked acts of those* that rebel have *reached the maximum limits*, a king of fierce *appearance*, and who also *understands the working of evil plans*, shall arise.

[24] And his power shall be very strong, but not by his own strength: and he shall bring astonishing devastation, and shall prosper in everything he does, and shall destroy mighty men and the saints.

[25] And through his policy he shall also cause *deception* to prosper; and he shall be *overly conceited* in his heart, and when peace *gives a sense of security*, he will take a stand against the Prince of princes; but he shall be destroyed *without a human hand touching him.*
(EKJV)

Commentary

At the time when **"*those* that rebel** (the devil and his angels) **have become completely wicked, a king of fierce *appearance*, who also *understands the working of evil plans*** (the second beast from the earth) **shall arise."** (Dan. 8:23). He becomes very strong **"but not by his own strength"** (it is given to him by the antichrist). Therefore he **"shall destroy mighty men and the saints."** Yet **"he shall be destroyed *without a human hand touching him.*** His destruction will be by God and his angels. God's people will face a terrible test, but in the end they will receive the crown of life.

194

Daniel's Amazing Details of the Antichrist

> He *understands the working of evil plans* (8:23).
> He will speak against the Most High and oppress his saints (7:25).
> His power shall be very strong, but not by his own strength (8:23).
> He shall bring astonishing devastation (8:24).
> He shall destroy...the saints (8:24).
> He shall cause *deception* to prosper (8:25).
> He will take a stand against the Prince of princes (8:25).
> He will devour the whole earth: treading it down and breaking it in pieces (7:23).
> He shall be destroyed by other than human hands (8:25).

Daniel's Prophecy of War Against the Saints

Dan. 7:21 *While I looked* the same horn made war with the saints, and *overcame* them; *(See Rev. 13:7)* ²² Until the Ancient of days came, and judgment was given to the saints of the most High; and the time came that the saints possessed the kingdom. (EKJV)

Key Points Introduced by Paul in 2 Thessalonians
The Following Questions Are for Personal Study
Paul Speaks of the Days of Antichrist
("the lawless one"-v.3)

1. What is meant by the rebellion that will take place (v. 3)?
2. What is meant by "that day will not come until"... (v. 3)?
3. Who holds it back or restrains it (v. 6)?
4. When will the "lawless one" be overthrown (v. 8)?
5. His coming will be accompanied by the rise of every kind of evil (vs. 9-10).

We should see the relationship between war against the saints in Daniel 7 and the campaign against the children (the saints) of the heavenly woman in Revelation 12. There can be no doubt from the inspired scripture of Revelation 12 and 13 that the devil and his associates are going to inflict great harm upon the saints. Just read this for yourself and you will see what both Daniel and John saw and understood.

Paul's Prophecy of Antichrist's Evil

The Man of Lawlessness

2 Thes. 2:1 Now concerning the coming of our Lord Jesus Christ, and our being gathering together to him, we ask you brothers [2] That you do not be *quickly unsettled* in mind, or troubled in spirit, nor by word, nor by letters as if they came from us, *saying* that the day of Christ has *already* come. [3] Let no *one deceive* you *at all*: for that day will not come, except the rebellion *take place* first, and that man of lawlessness be revealed, the son of destruction; [4] Who stands in *opposition and exalts himself* above all that is called God, or that is worshiped; so that he *sits* as God in the temple of God, *pretending that he is* God.

[5] *Don't you* remember, that, when I was still with you, I told you these things? [6] And now you know what *restrains* him that he might be revealed in his time. [7] For the *mystery* of lawlessness is already at work: only he who now *restrains* it will do so until he is taken out of the way. [8] And then that *lawless one* will be revealed, whom the Lord will kill with the *breath* of his mouth, and will destroy with the *splendor (or brilliance)* of his coming: [9] Even he whose coming is *in accord* with the working of Satan with *much* power and *false* signs and wonders, [10] And with all the *wicked deception that* is in those that perish; because they did not *accept* a love of the truth, that they might be saved. [11] And for this *reason* God may send them a strong delusion, so that they should believe what is false.

The Antichrist from 2 Thessalonians

1. He will prevail because **believers are deceived** (2:3).
2. He **opposes and exalts himself above God** (2:4).
3. He will **oppose true worship** (2:4).
4. He **sets himself up in the temple of God** (2:4). **Which temple?**
5. He **accepts the mystery of lawlessness** (2:7).
6. He **will be destroyed at Christ's coming** (2:8). This is a key.
7. He will **do the works of Satan** (2:9).
8. He **will perform counterfeit miracles, signs and lying wonders** (2:9).
9. He **will deceive people who are not saved** (2:10).
10. They **will accept strong delusions** (2:11).

John Is the Originator of the Actual Term "Antichrist"

The title antichrist used only in 1 and 2 John is one of several titles for this super-diabolical world leader who will appear at the end of time. John makes it clear that there are always antichrists in the world as he noted in his own day. We have wicked, violent, evil, deceiving, destructive, world leaders in every age that defy God and all spiritual things. They also defy the basic human rights of entire classes of people. Those who meet with their displeasure are slaughtered including men, women, children and babies.

Paul called him the man of lawlessness. Daniel described the coming one as "...**a king of fierce *appearance*, and who also *understands the working of evil plans*, shall arise.**" (Dan. 8:23). Daniel also described him as "***different* from all the others, exceedingly dreadful, whose teeth were of iron, and his claws of brass; who devoured, broke in pieces, and *trampled the rest* with his feet**" (Dan. 7:19). All are in agreement as to the wicked, evil, treacherous, dangerous and destructive nature of this one that we now refer to as **"antichrist."**

1 John 2:18 **Dear children, this is the last hour; and as <u>you have heard that the antichrist is coming</u>, even now many antichrists have come. This is how we know it is the last hour.** (KJV)

1 John 2:22 **Who is the liar? It is the man who denies that Jesus is the Christ. <u>Such a man is the antichrist</u>—he denies the Father and the Son.** (KJV)

1 John 4:3 **...but every spirit that does not acknowledge Jesus is not from God. <u>This is the spirit of the antichrist</u>, which you have heard is coming and even now is already in the world.** (KJV)

2 John 1:7 **Many deceivers, who do not acknowledge Jesus Christ as coming in the flesh, have gone out into the world. <u>Any such person is the deceiver and the antichrist</u>.** (KJV)

1. **He is coming at the last hour (1 John 2:18). "Last hour"** is the end or climax (in our case, the coming of Christ and the time of judgment.)

2. **He is the liar who denies that Jesus is the Christ (1 John 2:22).**
3. **He does not acknowledge Jesus (1 John 4:3).**
4. **He is a deceiver (2 John 7).**

This is the Conclusion of This Select Section on the Anti-christ

---

THE THIRD MYSTERY
THE MONSTER FROM THE EARTH (13:11-18)
Text: Rev. 13:11-18
Rev. 13:11 And I *saw* another beast coming up out of the earth; and he had two horns like a lamb, and he *spoke like* a dragon. (EKJV)

The third figure (antagonist against Christ and His Church) is another beast that comes up out of the earth. We see a battle between Christ and Antichrist, between God and Satan shaping up. The mark of the beast: those **branded** for Satan are contrasted to the ones "**sealed**" by God. We are in a battle against evil. We are in a war against Satan. If he tested Jesus, he will certainly work on you. Sometimes we say, "It can't get any worse." In my understanding of Revelation, there is coming a time of intense evil similar to past events, but far greater in influence and effect than anything we have ever known. 1 John was warning the believers of that day and the days that follow that Antichrist will surely come.

The Second Beast is "coming out of the earth" (13:11). He is a pretense of Christ (13:11). He is an evil mockery of the Holy Spirit. He is opposite of the Holy Spirit in every way. In the cause of righteousness, he stands against the Holy Spirit and fights against God. He represents the power of religion disassociated with God. He has two horns. Christ has seven horns (Rev. 5:6). This beast (Rev. 13:11) had two horns like a lamb, but he spoke like a dragon. Very clearly, he is a diabolical false Messiah. Christ is the Lamb of God and this beast is the lamb of the devil.

What we are seeing is the religion designed by and for the world, not of the Spirit. That should cause us to be very alert. This is Satan's last diabolical attempt to take over the world. The authority of the second beast is that of the first beast.

Text—Rev. 13:12-14
Rev. 13:12 **And he exercised all the power of the first beast before him, and caused the earth and *those that live in the earth* to worship the first beast whose deadly wound was healed. 13 And he *performs amazing* signs, so that he *caused* fire to come down from heaven on the earth in *full* sight of *mankind*. 14 Because of the signs it *was enabled to perform* on behalf of the first beast, it was able to deceive the people of the earth; and *it ordered them to set up an image* of the first beast that had been wounded by a sword, and yet *was alive*.** (EKJV)

His Powers of Magic

He performed what appeared to be great and miraculous signs (13:13). He caused **"fire to come down from heaven"** (13:13). **"He deceived the inhabitants of the earth"** (13:14). **"He ordered them to set up an image in honor of the beast that was wounded by the sword and yet lived"** (13:14). He is a one man show. He can do false miracles and magic, and he can force people to do what they do not want to do. He works through deception. He will deceive **"the inhabitants of the earth"** (v. 14), and force them **"to set up an image** (idol) **in honor of the beast"** so that people can worship him.

The second Beast is not the "man of Sin." The second Beast causes the earth to worship the first Beast (Rev. 13:12), whereas the **"man of Sin exalts himself"** (2 Thes. 2:4); see also Dan. 11:36: **"And he exalts himself."** His authority is the authority of the first beast from the sea. It is granted to him and permits him to carry out the commands of the Antichrist. As already intimated, there are several things which show plainly that the second Beast is the third person in the Trinity of Evil. Now we are given further confirmation. There is nothing in Rev. 13 or elsewhere to show that this second beast is worshiped. Rather he directs believers to worship not himself, but the first Beast.

He comes from the earth, not heaven. However, the land monster is a partner with the monster from the sea. He represents the religion that speaks to Antichrist and Satan. He functions to make the world the church of Satan. These two represent Satan's last desperate attempt to take over the world. Satan and those who follow him are judged. Jesus taught us that we should not fear the workmen of Satan, but to fear God.

Luke 12:4 "I tell you, my friends, do not be afraid of those who kill the body and after that can do no more. ⁵ But I will show you whom you should fear: Fear him who, after the killing of the body, has power to throw you into hell. Yes, I tell you, fear him."

This Beast Is Counterfeit, But Christ Is the True Lamb of God

The beast from the sea mimics Satan. The beast from the earth is Satan's lamb. He bears some resemblance to a lamb. But when he opens his mouth he reveals his demonic nature: **"He speaks like a dragon."** Notice that the dragon gives authority to the beast from the sea and the beast from the sea transfers power to the beast from the earth.

The Antichrist's Number

His symbol is the number 6 "heaped up" or 666.
Text: Rev. 13:15
Rev. 13:15 The second beast was given power *to give life* to the image of the first beast so that its image *was able to speak* and to *cause* all that would not worship the image to be killed. (EKJV)

He (the beast from the earth) **gave breath to the image of the beast** (from the sea—the antichrist). It will be a devastating matter to worship Christ rather than the beast. You forfeit your life violently and will become a martyr just as many believers in the first days of Christianity did. You will have to decide in one moment where you stand and with whom you stand. To stand with Christ will mean certain death by public execution.

The Mark of the Beast
Text: Rev. 13:16
Rev. 13:16 It also forced *everyone,* small and great, rich and poor, free and slave, to receive a mark on their right hand, or on their foreheads: ¹⁷ And no one could buy or sell, except those that had the mark, or the name of the beast, or the number of its name.

He forced everyone...to receive a mark."

The antichrist will have such power that you will have to get a special mark to buy or sell. Notice that there are no exceptions. It says: **"everyone small and great."** That is a biblical term frequently used to express completeness (In Revelation: 11:8; 13:16; 19:5, 18; 20:12). No doubt one is omitted. Without the mark of the beast no one will t be able to buy anything or sell anything in order to earn money, or for food and daily needs. Here is a fearful aspect of the work of the Antichrist.

How Could the Mark of the Beast Work?

We should be concerned at how technology has brought us to a place as described in this scripture. Credit cards have a chip implanted. Computers keep a record of where you go, and what you purchase. Fingerprints are common in banks today. Many of us have a food market or drug store discount card. These are not evil in and of themselves, but it will be so easy when the evil beast appears to control the lives of all those on the earth. These are examples of your name, address, and much more information already held as records in computers. The saints who defy his demand will face persecution and execution. But they receive a glorious resurrection to eternal life in the city of our God.

Compare the people bearing the mark of the beast to the 144,000 who stand with the Lamb. We decide where we will stand on all vital issues. Spiritual leaders take spiritual stands regardless of the popularity of their choice. Someone said, "When you ride the fence you get hung up on barbed wire." It is a very uncomfortable place to be.

OUR LIVES ARE NUMBERED

The Antichrist figure represents, in a human personality, the totality of evil in its most antagonistic and violent form. His symbol is the number 6 "heaped up" or 666. In contrast to the limited period of the dominance and power of the Antichrist (1260 days, 3 and ½ years, or 42 months), John will demonstrate the eternal reign of the Lamb of God.

The number **"666"** represents the ultimate evil. Each number of the alphabet equaled a number. If you assign "A" the number 100;

"B" = 101; "C"= 102, etc. you can add a total of 666 and spell "Hitler." The number of Messiah is 888. People attempt to identify the antichrist by all kinds of mathematical formulas. No one knows the meaning of the number. If we could discover his name, we could possibly predict the coming of Christ, and the scripture tells us that no man will know the time or the season. We will, however, undoubtedly recognize him when he appears due to his world domination and his persecution of the faithful in Christ.

Matt. 24:36 But of that day and hour no man knows, no, not the angels of heaven, but my Father only. (KJV)
Matt. 24:42 Watch therefore: for you *don't* know what hour your Lord will come. (KJV)

SS

Select Section on the Saints

SAINTS YOU MAY KNOW

The Saints Are Classified

Rev. 14:12 Here is the patience of the saints: here are *the ones that keep the commandments of God and the faith of Jesus*. (EKJV)

The verse above is the definition of a saint. Therefore, you may know many people that you interact with in your life who are saints. In fact, you may be a saint.

To begin, the King James Version **"saints"** is a very appropriate term. In the Catholic Church, a saint designates a kind of super church leader, when there is nothing of that in the New Testament. Saints are born-again believers in Christ who are obedient to Him. Saints are always believers. All true believers are saints. At least 33 times in Acts, the letters of Paul and in Jude **the term "saints" is used of believers <u>then living on the earth</u>. Check these scriptures with a concordance.** This is a critical and crucial distinction.

In Revelation we see the saints alive before, and also after their death celebrating their resurrection together with the Lamb of God. This is a wonderful and glorious picture of what is ahead.

The Saints in Acts and Romans

Acts speaks of the **"saints"** in Jerusalem.

Acts 9:13 **Then Ananias answered, Lord, I have heard *from* many *people* of this man, *and* how much evil he has done to your saints at Jerusalem:** (EKJV)

Acts 26:10 **And that is just what I did in Jerusalem. On the authority of the chief priests I put many of the saints in prison, and when they were put to death, I cast my vote against them.** (KJV)

Acts 9:32 **As Peter traveled about the country, he went to visit the saints in Lydda.** (KJV)

Rom. 1:7 **To all in Rome who are loved by God and called to be saints:** (KJV)

> Rom. 8:27 **And he who searches our hearts knows the mind of the Spirit, because the Spirit intercedes for the saints in accordance with God's will.** (KJV)

It is notable that the saints were rounded up, placed in prison and executed just as will happen in the last great tribulation yet to come. Paul makes clear his part in the rounding up and execution of the saints in his life as Saul before Christ appeared to him on the Damascus Road and ordained him to become the missionary to the Gentiles (Acts 9:13; 26:10).

The Saints in Revelation are those whose names are in the Lamb's Book of Life, those who refuse to worship the Antichrist. And they are faithful even to the point of death. He gives them the power of His Spirit to endure persecution.

The Saints in Revelation

> The Saints lifting up their prayers (Rev. 5:8; 8:3, 4)
> The Saints receive their reward (Rev. 11:18)
> The Saints, and Antichrist's war against them (Rev. 13:7)
> The Saints are persecuted (Rev. 13:10)
> The Saints demonstrate enduring patience (Rev. 14:12)
> The Saints and their bloodshed (Rev. 16:6)
> The Saints and the harlot woman drunk with their blood (Rev. 17:6; 18:24)
> The Saints and their righteousness (Rev. 19:8)
> The Saints after the Millennium (Rev. 20:9)

When Will the Saint's Bloodshed Take Place?

A great portion of it will be during the great tribulation. In Revelation 18:20 the saints, prophets and apostles are called upon to rejoice because their suffering, persecution and death have been avenged by God. **Rev. 18:20 "Rejoice over her, O heaven, and you saints, apostles, and prophets; for God has judged *your case against her in your favor.*"**

Revelation 14:12 is the final mention of <u>living saints on the earth</u>. There is no further mention of living saints. The very next verse is the epitaph of the saints: **Rev. 14:13 Then I heard a voice from heaven say, "Write: Blessed are the dead who die in the Lord from now on." "Yes," says the Spirit, "<u>they will rest from their labor</u>, for their deeds will follow them."**

What labor? Their labor was when these faithful witnesses for Christ served the Lord on earth.
What deeds? Their deeds are their willingness to bear His name even if it meant death such as He died. The deeds of the righteous saints go with them into eternity.

And the next verse tells of **the harvest of the earth** by the One seated on the cloud (14:14ff). In 14:17 the harvest of the wicked is reported. Then we have the marvelous anthem of the redeemed saints in heaven:

Rev. 15:1 And I saw another great and *amazing* sign in heaven, seven angels having the seven last plagues; for with them the wrath of God is *completed.* ²And I saw a sea of glass mingled with fire:

and those that had won the victory over the beast, and over its image, and over its mark, and over the number of its name, stood on the sea of glass, *holding in their hands the harps* of God. (EKJV)

³ And they *sang* the song of Moses the servant of God, and the song of the Lamb, saying, Great and *amazing* are your works, Lord God Almighty; just and true are *your* ways, King of saints. ⁴ Who shall not fear you, O Lord, and glorify *your* name? for you alone are holy: all nations will come and worship before you *because* Your judgments are revealed. (EKJV)

The saints suffered indescribable punishment because of the unwavering adherence to their faith in Christ and His death for sinners. These saints are going through the same kind of tribulation as was experienced by Peter, Paul and the early church. Believers in the early church suffered indescribable pain and death, and many of them experienced vile and violent death because of their refusal to retract their faith in the Lord Jesus Christ.

John 16:33 **I have spoken these things to you, that in me you might have peace. In the world you will have tribulation: but be of good cheer; I have overcome the world.** (KJV)

1Thes. 3:4 **For truly, when we were with you, we told you then that we would suffer tribulation; even as it *happened*..."** (EKJV)

Acts 9:15 **But the Lord said to Ananias, "Go! This man is my chosen instrument to carry my name before the Gentiles and their kings and before the people of Israel. ¹⁶ <u>I will show him how much he must suffer for my name.</u>"** (EKJV)

Revelation was written to encourage these early Christians in a time of tribulation and suffering. It is said of them: **"No lie was found in their mouths; they are blameless"** (Rev. 14:5).

The Glory of the Saints

The first verse of Revelation 14:1 reveals a wonderful and glorious portrayal of the Lamb of God and the saints on the heavenly Mount Zion.

Rev. 14:1 **And I looked, and, behold, a Lamb stood on mount Zion, and with him a hundred and forty-four thousand, who had his name and his Father's name written on their foreheads. ²And I heard a sound from heaven, like the sound of *rushing* waters, and like the sound of *continuous* thunder: and I heard the sound of harpists playing their harps: ³And they sang a new song before the throne, and before the four creatures, and the elders: and no one could learn that song but the hundred and forty-four thousand, that were redeemed from the earth.** (EKJV)

Those who fail to take a spiritual stand today have no hope in the time of tribulation and persecution. In Chapter 14 we have a beautiful view of what will happen to the Israelites who believe and to the Gentiles who believe. We see the glory laid out for us by our God, and we can truly rejoice.

Chapter 14

THE EVERLASTING GOSPEL AND THE FINAL HARVEST

Snapshot of Chapter 14

This chapter is full of events. First, John sees the 144,000 that we met in Chapter 7. They are with the Lamb on Mt. Zion, and now they have been sealed. These have been redeemed from the earth. They are completely obedient to Christ. We have a preview announcement of the fall of New Babylon, the city of the Antichrist. We also see two harvests. The first is by Christ of the redeemed. The second is a harvest of grapes that are thrown in the winepress where Christ (see Chapter 19) treads the grapes of God's wrath, and blood, not grape juice, flows for 200 miles as deep as a horse's bridle. The final condition of the wicked is thus revealed.

The first part of the chapter gives us a view of the 144,000 out of the twelve tribes of Israel who, during the last 3½ years of human history, will complete the number of the elect among the Israelites that believe in Jesus as the Messiah.

They are with the Lord on Mount Zion. They are going to reign with Christ. This scene is just before the rapture and the final harvest of the wicked (all in Chapter 14). Christ is coming again in glorious fashion.

Chapter 14 is comprised of **seven vivid scenes** that fit well after the revelations in Chapter 13. Verse 13 is unattached to the seven. The chapter concludes with the *parousia* of Christ and the final judgment of mankind.

In Chapter 14 the scene moves from a view of the beast back to Mt. Zion. Mt. Zion was profoundly in the hearts of the Israelites in the Old Testament. The Spirit permitted John to see beyond death. His words are encouraging to those of us who have loved ones on the other side. In verse 13 we will find the second beatitude as it applies to the saints mentioned in v. 12. We are also shown the blessedness of the 144,000.

FIRST SCENE: THE 144,000 ARE WITH THE LAMB ON MT. ZION (14:1-5)

Text: Rev. 14:1-5

Rev. 14:1 **And I looked, and, behold, a Lamb stood on mount Zion, and with him a hundred and forty-four thousand, who had his name and his Father's name written on their foreheads. ² And I heard a sound from heaven, like the sound of *rushing* waters, and as the sound of *continuous* thunder: and I heard the sound of harpists playing their harps: ³ And they sang a new song before the throne, and before the four creatures, and the elders: and no one could learn that song but the hundred and forty-four thousand, which were redeemed from the earth. ⁴ These are the ones that were not defiled with women; for they are virgins. They follow the Lamb wherever he goes. They were redeemed from among men, and are the first fruits to God and to the Lamb. ⁵ And there was no lie found in their mouth for they are without blame before the throne of God.** (EKJV)

We have a beautiful picture of the heavenly Mount Zion in Hebrews 12:22-24. This is the Mt. Zion in John's vision. It is the ultimate Mt. Zion prepared for the saints.

Heb. 12:22 **But ye are come unto mount Zion, and unto the city of the living God, the heavenly Jerusalem, and to an innumerable company of angels, ²³ To the general assembly and church of the firstborn, which are written in heaven, and to God the Judge of**

all, and to the spirits of just men made perfect, ²⁴ And to Jesus the mediator of the new covenant, and to the blood of sprinkling, that speaks better things than that of Abel. (EKJV)

When John takes us to the heavenly Mt. Zion in his vision, we have the character of the 144,000 revealed to us as is recorded below. They have the name of Christ and of God on their foreheads. They are marked for God. They belong to Him just as the others are marked for the beast. In Revelation 7 we are only introduced to the 144,000, but then the scene transports us to a great multitude. John says:

Rev. 7:9 After this I looked, and there was a great multitude, that no man could number, of all nations, and *tribes*, and people, and *languages*, stood before the throne, and before the Lamb, clothed with white robes, and palms in their hands... (EKJV)

It is vital to keep the two groups in our focus. One of the elders discussed the identity of this enormous multitude with John, and at John's request, the elder supplies the answer. The major thought is that they have come out of the terror of the great tribulation. You notice in Revelation 7:9 that their filthy garments worn in the suffering of the Great Tribulation have been discarded, and they are dressed **"with white robes"** (7:9, 14). Their garments are **"made...white in the blood of the Lamb."**

Rev. 7:14 "And I said unto him, Sir, you know. And he said to me, These are they which came out of great tribulation, and have washed their robes, and made them white in the blood of the Lamb. (EKJV)

What are they doing?
Rev. 7:15 "Therefore they are before the throne of God, and serve him day and night in his temple: and he that sits on the throne will dwell among them." (EKJV)

The Levites had the responsibility of serving in the temple **"day and night"** by providing music and other responsibilities of the temple (as recorded in: 1 Chr. 6:29 ff; 1 Chr. 9:33). In the New Jerusalem of God we will have definite responsibilities, and we will render perfect service joyfully in the everlasting kingdom.

THE HOLY CHARACTER OF THE 144,000

- They are under the care of the Lamb of God on Mt. Zion (v. 1).
- They bear His mark and insignia on their foreheads (v. 1).
- They produce an earth-shaking sound (v. 2).
- They are playing stringed harps and they are singing a new song (vs. 2-3).
- They always follow the Lamb wherever He goes (v. 4).
- They were purchased (by the blood of the Lamb) from among men (v. 4).
- They are first fruits (the proof of the harvest to come) of God and the Lamb (v. 4).
- They speak no lies, or anything false, and they are found blameless (v. 5). (cf. Ps. 15:2; 19:13; 26:1; 84:11; 119:1; 1 Cor. 1:8; Eph. 1:4; 5:27; Phil. 1:10; 2:15; 1 Thes. 3:13; 5:23; 2 Pet. 3:14)

You should notice that the first verse in Chapter 14 tells an important fact concerning the 144,000. And they [14:1] **"...had his name and his Father's name written in their foreheads."** (KJV)

The others who have the mark of the beast and have rejected salvation are excluded. But these have the name of Christ and His Father written on their foreheads. This means that they are covered by the blood of Jesus shed on the cross of Calvary. And more than that, He knows them all by name because they are His very own.

What is the meaning of Mt. Zion? Mt. Zion was the old name for Jerusalem. With Him are the 144,000. They are called **"firstfruits"** and are offered to God and the Lamb. The giving of the firstfruits sanctified the rest of the harvest.

In Chapter 7, the sealing of the servants should be accomplished. In Chapter 14, it is after the troubles (persecution/tribulation). They are singing—a new and triumphant song (14:3). It is a song of celebration. Only these could learn this song because they belong to God.

Compare this scene to Rev. 15:1-3 where the scene is the counterpart of the Israelites by the Red Sea. To say that they have been **"redeemed"** means that they are freed from bondage for their ultimate and eternal salvation (cf. Ps. 110:4).

In verse 4 we read: **⁴ These are the ones that were not defiled with women; for they are virgins.**
They are dedicated. These are virgins or celibate. This term is not normally applied to males. These are the army of the Lord sharing His victory. Men in Israel must forego sexual relations when they go to war, just as when they go to the temple.

Text: Rev. 14:4
¹⁴:⁴ They were redeemed from among men, and are the first fruits to God and to the Lamb. (KJV)

The firstfruits were for the first days of harvest and were presented to the Lord as a **"wave offering"** (Lev. 23:10, 17). Upon the return from the Babylonian Exile, Nehemiah commanded them to resume the practice of this offering (Neh. 10:37). Revelation 14:4 should be read in light of 1 Cor. 15:21-24. Those who are alive in Christ are singled out. Paul says:
1 Cor. 15:21 For since by man came death, by man came also the resurrection of the dead. ²² For as in Adam all die, even so in Christ shall all be made alive. ²³ But every man in his own order: Christ the firstfruits; afterward those that are Christ's at his coming. ²⁴ Then comes the end, when he shall have delivered up the kingdom to God, even the Father; when he shall have put down all rule and all authority and power. (KJV)

Pay attention to Paul's summary of salvation and the end time. The situation is that death came through Adam. But the resurrection from the dead (the release from the power of death) comes through Jesus Christ. In the first man, Adam, all men die. In Christ all will be made alive. They will be resurrected. When Christ died and was resurrected He became the firstfruits of the dead. When He returns (His second coming or *Parousia)* those who belong to Him will come alive.

At that time and in that immediate span of God's time, the end will come. Simultaneously, Christ, the Victor and Son of God is going to **"hand over the kingdom to God the Father."** He will have accomplished God's great purpose. He will have **"destroyed all dominion, authority and power."** We see this concurring in Revelation 19 when Christ is victorious over all the kings of the earth, and over Satan and his domain, and over all the evil powers. So in

Chapter 14 we see Christ, the Lamb of God standing on Mt. Zion with the 144,000, and John says that they are the firstfruits of the dead. Further we are shown the harvest of the righteous and the gathering of the unrighteous to be thrown into the winepress. We see in Rev. 19 again that it is Christ who treads the winepress. These two chapters are locked together. James 1:18 says:

James 1:18 Of his own will he *gave us birth* with the word of truth, that we should be a kind of firstfruits of his creatures. (EKJV)

James uses the **"we"** in speaking of the first Christians in his own day. Paul uses the term firstfruits in referring to the first believers.

1 Cor. 16:15 I beseech you, brethren, (you know the house of Stephanas, <u>that it is the firstfruits of Achaia</u>, and that they have addicted themselves to the ministry of the saints). (KJV)

These saints are **truthful and blameless** (14:5). That is how Christ, through His blood, will present these to the Father.

SECOND SCENE: THE PROCLAMATION OF THE ETERNAL GOSPEL (14:6-7)

Text: Rev. 14:6-7
⁶ And I saw another angel fly in the middle of heaven, having the everlasting gospel to preach to all that live on the earth, and to every nation, and tribe, and language, and people, ⁷ Saying with a loud voice, Fear God, and give him glory; for the hour of his judgment has come: and worship him that made heaven, and earth, and the sea, and the fountains of waters. (KJV)

John sees an angel proclaiming the eternal gospel. The meaning of the sentence **"to preach unto them that dwell on the earth, and to every nation, and kindred *(or tribe),* and tongue *(or language),* and people"** (14:6) means that the gospel is for **all** people. Revelation 14:7-12 point to the imminent approach of the judgment of God. The angel issues a final warning and invitation:

The people of the world did not **"give him glory"** (see Rev. 16:9)—**"they did not repent to give him glory."** The hour of his judgment has come. Even now, **"Fear God and give him glory..."** In Rev. 10:6 John is told **"there will be no more delay"** (cf. Heb. 10:37). We should see these two warnings in keeping with one another.

THE ANNOUNCEMENT OF GOD'S JUSTICE: BABYLON THE GREAT WILL FALL

Text: Rev. 14:8

Rev. 14:8 **And there followed another angel, saying, Babylon is fallen, is fallen, that great city, because she made all nations drink of the wine of the wrath of her sexual immorality.** (KJV)

This is not one of the scenes or visions as outlined in Chapter 14, but it is an announcement inserted concerning the scenes in Chapter 18. Some commentators feel that this announcement is out of place in Chapter 14. But this special scene is here for a very specific reason. The saints are being informed that God's righteous judgment upon Babylon is certainly being carried out.

This special scene immediately precedes the scene of the saints who die and find rest in the Lord, and the final harvests of the righteous and the unrighteous. These events are taking place in close proximity to one another. Rather than attempting to determine a time line, we should see them all as imminent. There will be a sudden conclusion to earth, judgment of the wicked, and victory for the saints as in verse 13 below.

Old Testament Connection
Babylon's Fall in Ancient Prophecy

Isa. 47:1 **"Come down, and sit in the dust, O virgin daughter of Babylon, sit on the ground: there is no throne, O daughter of the Chaldeans: for you shall *never again* be called tender and delicate.** (EKJV)

Babylon is mentioned approximately 360 times in scripture; more so in Jeremiah than in any other book. This is the first announcement in Revelation of symbolic Babylon, who represents the sinful, decadent, and unremorseful city of the world culture. This is the prelude to her final doom. Below are the other passages from Rev. 16, 17, and 18 regarding this angel's announcement. The next chapters lead up to the fulfillment of this announcement. Rev. 16:19 **And the great city was divided into three parts, and <u>the cities of the nations fell</u>: and great Babylon came in remembrance before God, to give to her the cup of the wine of the fierceness of his wrath.** (KJV)

^{Rev. 17:5} And upon her forehead was a name written, MYSTERY, BABYLON THE GREAT, THE MOTHER OF HARLOTS AND ABOMINATIONS OF THE EARTH. (KJV)

^{Rev.18:1} And after these things I saw another angel come down from heaven, having great power; and the earth was *illuminated* with his glory. ²And he *shouted loudly* with a strong voice, saying, <u>Babylon the great is fallen, is fallen</u>, and has become the habitation of *demons,* and the hold of every foul spirit, and a cage of every unclean and hateful bird. (EKJV)

^{Rev. 18:9} And the kings of the earth, who have committed adultery and lived luxuriously with her, shall wail for her, and lament for her, when they shall see the smoke of her burning *rising up,*

¹⁰Standing afar off for the fear of her torment *falling on them,* saying, <u>Alas, alas that great city Babylon, that mighty city! for in one hour your judgment has come</u>." (EKJV)

^{Rev. 18:21} And a mighty angel took up a stone like a great millstone, and threw it into the sea, saying, Thus <u>shall that great city Babylon be thrown down with violence, and will</u> *never* <u>be found</u> *again.*" (EKJV)

THIRD SCENE: THE THIRD ANGEL'S AWESOME WARNING

Text: Rev. 14:9-10
^{Rev. 14:9} And the third angel followed them, saying with a loud voice, If any man worships the beast and his image, and receives his mark on his forehead, or on his hand, ¹⁰He shall drink of the wine of the wrath of God that is poured out without mixture into the cup of his indignation; and he shall be tormented with fire and sulfur in the presence of the holy angels, and in the presence of the Lamb:

No Rest for the Wicked (14:11)

Text: Rev. 14:11
^{Rev. 14:11} And the smoke of their torment ascends up forever and ever: and those, who worship the beast and his image, and whosoever receives the mark of his name, have no rest day nor night. (KJV)

The third angel issues the ultimate warning concerning those who worship the beast and his image and receive his mark. The punishment is spelled out in verse 10. The thought of **"no rest"** indicates that the senses are fully active during the suffering delivered by

God. This prepares us for the coming of the Christ, God's Lamb, but also the One who dispenses God's vengeance. Here we have a warning of terrible judgment to come.

This is a special message for the saints. They receive the promise of God's ultimate blessing while those who worship the beast will **"drink of the wine of the fury of God's wrath"** (v. 10). There is nothing but despair and enormous suffering and separation when the wrath of God falls upon them. This is Isaiah's prophecy as follows: ^{Isa. 66:14b} **"...the hand of the LORD shall be known toward his servants, and his indignation toward his enemies. ¹⁵ For, behold, the LORD will come with fire, and with his chariots like a whirlwind, to render his anger with fury, and his rebuke with flames of fire. ¹⁶ For by fire and by his sword will the LORD plead with all flesh: and the slain of the LORD shall be many.** (KJV)

Ultimately, the evil city will receive the full fury of God's wrath. Ironically, the harlot woman gives a cup filled with all manner of wickedness, but God's cup is a cup of unrelenting fury (cf. Rev. 16:19 above).

The harlot city dishes out her cup of evil, but she is repaid with God's **"cup filled with the wine of the fury of his wrath."** To worship the beast or to receive his mark is to permanently mark one to receive the fury of God's everlasting wrath.

God Cares for His Saints

Text: Rev. 14:12
¹² Here is the patience of the saints: here are those that keep the commandments of God, and the faith of Jesus. (KJV)
No doubt they are disturbed by the pain and suffering in their world and the martyrdom of their number. Verse 13 is meant to assure them that they are remembered and they will reside in the presence of the Lord. It is extremely difficult to live and suffer under great persecution. It is so easy to lose heart. They are encouraged to **"remain faithful to Jesus"** who suffered tremendously for the sins of the world. We should remain faithful in our day. Our suffering is small compared to theirs.

FOURTH SCENE: THE EPITAPH OF THE SAINTS (14:13)
Text: Rev. 14:13

Rev. 14:13 **And I heard a voice from heaven saying to me, Write, Blessed are the dead who die in the Lord from henceforth: Yes, says the Spirit, that they may rest from their labors; and their works do follow them.**

We have yet another beatitude. This is one of the seven in Revelation. **"Blessed are the dead who die in the Lord"** (14:13). This beatitude is the blessed epitaph of the saints. John reports from the other side. They are in the Lord's hands and He will take care of them. What we see as darkness is in reality **GLORY**. But this glory and this joy and this ever blessed world is reserved for believers. Salvation is a volitional act of the human will acted upon through faith in Christ crucified and resurrected. Salvation is for those with a lasting and earnest faith in the Son of God. Note: There are seven beatitudes in Revelation: Rev. 1:3; 14:13; 16:15; 19:9; 20:6; 22:7, 14. The psalmist wrote with inspiration:

Ps. 116:15 **Precious in the sight of the LORD is the death of his saints.** (KJV)

The Saint's Wonderful Rest

Regarding the saints we are told in verse 13: **"they may rest from their labors; and their works do follow them."** But in radically sharp contrast we see the judgment of those who follow and serve the beast and receive his mark of identification.

What a contrast! The one thing that most people long for will be denied to those who worship and identify with the beast. However, the redeemed saints who followed the Lamb will enter eternal rest. Hebrews 4 explains this reward: Heb. 4:9 **There remains therefore a rest to the people of God. [10] For he who has entered into his rest, he also has ceased from his own works, as God did from his. [11] Let us labor therefore to enter into that rest, lest any man fall after the same example of unbelief.**
(cf. Heb. 4:1-11 KJV; Ps. 95:11; Ps. 91:1; 1 Cor. 3:8; 15:58).

Sometimes we are overwrought with suffering, pain or grief. We may think no one knows or cares, but the one who has labored in the will and calling of God will be eternally remembered, for the record of that faithfulness is recorded in heaven.

FIFTH SCENE: THE HARVEST OF THE RIGHTEOUS (14:14-16)

There are Two Harvests (Resurrections)

Text: Rev.14:14-16

¹⁴ And I looked, and *I saw* a white cloud, and on the cloud *there* sat one like the Son of man, having a golden crown on his head, *and* a sharp sickle in his hand. ¹⁵ And another angel came out of the temple, crying with a loud voice to *the one* that sat on the cloud, Put in your sickle, and reap: for the time has come for you to reap; for the harvest of the earth is ripe. ¹⁶ And he that sat on the cloud put in his sickle on the earth; and the earth was reaped. (EKJV)

Acts 24:15 "...and I have the same hope in God as these men themselves have, that there will be a resurrection of both the righteous and the wicked. ¹⁶ So I strive always to keep my conscience clear before God and man." (KJV)

The Son of Man comes on a cloud. The figure in 14:14 obviously represents Christ. It is the same figure we saw in Daniel—"**one like a son of man**" (Dan. 7:13). He wears a **"golden crown"** (v. 14). The golden crown suggests a royal figure—one who is a king. His coming on a cloud links the Son of Man figure here with the parousia (Gk. For the coming of

> Luke 21:25 "**And there shall be signs in the sun, and in the moon, and in the stars; and upon the earth distress of nations, with perplexity; the sea and the waves roaring; ²⁶ Men's hearts failing them for fear, and for looking after those things which are coming on the earth: for <u>the powers of heaven shall be shaken.</u> ²⁷ <u>And then shall they see the Son of man coming in a cloud with power and great glory.</u>**" (KJV)

The twenty-four elders also wear **"crowns of gold"** (Rev. 4:4) which signifies their reign with Christ on thrones in the vicinity of the throne of God. Jesus promised this rule to his disciples.

Matt. 19:28 **And Jesus said to them, Verily I say unto you, That you that have followed me, in the regeneration when the Son of man shall sit in the throne of his glory, you <u>also shall sit upon twelve thrones, judging the twelve tribes of Israel</u>.** (KJV)

The first harvest is the ripe harvest of grain or wheat (Mt. 3:12; Mt. 13). We are prone to see this harvest as the gathering of the righteous. Both harvests are said to be **"ripe."** Grain represents the righteous. They are those who belong to Christ and they are harvested in one sweep. This is what we call the Rapture. And Jesus foretold this scene in the days when He walked on earth with men.

There Is Tragic Sorrow for the Unbelieving When They See Christ Coming

Matt. 24:30 **At that time the sign of the Son of Man will appear in the sky, <u>and all the nations of the earth will mourn. They will see the Son of Man coming on the clouds</u> of the sky, with power and great glory. [31] And <u>he will send his angels with a loud trumpet call, and they will gather his elect</u> from the four winds, from one end of the heavens to the other.** (KJV)

1 Thes. 4:15-18 **For this we say unto you by the word of the Lord, that we which are alive and remain unto the coming of the Lord shall not prevent those that are asleep. [16] For the Lord himself shall descend from heaven with a shout, with the voice of the archangel, and with the trump of God: and the dead in Christ shall rise first: [17] Then we which are alive and remain shall be caught up together with them in the clouds, to meet the Lord in the air: and so shall we ever be with the Lord. [18] Therefore comfort one another with these words.** (KJV)

Notice that he has **"a sharp sickle in his hand"** (Rev. 14:14) as does the angel in the second harvest. In Revelation 20 we see the glorious joy of the righteous during the Millennium. The inspired word says that they **came to life and reigned with Christ a thousand years.** It tells us twice that they reigned with Christ (vs. 4 and 6).

Rev.n20:4 **And I saw thrones, and they sat upon them, and judgment was given unto them: and I saw the souls of them that were be-**

headed for the witness of Jesus, and for the word of God, and that had not worshipped the beast, nor his image, nor had received his mark on their foreheads, or on their hands; and <u>they lived and reigned with Christ a thousand years</u>.

[6] Blessed and holy is he that has part in the first resurrection: on such people the second death has no power, but <u>they shall be priests of God and of Christ, and shall reign with him a thousand years</u>. (KJV)

SIXTH SCENE: THE HARVEST OF THE UNREPENTANT (14:17-19)

Text: Rev. 14:17-19
Rev. 14:17 And another angel came out of the temple which is in heaven, he also had a sharp sickle. [18] And another angel came out from the altar that had power over fire; and cried with a loud *voice* to the angel that had the sharp sickle, saying, *put in* your sharp sickle, and gather the clusters of the *grape harvest* of the earth; for her grapes are fully ripe. [19] And the angel *put in* his sickle and gathered the grape harvest of the earth, and threw it into the great winepress of the wrath of God. (EKJV)

THE SECOND ANGEL ALSO HAS A SHARP SICKLE

John now sees the vision of the harvest of the wicked, the rebellious, and unrepentant. Another angel appears with a sharp sickle in hand. He is joined by yet another angel who gives the command to harvest the vintage of the earth. The harvest of grapes in prophetic scripture is the gathering of those who have not repented and placed their everlasting future in the hands of Christ.

This harvester is an angel, here called **"another angel."** He receives his instructions from yet another angel who emerges from the Temple. John has lost count of the many angels who appear in these scenes. All the angels come from the temple in heaven. But this angel comes from **"the altar"** that is before the temple.

Observe that while Christ is on the cloud, the exact moment of the rapture is not fully known to him until the angel brings the final command from the altar of God. Naturally the altar is mentioned seven times in Revelation. It was said to be established in front of the temple. It is the same altar under which John heard the sounds of those who had been slain for the word of God and for their testimony (Rev. 6:9). In Revelation 8:5, the angel took the censor with blazing coals from the altar and hurled them upon the earth.

SEVENTH SCENE: THE WINEPRESS OF GOD'S WRATH (14:20)

Text: Rev. 14:20
20 And the winepress was trodden outside the city, and blood came out of the winepress, up to the horse's bridles, for a distance of 1600 stadia (200 miles).

John watches as the harvest takes place instantaneously. In one swing, the angel completes the harvest of the earth. Both harvests are accomplished with a single swing of a sickle. This is a remarkable picture of how it will be when Christ reappears with His angels to harvest the earth.

There is a strong prophecy from the prophet Joel. Notice how the explicit details of this prophecy coincide with Revelation 14. Read it with Revelation 14:17-19. In Joel 3:15 all of the heavenly lights go out at the time of the winepress judgment.

Joel 3:13 *Swing* **the sickle, for the harvest is ripe: come** *and help*, **for the winepress is full, the vats overflow; for their wickedness** *is* **great!** **14 Multitudes, multitudes in the valley of decision: for the day of the LORD** *is* **near in the valley of decision.** **15 The sun and the moon shall be darkened, and the stars shall** *cease their* **shining.**

Again we see the prophet Isaiah nearly nine hundred years earlier telling us that this great judgment will happen when Christ treads the winepress of God's wrath.

Isaiah 63

Isaiah 63:1 **Who** *is* **this coming from Edom, from Bozrah, with his garments stained crimson?** *Who is this one* **glorious in his apparel,** *striding* **in the greatness of his strength?** *It is* **I that speak in righteousness, mighty to save.** **2 Why are your** *garments* **red like the one that treads the winepress?** **3 I have trodden the winepress alone; and** *out of the nations there was* **no one with me: for I will tread them in mine anger, and trample them in my fury; and their blood will be sprinkled upon my garments, and I will stain all my raiment.** **4 For the day of vengeance** *is* **in my heart, and the year of my redeemed has come.** **5 And I looked, and** *there was* **no one to help; and I was amazed that** *there was* **no one to uphold: therefore mine own arm brought salvation unto me; and my own wrath upheld me.** **6 And I will tread down the nations in my anger, and**

make them drunk in my fury, and I will bring down their strength to the earth. (EKJV)

The Winepress Is Trodden Outside the City

The winepress is trodden outside the city, most likely Jerusalem. The death of Christ took place outside the city of that day. In Revelation 14 the blood flowed out of the winepress for **"by the space of a thousand and six hundred furlongs"** (about 200 miles) and it reached up to the horses' bridles. The blood reminds us that this chapter is about human punishment, not about grapes which are likened to blood in numerous biblical examples. We cannot imagine a scene like this. When the Romans destroyed Jerusalem and the temple in 70 A.D., the streets were said to be filled with flowing blood because so many men, women and children had been slaughtered. What men have given they will receive in return.

We are given more information concerning the one who treads the winepress in Revelation 19. It is our risen Lord and Savior who comes riding a white horse who treads the winepress **"of the fury of the wrath of God Almighty."**

Who Treads the Winepress?

Christ is clearly identified in the scripture below.

Rev. 19:15 **And out of his mouth goes a sharp sword, that with it he should smite the nations: and he shall rule them with a rod of iron: and he treads the winepress of the fierceness and wrath of Almighty God. 16 And he has on his *robe* and on his thigh a name written, KING OF KINGS, AND LORD OF LORDS.** (EKJV)

Jesus taught the parable of the one that sows and the harvest.

Matt. 13:36 **Then he left the crowd and went into the house. His disciples came to him and said, "Explain to us the parable of the weeds in the field." 37 He answered and said to them, "He that sows the good seed is the Son of man; 38 The field is the world; the good seed are the children of the kingdom; but the tares are the children of the wicked one; 39 The enemy that sowed them is the devil; the harvest is the end of the world; and the reapers are the angels."**

Jesus explains the final harvest as we see in Revelation complete with the angel harvesters. And so we have the great gospel of Christ in its glorious blessedness upon the righteous saints, and in its awesome fulfillment on unrepentant mankind. There is the searching question from the Lord's disciples: **Matt. 19:25** **When his disciples heard it, they were exceedingly amazed, saying, "Who then can be saved?"** (KJV)

But Christ the Redeemer gives us the answer regarding the power of our great God: **Matt. 19:26** **" But Jesus looked *at* them, and said to them, With men this is impossible; but with God all things are possible."** (KJV)

We see the Lamb of God three times in Revelation 14. We see God's Lamb 27 times in Revelation. **Rev. 6:15** **And the kings of the earth, and the great men, and the rich men, and the chief captains, and the mighty men, and every *slave*, and every free man, hid themselves in the dens and in the rocks of the mountains; ¹⁶ And said to the mountains and rocks, Fall on us, and hide us from the face of him that sits on the throne, and from the wrath of the Lamb: ¹⁷ For the great day of his wrath is come; and who shall be able to stand?** (EKJV)

But the defining scene is here. What God has warned mankind throughout earth's history will surely come to pass in His proper time. And so with this one sweep of the sickle we are left with a sea of blood stretching for over 200 miles. Such is the vastness of God's judgment on evil.

Chapter 15

CELEBRATION ON A SEA OF GLASS

> ### *Snapshot of Chapter 15*
> We are introduced to the seven angels of the seven plagues. They hold beautiful bowls but the contents are terrifying to the earth. Heaven opens up with a great hymn of praise to our God. Then John sees the heavenly temple open, and the marvelous glory of God's power. The bowls signify God's extensive and righteous wrath that will soon fall upon the earth and its remaining people.

Seven Angels with Seven Plagues

Text: Rev. 15:1-3

^{Rev. 15:1} **And I saw another great and marvelous sign in heaven, seven angels having the seven last plagues; for in them the wrath of God is *completed*. ² And I saw a sea of glass mingled with fire: and those that had *won* the victory over the beast, and over his image, and over his mark, and over the number of his name, were standing on the sea of glass, *holding* the harps of God. ³ And they sang the song of Moses the servant of God, and the song of the Lamb, saying, Great and marvelous are your works, Lord God Almighty; just and true are your ways, O King of saints.** (EKJV)

For clarification, are the saints standing **"by"** the sea of glass, as some translations state, or are they standing **"on"** it as *epi (Greek)* with the accusative indicates? Most believe that the raptured saints are in heaven since they have received harps from God (15:2), the sea of glass is in heaven (4:6) where the host of people is standing, and the seven bowls of wrath are given out by one of the four living creatures (15:7). Every single one is equipped to sing and play the music of heaven.

John refers to this next vision of heaven as **"another great and marvelous sign."** Note that he refers to the sign as **"great and marvelous"** twice in verses 1 and 3. The scene of these redeemed is almost more than he can take in. They are the angels of the **"seven angels having the seven last plagues; for in *(with)* them is completed the wrath of God."** What God has promised for thousands of years is now to be completed. In fact, the praises in this song are drawn from Ps. 111:2-3; Deut. 32:4; Jer. 10:7; Ps. 86:9; 98:2. John states in this same passage that the seven angels sang **"the song of Moses the servant of God, and the song of the Lamb"** (15:3). They sing the song in light of the judgments spelled out in Rev. 14. Observe how Psalm 110 and Deut. 32 address the same judgment.

Old Testament Connection

In Deut. 32:22 we have **"the Song of Moses"** and it is describing the wrath of God: ^{Deut. 32:22} **For a fire is kindled in my anger, and shall burn to the lowest hell, and shall consume the earth with her *harvest*, and set the foundations of the mountains on fire.** (EKJV)

Psalm 110 is a wonderful Messianic Psalm pointing to the final battle when Christ comes on a white horse and subdues all opposition. It states in verses 5-6:

> ^{Ps. 110:5} **The Lord at your right hand shall strike through kings in the day of his wrath. ⁶ He shall judge among the heathen, he shall fill the places *(pile up the dead)* with the dead bodies; he shall wound the heads *(rulers)* over many countries.** (EKJV)

^{Isa. 34:1} **Come near, you nations, to hear; and hearken, you people: let the earth hear, and all that is therein; the world, and all things**

that come forth of it. ² For the indignation of the LORD is upon all nations, and his fury upon all their armies: he has utterly destroyed them, he has delivered them to the slaughter.

³ Their slain also shall be cast out, and their stink shall come up out of their carcases, and the mountains shall be melted with their blood.

> ⁴ And all the host *(stars)* of heaven shall be dissolved, and the heavens shall be rolled together as a scroll: and all their host *(stars)* shall fall down, as the leaf falls off from the vine, and as a fig falling from the fig tree. (EKJV)

Cf. Rev. 6:6 that quotes this verse.

John quotes verse 4 in Revelation 6:12-14. The scriptures line up in an accurate sequence. God has already explained what will happen at the end time. God has absolutely revealed the outcome and result of His divine wrath thousands of years before the crucial and climatic end.

Text: Rev. 15:3-8
Rev. 15:3 And they are singing the song of Moses the servant of God, and the song of the Lamb, saying, Great and marvelous are your works, Lord God Almighty; just and true are your ways, O King of saints.

⁴ Who shall not fear you, O Lord, and glorify your name? for you only are holy: for all nations shall come and worship before you; for your judgments are made manifest.

⁵ And after that I looked, and the temple of the tabernacle of the testimony *(or covenant)* in heaven was opened:

⁶ And the seven angels came out of the temple, having the seven plagues, clothed in pure white linen, and having their breasts girded with golden *belts.*

⁷ And one of the four beasts gave the seven angels seven golden *bowls full* of the wrath of God, who lives forever and ever.

⁸ And the temple was filled with smoke from the glory of God, and from his power; and no man was able to enter the temple, till the seven plagues of the seven angels were fulfilled. (EKJV)

The Seven Angels and the Heavenly Temple

We observe these seven angels in the heavenly temple—the tabernacle of the covenant *law (called **"the testimony" in the KJV)— and it was opened"** (Rev. 15:5). This would certainly raise a question in John's mind for we read in Num. 1:50-51.

> **Num. 1:50 But you shall appoint the Levites over the tabernacle of testimony, and over all the vessels, and over all things that belong to it: they shall *carry* the tabernacle, and all the vessels *within it*; and they shall minister to it, and shall camp *close by* the tabernacle.** (EKJV)
>
> **⁵¹ And when the tabernacle *moves* forward, the Levites shall take it down: and when the tabernacle is to be pitched, the Levites shall set it up: and the stranger that *comes near* shall be put to death.** (EKJV)

No one, other than the Levites, could approach the tabernacle and survive, yet John sees the tabernacle in heaven and it was **OPENED** so that he could view everything inside. The tabernacle was a wonderfully designed tent that served Israel until the days of Solomon's temple. So John sees the tabernacle within God's heavenly temple. Remember when we get to Revelation 21, there will be no temple in heaven, because the earth and its inhabitants are gone. All of the redeemed are in heaven by the shedding of Christ's blood and their obedient faith in Him.

The Terrible Contents of the Beautiful Bowls: God's Final Wrath

The first thing that John observes is seven angels with the seven plagues, and they are carrying these plagues in **"seven golden bowls full of the wrath of God"** (15:7). In Rev. 5:8 the four living creatures and the twenty-four elders are around the throne. Each had a golden bowl full of incense offered to the Lamb **"which are the prayers of God's people."** What a contrast!

These **four living creatures** appear in Chapters 4, 5, 6, 14 and here in Chapter 15, and finally in Chapter 19. We see scenes like this in the call experience of Isaiah (Isa. 6:3), and in the cherubim in Ezekiel (1:5-25 and also in 10:1-22). To refresh our memory, these four living creatures praise God without ceasing. See Revelation 4:6-8.

The angels are immaculate and are dressed in clean, white linen and wore golden belts around their chests (15:6). They are dressed in a priestly fashion. However, their bowls are filled with the awful and terrible wrath of God to be poured out upon the earth. Moreover, the temple **"was filled with smoke from the glory of God, and from his power"** (15:8). While the angels were pouring out the awesome contents of the seven golden bowls **"no man was able to enter into the temple"** (15:8). Follow with me to Exodus 40 where we see this amazing scene in the days of Moses:

Old Testament Connection

Ex. 40:33 **And he *set* up the *courtyard around* the tabernacle and the altar, and set up the hanging of the court gate. So Moses finished the work.** [34] **Then a cloud covered the tent of the congregation, and the glory of the LORD filled the tabernacle.** [35] **And Moses was not able to enter into the tent of the congregation, because the cloud *on it,* and the glory of the LORD filled the tabernacle.** (EKJV)

The same phenomenon occurred during the days of Solomon's temple in Jerusalem: 1 Kings 8:10 **And it came to pass, when the priests *came* out of the holy place, that the cloud filled the house of the LORD,** [11] **So that the priests could not stand to minister because of the cloud: for the glory of the LORD had filled the house of the LORD.**

Chapter 16

THE SEVEN LAST PLAGUES

> ### *Snapshot of Chapter 16*
> The angel reveals the seven plagues to come upon the world (remember the seven trumpets of ChapterS 8-11). We see the drying up of the River Euphrates preparing for the crossing of the kings of the earth with 200 million troops. They expect that everything is going their way, but God is opening the pathway for the ultimate victory of Christ and their demise. Verse 15 presents the third of seven beatitudes. The beatitude issues the final invitation to repent, but mankind's evil is unrelenting, and they do not repent.

Text: Rev. 16:1
And I heard a *loud* voice out of the temple saying to the seven angels, "Go your ways, and pour out the *bowls of* the wrath of God upon the earth. (EKJV)

GOD'S WRATH IS RIGHTEOUS

John is shown the righteous wrath and justice of our God directed to unrepentant mankind. We view their absolute refusal to repent or demonstrate remorse for their evil, rebellion and sin. An unrepentant sinner cannot be saved. We are shown the prelude to the infamous battle of Armageddon (vs. 12, 16). John sees another great sign in heaven (15:1).

Rev. 15:1 And I saw another great and marvelous sign in heaven,, seven angels having the seven last plagues; for in them the wrath of God is *completed*.

God's Wrath Is Poured Upon the Earth

Now the seven angels commence pouring out their bowls upon the earth. They drench mankind with the contents of the bowl. God keeps His promise and He is fully capable of distributing His wrath upon the wicked and unrepentant. We should remember and consider the ten plagues God sent upon Egypt in the days of Moses leading up to the Exodus.

Rev. 16:2 And the first went, and poured out his *bowl* upon the earth; and a *festering* and *painful* sore fell on the men *that* had the mark of the beast, and on those who worshiped his image.

In Rev. 7:1 we read, **"And after these things I saw four angels standing on the four corners of the earth, holding the four winds of the earth, that the wind should not blow on the earth, nor on the sea, nor on any tree."** My Greek professor Dr. George Beasley-Murray said, "This wrath is against an age that has gone to the devil." We should note the similarity of the seven trumpet plagues to the seven bowl plagues.

The plagues lead up to the ***parousia*** of Christ. He is coming! Revelation is not always a chronological account. Through it all, mankind steadfastly refused to repent. There was no shame, remorse, or confession of notorious sins. Without repentance no person can be saved. Salvation is an actual lasting faith in the sacrifice of Jesus

Christ on the cross, His divine resurrection, and a lasting and true faith in Christ to forgive our total sinful nature and cleanse us from all sin.

Plagues in Perspective

THE FIRST PLAGUE—*Festering and painful* sores on those with the mark of the beast (16:2)
THE SECOND PLAGUE—The sea turned to blood (16:3)
THE THIRD PLAGUE—The fresh water also turned to blood (16:4)
THE FOURTH PLAGUE—Scorching heat (16:8-9)
THE FIFTH PLAGUE—Darkness on the kingdom of the beast (16:10-11)
THE SIXTH PLAGUE—Preparation for the great battle (16:12-16)
THE SEVENTH PLAGUE—Against the elements: air and the elements of earth resulting in a great earthquake (16:17-21)

The First Plague—Festering Sores Broke Out on Those Marked By the Beast (16:2)

Text: Rev. 16:2

Rev. 16:2 **And the first went, and poured out his *bowl* on the earth; and a *festering and painful* sore *came* on those *that* had the mark of the beast, and on those *who* worshiped his image.** (EKJV)

John points us back to the Exodus from Egypt and the Rapture from the earth (in the song of Moses—Rev. 15:3).

This content of the bowl only strikes those who **"had the mark of the beast,"** and had united with him by worshiping his image. The result was **"a *festering and painful* sore"** over their bodies. Note: **"mark of the beast"**—Rev. 13:16, 17; 14:9, 11; 16:2; 19:20; 20:4.

The mark of the beast marks one for God's wrath. All who give allegiance to the beast have this punishment in common. Believers do not experience God's wrath as Paul explains: 1 Thes. 5:9 **For God has not appointed us to wrath, but to obtain salvation by our Lord Jesus Christ, 10 Who died for us, that, whether we wake or sleep, we should live together with him.**

230

Old Testament Connection

The first connection was experienced in the plague of Egypt when Pharaoh refused to recognize the right of the Israelites to leave.

Moses listed a host of terrible afflictions that Israel would face for rebellion against the Lord:

> Ex. 9:8 **And the LORD said to Moses and to Aaron, Take hand-fuls of ashes of the furnace, and let Moses sprinkle it to-ward the heaven in the sight of Pharaoh. ⁹ And it shall be-come small dust in all the land of Egypt, and *festering* boils *will* break out on man, and on *cattle*, throughout all the land of Egypt. ¹⁰ And they took ashes *from* the furnace, and stood before Pharaoh; and Moses sprinkled it up toward heaven; and it became a *festering* boil breaking *out* on man, and on cattle.**

> Deut. 28:27 **The LORD will smite you with the *boils* of Egypt, and with *tumors*, and with *scurvy*, and with itch, *from which you cannot* be healed.**

Isaiah explained the affliction of devastating sores to the people of Judah and Jerusalem:
Isa. 1:5 **Why should you be stricken anymore? You will revolt more and more: the whole head is sick, and the whole heart faint. ⁶ From the sole of the foot even unto the head there is no sound-ness in it; but wounds, and bruises, and petrifying sores: they have not been closed, *nor* bound up, *nor* mollified with ointment.**

In verse 11 we find that even with the sores the people cursed God and refused to repent: Rev. 16:11 **And blasphemed the God of heaven because of their pains and their sores, and repented not of their deeds.**

But the plagues of God's wrath continue to be poured out. Now we see the plagues against the waters. The second is over the sea, and the third is over the rivers and springs.

The Second Plague—the Sea of Blood (16:3)
Text: Rev. 16:3

Rev. 16:3 And the second angel poured out his *bowl* on the sea; and it became *like* the blood of a dead man: and every living *thing* in the sea died.

Notice that death comes to every living thing in the sea. This great calamity affects hundreds of millions of people who draw their main food supply from the sea.

Old Testament Connection

Ex. 7:19 And the LORD spoke to Moses, Say unto Aaron, Take your rod, and stretch out your hand upon the waters of Egypt, upon their streams, upon their rivers, and upon their ponds, and upon all their pools of water, that they may become blood; and that there may be blood throughout all the land of Egypt, both in vessels of wood, and in vessels of stone. [20] And Moses and Aaron did as the Lord commanded; and he lifted up the rod, and smote the waters that were in the river, in the sight of Pharaoh, and in the sight of his servants; and <u>all the waters that were in the river were turned to blood</u>. [21] And the fish in the river died; and the river stunk, and the Egyptians could not drink of the water of the river; and there was blood throughout all the land of Egypt.

The Third Plague—the Fresh Water Also Turned to Blood (16:4)
Text: Rev. 16:4-7

Rev. 16:4 And the third angel poured out his bowl upon the rivers and fountains of waters; and they became blood. [5] And I heard the angel of the waters say, "You are righteous, O Lord, who are, and was, and shall be, because you have judged thus. [6] For they have shed the blood of saints and prophets, and you have given them blood to drink; for they are worthy." [7] And I heard another voice out of the altar say, "Even so, Lord God Almighty, true and righteous are *your* judgments."

Old Testament Connection

Refer to the plagues of Egypt above. This time it is the fresh water and the drinking and bathing water that we may take for granted in our daily life until it is ruined.

The angels recognize the fact that God is in no way unjust in this punishment, for these are people who slaughtered the saints and the prophets. The third plague is accompanied by an affirmation by the angel of God's righteous judgment upon those who have murdered the saints and the prophets. Those who have shed the blood of God's people **now have only waters of blood.**

Rev. 16:6 **For they have shed the blood of saints and prophets, and you have given them blood to drink; for they are worthy.**

Dr. Frank Stagg was professor of one course on Revelation that I took in the seminary. He said in his lecture: "Hell is the last tribute that God pays to the dignity of man."

The Fourth Plague—A Scorching Heat (16:8-9)
Text: Rev. 16:8-9
Rev. 16:8 **And the fourth angel poured out his bowl upon the sun; and power was given to him to scorch men with fire. ⁹ And men were scorched by the *extreme* heat, and they blasphemed the name of God, *that* had power over these plagues: and they did not repent to give him glory.**

Old Testament Connection
Moses warned the people of what God would do to those who were willfully rebellious: Deut. 28:22 **The LORD shall smite you with consumption, and with fever, and with inflammation, and with extreme burning, and with the sword, and with blight and with mildew; and they shall pursue you until you perish.**

In John's vision **"They were seared by the extreme heat"** of the sun (16:9). The Greek means **"extreme"** or **"intense"** heat. Did you ever touch an iron that was hot when you were unaware? They were really being scorched by this heat. This is not a heat wave. It is an astronomical beaming of solar heat upon the wicked ones. Here is where we see their wickedness and perversion. Although they knew themselves to be guilty, yet they blasphemed by cursing **"the name of God."** And God is the One **"who had power over these plagues."** More than that, **"they did not repent to give him glory."** Nothing remains of remorse or civility. They belong to Satan in totality.

When is it too late to repent? We never know, but when the Lord God is pouring out His most vehement wrath on someone, it is a great time to repent. Who knows if God will accept this late confession as an act of submission? When Jonah preached in Nineveh, their king issued a decree and asked a question: ^{Jonah 3:9} **Who can tell if God will turn and repent, and turn away from his fierce anger *so* that we *will not* perish?"**

We have the name of Hezekiah, king of Judah, 117 times in Scripture, and when Isaiah was sent by the Lord to tell him that his life was required it says: **"he turned his face to the wall and wept *his heart out"*** (Isa. 38:3—KJV). In his repentance, God gave him additional years. But these wicked people just cursed God's name. Their refusal to repent justified their punishment.

The Fifth Plague—the Light Goes Out in the Kingdom of the Beast (16:10-11)

Text: Rev. 16:10-11

^{Rev. 16:10} **And the fifth angel poured out his *bowl* on the *throne* of the beast; and his kingdom was *completely dark*; and they gnawed their tongues *because of* pain, ¹¹ And blasphemed the God of heaven because of their pains and their sores, and *did not* repent of their deeds.**

When the angel pours out the fifth bowl, it is upon the very kingdom of the beast **"on the** *(throne)* **of the beast and his kingdom..."** The evil partner of Satan is now receiving pay back. The people were in darkness 24 hours a day. They had served the representative of darkness and now they were in the blackness of night. With no light, they were lost in a maze of sin-filled people with all of their evil boiling to the surface. More than that, they had no direction to find home, food or water. They wore darkness as a shroud. There could be no commercial transactions. They were enveloped by darkness. The connection of Satan and his beast opposed God and His people in every way. It says: **"they gnawed their tongues *because of* pain"** (v. 10). But this is not hell! It is only a prelude. They refused the light and God has given them what belongs to their goal in life.

Old Testament Connection

^{Ex. 10:21} **And the LORD said unto Moses, Stretch out your hand toward heaven, that there may be darkness over the land of Egypt, even darkness which may be felt. ²² And Moses stretched out his hand toward heaven; and there was a thick darkness in all the land of Egypt three days: ²³ They *could not see* one another, *nor***

could anyone move from his place for three days: but all the children of Israel had light in their dwellings.

Egypt only experienced a foretaste of this darkness, but John sees a lasting and consuming darkness that ultimately precludes life. At this point the seas are lifeless, there is no water for personal use, there are festering sores on all these people, and now they are in total darkness wandering about and crashing into objects and people, and unable even to attempt to attend to their horrible sores.

The Sixth Plague—Rounding up the Kings of Earth for the Great Battle of Armageddon (16:12-16)

This is the battle of Armageddon.

Text: Rev. 16:12-16

Rev. 16:12 **And the sixth angel poured out his *bowl* upon the great river Euphrates; and *its* water was dried up, that the way of the kings of the east might be prepared. ¹³ And I saw three unclean spirits like frogs come out of the mouth of the dragon, and out of the mouth of the beast, and out of the mouth of the false prophet. ¹⁴ For they are the spirits of devils, working miracles, *and they* go _out_ <u>to the kings of the earth and of the whole world, to gather them to the battle of that great day of God Almighty.</u>**

¹⁶ **And he gathered them together into a place called in the Hebrew tongue <u>Armageddon</u>.**

John's vision now reveals the sixth plague: drying up **"the great river Euphrates."** The Euphrates traveled from its headwaters near eastern Turkey, through eastern Syria and through the middle of Iraq for a distance of 1800 miles before connecting with the Tigris River flowing from modern Baghdad. The area between the rivers was known as Mesopotamia (between the rivers). The area was the center of civilization where writing was developed. It is mentioned numerous times in the Bible from the creation account (Gen. 2:14), where it was one of the four rivers that flowed from the Garden of Eden; and in Gen. 15:18 when the Lord discussed the boundaries of the Promised Land in regard to the river. Abraham traveled from his home in Ur located on the river.

Don't be confused. The reason the Euphrates was dried was so the kings of the nations could cross with great masses of troops to wage the battle of Armageddon. It would take weeks for 200 million troops to cross the river even with a hundred bridges. They saw the drying up of the river as a positive sign. They undoubtedly thought it to their advantage, but it only hastened their demise and defeat. **"and the water of *it* was dried up, that the way of the kings of the east might be prepared"** (v. 12). We could imagine Iran, Pakistan, India, China, North Korea, Russia, the terrorists in Afghanistan and many smaller countries sending hundreds of thousands of troops for this battle.

There is some confusion regarding the biblical **"Har Mageddon"** ("har" means "mountain"). The question: Is this a place name or does it describe the final event known as Armageddon. Mageddon (Megiddo is near the Esdraelon Plain—the location of some of Israel's fiercest battles). It is a beautiful place to see and I can understand how great battles were fought in this spacious plain.

But Obviously Megiddo is not a mountain according to my personal experience. We should think of the final war against God in such a place. The battle takes place when Christ comes riding a white horse (Rev. 19). This is the second and final war in Revelation. The first war is in Chapter 12 where Michael and his angels defeat Satan and his evil angels. There will never be another war after this war. Satan tried to establish a war after his thousand years in prison, but it ended before it started.

Now John sees evil spirits that look to him like frogs (16:13). They are three frogs like devils. From the mouth of these three—the **dragon (Satan),** the **beast (king or antichrist),** and the **false prophet (his chaplain)**—come these evil spirits. These evil spirits are performing **"miraculous signs."** And what is their purpose? They are attracting the attention of **"the kings of the whole world"** for the purpose of gathering **"...them to the battle of that great day of God Almighty.**

This demonic team is assigned to a world-wide roundup of kings. They are to plant evil seed in these kings to draw them together for a common evil battle against the power of God. Throughout scripture, the day of the Lord is anticipated. It is certainly not a day to be cherished, but a day of God's wrath upon the wicked. It is ironic that the demonic spirits now are gathering these kings for the wrath due them from God Almighty. We read these things and we come to understand that what man has felt was impossible is only an instant away for God to carry out.

In summary, the dragon, the beast and the false prophet vomit up three evil spirits (v. 13). These three spirits are sent out to the kings of the earth to deceive them and gather them in a battlefield called **"Har mageddon."** This battle is the last rebellion that precedes the coming of the Kingdom of God in fullness and completeness.

The river Euphrates is dried up so that the kings the demonic spirits are drawing can cross to their final end in the battle of Armageddon. There will never be another such war. Everything that would prevent such a war has been removed; and John watches breathlessly as it unfolds before his eyes. All hindrances and defenses against these nations in history's final battle are removed. The way is open for the final battle called the battle of Armageddon. But the battle will mark their day of death and judgment.

Rev. 19:19 **And I saw the beast, and the kings of the earth, and their armies, gathered together to make war against *the one* that sat on the horse, and against his army. [20] And the beast was taken, and with him the false prophet that *worked* miracles, *by* which he deceived *those* that had received the mark of the beast, and that worshiped his image. These both were cast alive into a lake of fire burning with brimstone. [21] And the *rest* were slain with the sword of *the one* that sat on the horse; *with the* sword *that came* out of his mouth: and all the fowls were filled with their flesh.**

The Seventh Plague—an Astronomical Earthquake, the Collapse of Cities and Nations, and the Disappearance of Islands and Mountains (16:17-21)

Text: Rev. 16:17-21
Rev. 16:17 **And the seventh angel poured out his *bowl* into the air; and there came a *loud* voice out of the temple of heaven, from the throne, saying, It is done. [18] And there were voices, and *peals of* thunder, and *flashes of* lightning; and there was a great earthquake, *and there* was nothing like it since men were upon the earth, because it was so mighty and so great an earthquake.**

It is poured out *into the air*—the abode of the demons. The evil spirits are attacked in their own domain.

237

> **Eph. 6:12** **For we wrestle not against flesh and blood, but against principalities, against powers, against the rulers of the darkness of this world, <u>against spiritual wickedness in *heavenly* places</u>.**

> **Rev. 16:19** **And the great city was divided into three parts, and the cities of the nations fell: and God remembered great Babylon, and *gave* her the cup of the wine of the fierceness of his wrath. ²⁰ And every island fled away, and the mountains were *all gone*. ²¹ And great hail fell out of heaven upon men, every stone was about *a hundred pounds* and men blasphemed God because of the plague of hail; and *because* the plague was exceedingly great.**

Phenomenon of the Seventh Plague of God's Wrath
in Revelation 16

- The source of these phenomena is God's throne (Rev. 4:5).
- There were flashes of lightning, rumblings and peals of thunder.
- Thee was a severe earthquake greater than any man has ever experienced.
- The great city split into three parts,
- The cities of the nations collapsed.
- The islands disappeared ("fled away;" see 20:11).
- The mountains could not be found (But actually, the earth is disintegrating).
- Hundred-pound hailstones fell upon men and they cursed God (v. 21).

- **Obviously, no one could survive a blow from a hundred-pound hailstone.**
- **The universe is striking back and man is the target.**
- **And yet there is no repentance.**

This raises the question that every person should answer immediately. If the love and sacrifice and devotion of the Lord Jesus Christ do not move me, what is left? Many people give up on life because they have no hope. They have no sense of eternal relationship. God has no place in their lives and they have so committed themselves to Satan, the great dragon, that they have absolutely lost sight of God.

The women were weeping over the abuse heaped upon our Lord leading up to the crucifixion. Jesus told them not to weep now because something far worse was coming upon the world, and He said: Luke 23:30 "Then **shall they begin to say to the mountains, Fall on us; and to the hills, Cover us. [31] For if they do these things *to* a green tree, what shall be done *when it is* dry?"**

John in his vision in Revelation sees a scene of awesome magnitude. Rev. 6:15 **And the kings of the earth, and the great men, and the rich men, and the chief captains, and the mighty men, and every *slave*, and every free man, hid themselves in the dens and in the rocks of the mountains; [16] And said to the mountains and rocks, "Fall on us, and hide us from the face of *the one who* sits on the throne, and from the wrath of the Lamb: [17] For the great day of his wrath *has* come; and who shall be able to stand?"**

Therefore, we are brought down to Revelation 16:15 **where we have the final invitation.**

A Warning and a Final Invitation: The Third Beatitude

Text: Rev. 16:15
Rev. 16:15 **"Behold, I come as a thief. Blessed is he that watches, and keeps his garments, lest he walk naked, and they see his shame** *(or he be exposed)*."

Luke 12:39 **"And know this, that if the *owner* of the house had known *at* what hour the thief would come, he would have watched, and *would* not have *permitted* his house to be broken through. [40] *You***

***also must be ready**: for the Son of man comes at an hour when you do not expect him."*

In verse 15 we find a beatitude. The Lamb of God intercedes with mankind to always remain ready for his coming. We are to be awake, alert and ready to be clothed at all times. When I served as a county fire chief, everything was laid out at night by the bed (boots, bunker pants, suspenders, and fireman's coat and helmet in the car).

Shameful exposure points to those who are unprepared for the coming of Christ. This means far more than mere embarrassment. The two passages reflect on the same moment. It is the appointed hour and the Lord is coming, and the unrepentant and wicked are in view. Some of them intended to do something—heaven only knows what. Men who don't get ready today will likely never find a convenient time. And suddenly the moment is upon us—do you not really believe that time will come?

We don't really believe in the Lord's coming when we spend so much time on the structural issues of the church and on our own needs instead of Christ's great world-wide purpose.

Some people may have been baptized but they have no fruit in their lives. Their lives are a sordid and fruitless and unconcerned testimony to their lack of faith. They have no evidence of a revolutionary change that Christ makes when one repents. The Lord's Day is just another day and they can think of a thousand things to do rather than worship the King of kings. And they are going to be shamefully exposed.

The startling suddenness of His coming is powerfully communicated through this verse. In the midst of the plagues we are reminded that Jesus is coming. Jesus is coming and we are to be ready.

Man's Unrelenting Evil

Men continue in their evil ways during the plagues. In fact they became more evil, unbending, and set against God. They are like Pharaoh. Pharaoh hardened his own heart. To harden one's heart is to blaspheme against every word God has ever spoken, every prophet He has ever sent and the great sacrifice of His own Son. They don't serve Him, don't love Him, and don't consider His claims on their lives, but they curse Him with all of their might. Their mouths spew forth the venom that resides in their hearts. And they are naked and exposed before Almighty God. They recognize that God has sent the plagues and they curse Him. This is a dramatic illustration of their failure to repent of their sin and unbelief. Three times in this chapter we are reminded that they refused to repent (16:9; 16:10b; 16:21).

In the final days of earth, the people continued to blaspheme against God in the face of the sufferings he sent to warn them of His approaching wrath. Whatever your heart's attitude it will become more so in times of suffering. Suffering arouses a desire for God on the part of some, but it causes others to curse Him. And so we see after thousands of years of God calling His people to repentance, He will finally bring His ultimate wrath to bear upon those who continue in their sin and rebellion.

EXAMPLES OF TERRIFYING DISASTERS

2010—Volcanic Ash from Iceland blotted out the sun and halts European air traffic. Oil gushed uncontrolled from a well in the Gulf destroying marine life and bringing economic hardships and often disaster to hundreds of thousands in the U.S.

2010—Earthquake in Haiti killed more than 220,000.

2005—Earthquake and tsunami in South Asia killed between 238,000 and 285,000.

2003—Power outage darkened much of Northeastern U.S. for days including New York City.

1991—Floods in Bangladesh killed about 139,000.

1991—Floods in China disrupted the lives of 200 million people, sweeping over a million homes away in one province alone.

1981-84—Many millions perished in Africa from famine and drought.

1976—The planet's deadliest earthquake of the century, by far, was a magnitude 8.0 that struck Tianjin, China, on July 27, 1976. The official casualty figure issued by the Chinese government was 255,000, but unofficial estimates of the death toll were as high as 655,000. (US Geol. Survey)

1918-19—Over 50 million perished from the worldwide influenza outbreak.

When you sum up all of these and the thousands of other natural disasters, they are only a tiny drop in the bucket to what Revelation is talking about.

EZEKIEL DID NOT SEE AS FAR AS JOHN IN THE REVELATION. THERE ARE MANY SIMILARITIES, BUT ALSO MANY DIFFERENCES.

1) Ezekiel's heart is Israel. John is the beloved disciple of Christ the Lord.
2) Ezekiel, as a priest, finds fulfillment in temple worship, but John knows the crucified and resurrected Christ.
3) Ezekiel's reality is in Jerusalem, and John's is in the glorious return of Christ.
4) One looks at the Millennium redemption of Israel, and the other looks into the eternal glory of the redeemed of all nations.
5) Both Ezekiel and John are transported to a high mountain where they see their vision (Ezek. 40:1-4; Rev. 21:10).
6) Ezekiel does not see the New Jerusalem. Both see a man measuring, but the dimensions are far different.
7) Ezekiel does see a temple, but John sees a city that does not need a temple because the Lord God and the Lamb is its temple (Rev. 21:22).
8) Ezekiel sees twelve gates representing the twelve tribes. John also sees twelve gates with the names of the twelve tribes written on them (Rev. 21:12).
9) Ezekiel's Eastern gate is closed and belongs to the Prince. All of John's gates are wide open and never subject to being closed (Rev. 21:25).
10) Ezekiel sees a restoration of Israel, but John sees the "the glory and honor of the nations" entering into the New Jerusalem (Rev. 21:26).
11) Ezekiel sees a river flowing from the temple down to the sea (Ezek. 47:1ff); John sees a river, but he says there is no more sea (Rev. 21:1).
12) These are certainly not contradictions; they are looking at two different realities.

EZEKIEL IS LOOKING INTO THE LIFE IN RESTORED ISRAEL DURING THE MILLENNIUM, AND JOHN IS LOOKING INTO THE ETERNAL REWARD OF ALL THE SAINTS

THE THIRD VISION: Rev. 17:1-21:8

Each vision begins with "I was in the Spirit..."
(cf. 1:10; 4:2; 17:3; and 21:10)

OPPOSITE SYMBOLS IN REVELATION

Revelation is written with what is often called parallel symbolism applied in an apocalyptic fashion.

There are Two Mothers

The heavenly mother (12:1-17) who represents the people of Israel in covenant with God; and...

The harlot mother (17:1-19:1) who represents Rome and her nature of sin and evil fulfilled in the Roman Empire, and the coming ultimate evil kingdom of the end time. She is the unholy city in contrast to the holy city.

There are Two Animals

The Lamb of God (Rev. 5:6, 12, 13; 6:1; 7:10, 14, 17; 12:11; 13:8; 14:1, 4, 10; 15:3; 17:14; 19:7, 9; 21:14, 22, 23; 22:1, 3); and

The Great Beast (Rev. 13:11)

There Are Two Harvests (Rev. 14:14-20)

The harvest of grain or wheat (the righteous) and
The harvest of the vineyard (the wicked)

There Are Two Suppers or Feasts

The Marriage Supper of the Lamb (19:9) and
The Fleshly Feast of God (19:17-18; the birds devour the flesh of the wicked)

There Are Two Resurrections

The Resurrection of the Righteous (20:4-6) and
The Resurrection of the Wicked (20:11-15)

There Are Two Thrones

The Great Throne of God (4:2) and
The White Throne of Judgment (20:11)

There Are Two Battles

The Battle of Armageddon (19:11-21) and
The Battle of Gog and Magog (20:8; cf. Ezek. 38-39)
The two are a thousand years apart.

There Are Two Sets of Books

The Deeds of the Wicked (20:12) and
The Lamb's Book of Life (20:12)

There Are Two Final Outcomes

The New Jerusalem (Rev. 21) andThe Second Death (Rev. 20)

Chapter 17

UNRAVELING THE MYSTERY OF NEW BABYLON

Snapshot of Chapter 17

In this chapter, John is shown the glamorous harlot, who stands for the final evil world system. She is wealthy, impressive, and is sought after by the evil kings of the world who will meet their end at Armageddon. In the end, the Beast (the Antichrist) will destroy her with the help of other kings. This prepares us to understand Chapter 18.

Babylon, the Prostitute, Is Sitting on the Beast
Text: Rev. 17:1-2

^{Rev. 17:1} **And one of the seven angels which had the seven *bowls* , came out of heaven and talked with me, saying, Come *here*; I will show *you* the *punishment* of the great *prostitute* that sits on many waters: ² With whom the kings of the earth have committed *adultery*, and the inhabitants of the earth have been made drunk with the wine of her *adulteries*."**

In Revelation evil always stands violently opposed to the purpose of God and His gospel. In Chapter 17 we come to the judgment of the Great Harlot.

17:1-2 Commentary

"One of the seven angels" of the bowls of wrath summoned John. In verse 1 we see the judgment of the harlot. **"Come, I will show you the punishment of the great prostitute."** There is every reason for her to conclude that she has escaped her certain fate, but God does not forget. To John, Rome is really old Babylon come back. But it will be at the end time when the ultimate scene of infidelity to God is punished in the evil nation. All efforts to identify the future harlot nation or city are futile until God's perfect timing.

The first charge: the kings of the earth were seduced by her wealth (18:15-19). She has displayed her wealth and wares to the kings, and they have been attracted to them with an inordinate love. These are the apostate nations of verse 2. In her pursuit of evil, she purposely led kingdoms and the world's people astray.

In the Old Testament it is said of Jerusalem: **"How *has* the faithful city become a harlot?"** (Isa. 1:21). In Ezekiel 16:15—**"*You did* trust in *your* own beauty and played the harlot."** Rome could be referred to as a **"harlot"** because she left her Creator and engaged with devils and demons. We commit spiritual adultery if we turn away from God and give anything else first place. God will never hold guiltless the one who seduces another into sin.

Text: Rev. 17:3-5

Rev. 17:3 **So he carried me away in the spirit into the wilderness: and I saw a woman sitting on a scarlet colored beast, *covered in* names of blasphemy, having seven heads and ten horns.**

⁴ And the woman was arrayed in purple and scarlet colors, and decked with gold and precious stones and pearls, *and she had* a golden cup in her hand full of abominations and filthiness of her *adulteries*: ⁵ And on her forehead was a name written, MYSTERY, BABYLON THE GREAT, THE MOTHER OF HARLOTS AND ABOMINATIONS OF THE EARTH.

17:3-4 Commentary
John Is Carried Away (Transported) into the Wilderness by the Angel

Verse 3 brings us to one of the four major divisions or visions in Revelation. John was **"carried away in the Spirit into a wilderness"** by the angel. In all four visions John is under the influence of the Spirit. (See division heading above this chapter). In 21:10 he is carried away into a high mountain. We are well aware that God often led His leaders into the wilderness: Moses, Elijah, John the Baptist, Jesus, and Paul certainly come to mind. Quiet and lonely experiences with God permit Him to mold and shape us.

The Harlot Woman on the Blasphemous Beast

In this vision, John saw a woman sitting on a blasphemous beast (cf. 13:1—the Antichrist). In Rev. 13:1 the beast arises from the sea with blasphemous names on his ten horns. In Rev. 17:3 the beast is covered with blasphemous names. He opposes everything related to God. He learned this from the Devil. These names are shameful in the presence of the living God. Jesus said:

Matt. 12:31 I *tell* you, All manner of sin and blasphemy will be forgiven: but blasphemy *against* the *Holy Spirit* will not be forgiven.

The beast represents both a city and the Antichrist. He has **"seven heads"** that represent seven mountains (17:9) which are the seven hills of Rome. She was elegant in her dress with clothing of purple and scarlet (the finest), and **"decked with gold and precious stones and pearls"** (v. 4). Scarlet was a symbol of great material wealth, and was considered very valuable.

Old Testament Connection

What Does Old Babylon Have to Do with This City?

Babylon is a pseudo-name like a nickname. It is representative of the worst of cities. Her name speaks to the ultimate evil against God and the Church expressed by evil nations and powers. The reckoning will take place in Revelation 19. Babylon destroyed the temple and Jerusalem, and killed multitudes of men, women and babies. God promised that she would pay. Babylon is Iraq today. The history of old Babylon's attack, siege and destruction of Jerusalem as well as the plans to rebuild are recorded in 2 Kings 24-25; 1 Chronicles 9:1; 2 Chronicles 32-36; Ezra 1-9; Nehemiah 7 and 13; Jeremiah; Ezekiel; and also Psalm 137. Israel in captivity prayed for the destruction of Babylon.

Ps. 137:8 **O daughter of Babylon, who *will* be destroyed; happy *will he be,* that rewards you as you have served us. ⁹ Happy *wil he be,* that takes and dashes your little ones against the stones.** (Referring to what Babylon did the babies of Israel).

God likens Babylon's destruction to the destruction of Sodom and Gomorrah. The attraction and the physical presence of City Sodom were removed in less than one hour.

Isa. 13:19 **And Babylon, the glory of kingdoms, the beauty and splendor of the Chaldees, <u>shall be as when God overthrew Sodom and Gomorrah</u>. ²⁰ It shall never be inhabited, neither shall it be dwelt in from generation to generation: neither shall the Arabian pitch tent there; neither shall the shepherds make their fold there.**

The phrase **"Babylon is fallen, is fallen"** is a direct quote of Isa. 21:9; see Jer. 51:8; Rev. 14:8; 16:19; 17:5 and 18:2, 10.
Isa. 21:9 **And, behold, here comes a chariot of men, *with* a couple of horsemen. And he answered and said, <u>Babylon is fallen, is fallen</u>; and all the graven images of her gods he has broken to the ground.**

Numerous passages describe her end. Therefore, the name Babylon is synonymous with evil, rampant sin, and rebellion against God and His people. Anyone familiar with the Old Testament accounts would quickly recognize this picture of an evil world city. While Babylon was destroyed, the fulfillment of Revelation 17-19 awaits God's ultimate destruction of an evil world city or future Babylon.

Jer. 51:35 **"The violence done to me and to my flesh be upon Babylon, the inhabitant of Zion shall say; and my blood upon the inhabitants of Chaldea, shall Jerusalem say. ³⁶ Therefore thus says the LORD; Behold, I will plead your cause, and take vengeance on your behalf; and I will dry up her sea, and make her springs dry. ³⁷ And Babylon shall become *piles of rubble,* a dwelling place for *lizards,* an astonishment, and an hissing, without *a single person living there."***

Her picture of wealth is further highlighted in verse 4. The **"golden cup"** in her hand reminds us of Jeremiah 51:7. She holds the golden cup, but it is really the Lord's cup and He permits her to live out her evil plans. Jer. 51:6 **Flee out of the midst of Babylon, and deliver** every man his soul: be not cut off in her iniquity; for <u>this *is* the</u> <u>time of the LORD's vengeance; he will render a recompense to</u> <u>her.</u> [7] Babylon *has been* <u>a golden cup in the LORD's hand</u>, that made <u>all the earth *drunk:* the nations have *drunk* her wine; there-</u> fore the nations are mad. [8] <u>Babylon *will be* suddenly fallen and</u> <u>destroyed.</u> (EKJV)

17:4—The Symbol of the Gold Cup in Her Hand

A golden cup leads us to think of a satisfying drink. The expensive container implies something that is the best. But the cup was "**a golden cup in her hand full of abominations and filthiness of her adulteries***"* (v. 4). What appeared to be her trophy had become her shame. She purposely gives birth to abominations against God.

17:5— Mystery Babylon
Text: Rev. 17:5
Rev. 17:5 **And on her forehead was a name written, MYSTERY, BABYLON THE GREAT, THE MOTHER OF PROSTITUTES AND THE ABOMINATIONS OF THE EARTH.**

Her name is a **"mystery"** (Greek: **musterion**), meaning a thing that is not known or understood. She is not only an evil harlot, but she spawns her own kind of evil. She is **"the mother of prosti- tutes and the abominations of the earth"** (v. 5).

Text: Rev. 17:6-8
Rev. 17:6 **And I saw the woman drunk with the blood of the saints, and with the blood of the martyrs of Jesus: and when I saw her, I wondered with great admiration. [7] And the angel said to me, Why did you marvel? I will tell thee the mystery of the woman, and of the beast that carries her, that has the seven heads and ten horns. [8] The beast that you saw was, and is not; and shall ascend out of the bottomless pit *(or abyss)*, and goes into perdition: and they that dwell on the earth, whose names were not written in the book of life from the foundation of the world shall wonder, when they *see* the beast that was, and is not, and yet is.** (EKJV)

She is drunk (satiated) with the blood of the saints and of the **mar- tyrs**. Rev. 17:6 (KJV) is the one single time the word **"martyr"** is used in the scripture; however there are numerous other terms used for those who are slain for the sake of Christ. These are the ones John sees in Rev. 20:4.

"...*I saw* <u>the souls of those that were beheaded for the witness of</u> <u>Jesus</u>, <u>and for the word of God</u>, and had not worshiped the beast, neither his image, neither had received *his* mark upon their fore-heads, or in their hands; and they lived and reigned with Christ a thousand years." (EKJV)

John the Baptist was beheaded (Mt. 14:1ff and the other gospels).

The Risen Christ's Promise to the Church at Smyrna:
Rev. 2:10 **Fear none of those things which you will suffer: look, the devil will cast some of you into prison, that you may be tried; and you shall have tribulation ten days: <u>be faithful unto death, and I will give you a crown of life</u>.** (See Rev. 2:13.)

When the fifth seal is opened there is this startling scene:
Rev. 6:9 **And when he had opened the fifth seal, I saw under the al-tar the souls of those that were slain for the word of God, and for the testimony which they held.**

Therefore in Chapter 17 we find the charge against the woman, the new Babylon and the wicked city, that she is the one who torment-ed and killed the saints.

17:6-7— The Harlot Is Not What John Expected
Her delight was in hounding Christians to death. She found sadistic pleasure in spilling the blood of the people of God. Now she falls completely into destruction and perdition while the faithful ones of Christ are eternally rewarded. John was **"greatly astonished."** She was impressive—not at all what he expected. She is dressed in finery: **"purple and scarlet"** (17:4; 18:16). There is a contradic-tion in her presence between her outward attractiveness and the inward evil of the cup she holds. Her beauty blinds many to the real person behind the façade.

If you have traveled to other continents you have perhaps visited structures, shrines, etc. that are pagan and ungodly to us, yet you might have marveled at the ability of ancient cultures to produce them. John said: **"...when I saw her, I wondered with great admiration..."** (17:6–KJV). The NIV has: **"When I saw her, I was greatly astonished."** Other translations have **"greatly amazed;" "great admiration;" "I mar-veled greatly;"** etc.

She is as much an enigma as the riddle that follows. She is almost beyond comprehension. In the heart of faith, she is completely evil. To worldly eyes she is a great attraction. Remember, we are not talking about a human, but an evil city at the end of history.
Text: Rev. 17:7
Rev. 17:7 **And the angel said to me, Why did you marvel? I will tell you the mystery of the woman, and of the beast that carries her, that has the seven heads and ten horns.**

Satan makes evil alluring, but he never shows the downfall of those who engage in evil. The harlot is not an old hag as we might expect. She is covered with the beauty of material wealth lavished upon her by the kings of the earth. They should have brought their wealth to the Lord, but they placed value in the wrong place. There are no winners in this drama.

17:8— John Is Presented with an Enigma Not Easily Understood

Text: Rev. 17:8
Rev. 17:8 **"The beast that you saw was, and is not; and shall ascend out of the bottomless pit** *(or the Abyss)* **and go into perdition: and those that dwell on the earth, whose names were not written in the book of life from the foundation of the world shall wonder, when they see the beast that was, and is not, and yet is."** (EKJV)

The beast **"was, *(now)* is not."** Christ **"was dead and is alive"** (Rev. 1:18). God is, and the beast is not. The lost of the earth that put their trust in the beast will look upon him with astonishment. These people are not in the book of life. The beast is going to his destruction (***apoleian***; v. 11). This Greek word can be translated destruction, or perdition. We are told this twice (verses 8 and 11). For us to understand this riddle **"calls for a mind with wisdom"** (v. 9). You need to think clearly, deeply and soberly. He means: put on your thinking cap.

Seven Heads Remind John of the Seven Hills of Rome

Remember that we said the **"seven heads"** are **"seven mountains"** (or hills). The woman was certainly not sitting on the heads. John is pointing to the empire. In John's day, it was the Roman Empire that was persecuting Christians, and perverting the ways of God. Hold the thought of verse 8.

We are told she is seated on the scarlet beast (17:3). By his description we recognize him as the Antichrist. From his appearance we know him as the beast from Rev. 13:1 (cf. **Leviathan**; Isaiah 27:1).

Rev. 13:1 **"And I stood upon the sand of the sea, and saw a beast rise up out of the sea, having seven heads and ten horns, and upon his horns ten crowns, and upon his heads the name of blasphemy."**

His Description Has Multiple Interpretations (17:9-11)
Text: Rev. 17:9-11

Rev.17:9 **And here is the mind *that* has wisdom. The seven heads are seven mountains, on which the woman sitts.**[10] **And there are seven kings: five are fallen, and one is, and the other is not yet come; and when he cometh, he must continue a short space.** [11] **And the beast that was, and is not, even he is the eighth, and is of the seven, and goes into perdition."**

Unpacking the Enigma
- **Seven heads are seven hills** (Rome).
- **Seven heads are also seven kings.**
- **The beast who once was, and now is not, is an eighth king. He belongs to the seven and is going to his destruction (Rev. 17:11).**
- **What does John's vision mean here?**
- **The beast is the eighth, but is also one of the seven.**
- **How can this be?**
- **The nature of the beast is reproduced in one of the emperors—that was the meaning for that time.**
- **They were expecting the return of Nero—the evil and diabolical emperor.**
- **But when Antichrist comes, he will be like Nero.**
- **There are five that have fallen.**

17:9-11 Commentary—The Return of the Beast
He is coming again for the final onslaught. Prophecy usually has two fulfillments: the first is immediate, and the second is the ultimate in the future. Verse 10 views the past, present and the fu-

ture. The beast is the eighth, and is also one of the seven (17:11). The one **"who was and is and is to come"** (17:8) is a ruler of the Roman Empire. The nature of the beast is reproduced in one of the Emperors just as will happen in the days of God's final wrath. We are looking for an evil and abominable world leader.

We could nominate several today, but when he appears, he will defy understanding. The sixth one is now. The seventh hasn't arrived and will only last a little while because his end is not far off. He embodies the characteristics of the final Antichrist and the traits of wicked Nero. Paul and Peter were executed in the days of Nero who was so evil he had his own mother killed. *"He used to spend hours in seclusion every day, doing nothing but catching flies and stabbing them with a keenly sharpened stylus."*

—Suetonius (his biographer)

This coming holds no dread for the faithful believers. First it is the dread judgments of a holy and righteous Christ toward a heedless and unrepentant people. The cross is the symbol of Him who reigns righteously on the throne of God, and the sickle (Rev. 14) is the symbol of judgment's great harvest. Christ comes as King and Judge.

Here is one example of how some scholars have attempted to solve this matter. The Antichrist will be someone like Nero.

THE FIVE RULERS OF THE ROMAN EMPIRE THAT HAVE FALLEN

Augustus (31 BC -14 AD)
Tiberius (14-37 AD - associated with the life of Jesus Christ)
Caligula (37-41 AD)
Claudius (41-54 AD)
Nero (54-68)
One Exits: **Vespasian** (AD 69-79)
Another Shall Come**: Titus** (AD 79-81)
The beast which was and is not, is itself the eighth:
Domitian (Nero *Redivius* – 81-96 AD)
He was said to embody the characteristics of the final Antichrist, and the traits of wicked **Nero.**

Not included are; Galba (68-69; Otho (January to April 69); Aulus Vitellius (July-December 69).

17:12-14 Commentary

The ten horns represent **yet ten other kings** who are yet to receive a
kingdom (17:12). Their authority will last but **"one hour"** (17:12).

Text: Rev. 17:12-14

Rev. 17:12 **And the ten horns which you saw** *are* **ten kings, which have received no kingdom as yet; but receive power as kings one hour with the beast.** [13] **These have one mind, and shall give their power and strength to the beast.** [14] <u>**These shall make war with the Lamb, and the Lamb shall overcome them: for he is Lord of lords, and King of kings: and**</u> *<u>those</u>* <u>**that are with him are called, and chosen, and faithful**</u>. (EKJV)

In Chapter 19 These Kings Bring an Enormous Army Against Christ

Rev. 19:19 **And I saw the beast, and the kings of the earth, and their armies, gathered together to make war against the one that sat on the horse, and against his army.** [20] **And the beast was taken, and with him the false prophet that** *performed* **miracles before him, with which he deceived** *those* **that had received the mark of the beast, and ...** *(those)* **that worshipped his image. These both were cast alive into a lake of fire burning with brimstone.** [21] **And the ...** *(rest)* **were slain with the sword of the one that sat upon the horse,** *(with the)* **sword ...** *(that came)* **out of his mouth: and all the fowls were filled with their flesh.** (EKJV)

- We know their purpose but not their identity
- But we will see them in history as certainly as we see this day.
- They will surrender their power and authority to the beast and make war against the Lamb who will overcome them.
- This all plays out in Chapter 19 as we shall come to see.

17:12—The Futile War and the Demise of Evil—The Lamb Triumphant

-+In verse 12, the ten horns represent ten kings. They do not yet have a kingdom, but when they do, it will only last for a brief time.

The symbolic time is **"one hour,"** a brief and insignificant moment in history because they will be totally destroyed in the battle of Armageddon (Rev. 19). Their only purpose is to **"give their power and authority to the beast."** Their intention is to **"...make war with the Lamb"** but **"the Lamb shall overcome them: for he is Lord of lords, and King of kings."**

He will be accompanied by His saints (Psalm 149; Dan. 7:18, 21-27; 1 Cor. 6:2; Jude 14—KJV; Rev. 19:8). Those with Him are called, chosen, and faithful (Gk. Keota, election, pistol). These wicked and unbelieving kings will rise up and make war against the Lamb (Rev. 17:14). He will overcome them in an instant. Look at the final victory. The beast will attack anything identified with God. But He (the Lamb) is the Lord of lords, and the King of kings.

17:15-18 Commentary
Text: Rev. 17:15-18
Rev. 17:15 **And he said to me, The waters that you saw, where the prostitute sits, are peoples, and multitudes, and nations, and *languages*. 16 And the ten horns which *you saw* upon the beast, these shall hate the *prostitute,* and shall make her desolate and naked, and shall eat her flesh, and burn her with fire. 17 For God has put in their hearts to fulfill his will, and to agree, and give their kingdom to the beast, until the words of God shall be fulfilled. 18 And the woman which *you saw* is that great city that *reigns* over the kings of the earth."** (EKJV)

Notice that God has put in their hearts (unknown to these short-term kings) to hand over their authority to the Antichrist. In verse 16 the word **"they" or "these"** means the other kings who join with the antichrist (the beast). They all hate the woman (the final evil world city).

This reminds us of Exodus, when God hardened Pharaoh's heart. In working against the woman, they serve God's plan and purpose (v. 17). They thought they were serving and working out their own purpose, but they were, in fact, working out the purposes of God. Righteousness will prevail over unrighteousness. In the last analysis, God is always "working things together for good."
Here it is: **"The 10 horns you saw, and the beast, will hate the prostitute."** (17:16 HCSB, ESB and many others are similar)—
NOT "the beast she rides, which has the seven heads and

ten horns." as we saw in 17:7 (NIV; KJV and other versions are similar). When John looked at the beast (v. 7) it had ten horns, but in v. 16 the ten horns are separate kings working against God with the beast (the antichrist). Even with a lot of help the antichrist is doomed to failure and destruction.

17:15 T—The Woman (the City) Comes to Her Ruin

Finally, the angel explains that the waters **"where the *prostitute sits*, are peoples, and multitudes, and nations, and languages** (v. 15). Ironically, the beast with ten horns hates the prostitute and **"shall make her desolate and naked"** (v. 16). The one she served will bring about her destruction.

These Kings Will Destroy the Prostitute City (17:16)

There is **irony in this fact.** To leave her **"naked"** (17:16) is to strip her of her dazzling apparel which marks her influence.

Rev. 17:17 **For God has put in their hearts to fulfill his will, and to agree, and give their kingdom to the beast, until the words of God shall be fulfilled.**

Rev. 10:7 **"...But in the days of the voice of the seventh angel, when he shall begin to sound, the mystery of God should be finished** (*or accomplished*), **as he has declared to his servants the prophets."** (EKJV)

The adulterous city is absolutely unfaithful to God (17:1-2; 4-5; 15-16). The phrase in verse 16 **"they shall eat her flesh, and burn her with fire"** is not cannibalism. It is part and parcel of her total destruction. John makes clear in verse 18 that the woman he saw is really the evil world city and not an actual woman. Such is the nature of apocalyptic scripture where the image is not the actual thing. The illustration is like a code. It represents the actual; in this case the woman is a city of an evil empire.

Where is this city? We cannot know until the time God has established, but then it will be obvious. All cities are notable candidates when one considers the successful work of Satan to thwart God's purposes and draw humankind into ruin.

Chapter 18

THE GLAMOROUS WOMAN'S DOOM

Snapshot of Chapter 18

John is shown the great harlot in what I refer to as "New Babylon" with all the sin, filth and degradation Satan can arouse in her. This chapter reveals how she seduced the world's people to follow her rather than God. She is seen in all earthly glory, but she is destroyed in an instant—**"one hour"**—never to rise again. This prepares us for the final battle between Christ and the earth's kings in Chapter 19.

We are brought to the spectacle of **the grand finale of the Great City.** Before us is the panorama of her final hour. Here is the moment when time shall be no more. The angel here illuminates earth **"with his glory"** and is marked by God's radiance (18:1). He spreads God's glorious light upon the earth in preparation for this spectacular act of the Father. Men stand far away gazing at the awesome spectacle just as they might have gazed at the destruction of Sodom.

The city is explained in Chapter 17. It is important that John brings two cities into focus in Chapter 18 and in Chapter 17. Babylon is the name used for this evil world city. This name is used because of what it did to God's people in 586 B.C. The same influence is still active in today's world. The other city is Rome. Rome is not identified by name, but it is obvious that she is the city of the multiple kings mentioned in Chapter 17. The angel that comes down from heaven had **"great power"** (18:1). In other words, the angel had the stamp of God's authority to act as necessary.

18:1-2 The Announcement From the Angel with Great Authority

Text: Rev. 18:1-2

Rev. 18:1 **And after these things I saw another angel come down from heaven, having great power; and the earth was *illuminated* with his glory.** ²**And he *shouted* with a *loud* voice, saying, Babylon the great is fallen, is fallen, and *has* become the *home* of *demons,* and the *lodging* of every *unclean* spirit, and *a roost for every unclean and detestable bird.*** (Easy KJV - See comments in Chapter 17 and the Old Testament Connection).

In Greek **"Fallen, Fallen"** is a prophetic perfect. It means that this announcement is absolutely certain to take place. We are familiar with this announcement which we read previously in Chapter 14. **"Fallen! Fallen is Babylon the Great!"'** The announcement hearkens back in the Old Testament to the watchman's warning in the prophecy of Isaiah (21:9).

Isaiah 21:9 *Look,* **here *comes men driving* a chariot with a couple of horsemen. And he answered and said, Babylon is fallen, is fallen; and he *has destroyed* all the graven images of her *idols!*'"**

God must bring justice to bear upon evil nations, and especially upon those that decimate His beloved people, even if they act as an instrument of God's justice toward Israel. Jeremiah provides the rationale for total judgment and vengeance upon Babylon.

Jer. 51:49 "**As Babylon *has* caused the slain of Israel to fall, so at Babylon the slain of all the earth shall fall**. (See Rev. 14:8; 17:10; 18:1-2).

In Revelation 14:8 the pronouncement of Babylon's fall seems almost as an interruption. It comes at an unlikely moment, and yet it comes with perfect timing when you consider the announcement about the harvesting of the earth (of both the righteous and the irredeemable).

18:3 The Notorious Sins of the Kings and the Merchants
Text: Rev. 18:3
"**For all nations have drunk of the wine of the wrath of her *adultery*, and the kings of the earth have committed *adultery* with her, and the merchants of the earth are *made* rich through the abundance of her *luxuries*.**" (EKJV)

18:4 God Commands His People to Flee
Text: Rev. 18:4
And I heard another voice from heaven, saying, Come out of her, my people, that you do not *share in* her sins, and that *you do not receive* her plagues. (EKJV)

The voices from heaven issue a warning: **"Come out of her, my people."** Obviously, God still has some people in the city. It is just like Lot leaving Sodom. Those who remain will be destroyed with the city. Flee to safety if there is time. Read Isaiah 52:11 (also the entire chapter; cf. Jer. 51:6; 2 Cor. 6:17) for God's call to **"come out."** Jeremiah tells them to come out of Babylon lest they experience her punishment.

Warning to Escape Babylon's Judgment
These men (the kings of the earth...and the merchants) are those that depended upon the commerce of the city for their wealth, economics and way of life. In a real sense, they worshiped the city. Before their eyes everything that marked her greatness and her glory has vanished. For the **"kings of the earth"** (18:3) also see Rev. 1:5; 6:15; 16:14 (KJV-the NIV omits **"of the earth"**); 17:2, 18; 18:3, 9; 19:19 and 21:24.

All those monuments to mankind that are so memorable have been violently removed. The astounding monument to man's achievement and self-glorification is but smoking ashes (18:8). All that remains is desolate emptiness.

Old Testament Connection
The Angel's Warned Lot: Flee for Your Lives
Gen. 19:17 "...Escape for *your* life; *do* not *look* behind *you, nor* stay in the plain; escape to the mountain, lest *you* be consumed. (Also 19:19, 20, 22). (EKJV)

Isaiah: Flee to the Crags and Caverns
Isa. 2:19 And they shall go into the holes of the rocks, and into the caves of the earth, for fear of the LORD, and for the glory of his majesty, when he *arises to violently shake the earth.* (Easy KJV)

Isa.2:21 *They will* go into the clefts of the rocks, and into the tops of the ragged rocks, for fear of the LORD, and for the glory of his majesty, when he *arises to violently shake the earth.* (Easy KJV)

Jeremiah: Flee from Babylon—Run for Your Lives!
Jer. 51:6 Flee out of...Babylon, and *save your lives:* do not be caught up in her iniquity *or sin*; for this is the time of the LORD's vengeance; he will render unto her a recompense *or what she deserves.* [7] Babylon has been a golden cup in the LORD's hand, that made all the earth *drunk*: the nations have *drunk* her wine; therefore the nations are mad. [8] Babylon is suddenly fallen and destroyed: howl for her; take *salve* for her pain, in *case* she may be healed. [9] We would have healed Babylon, but she is not healed: forsake her, and let us go every one into his own country: for her judgment *reaches* unto heaven, and is lifted up even to the skies.

Ezekiel: Flee to the Mountains
Ezek. 7:16 But those that escape, shall be on the mountains like doves of the valleys, all of them mourning for his iniquity.

John the Baptist: Flee from the Coming Wrath
Matt. 3:7 But when he saw many of the Pharisees and Sadducees *coming* to his baptism, he said to them, O generation of vipers, who *has* warned you to flee from the wrath to come?

Jesus Said: "Flee to the Mountains"

Jesus issued a warning in Matthew 24:16. What did He mean? What happens when God's warnings are ignored? Jesus warns concerning two events: the fall of Jerusalem in 70 A.D.; and the fall of the earth's cities at the consummation of this final age of history.

Matt. 24:15 **"So when you see 'the abomination that causes desolation standing in the holy place,' spoken of through the prophet Daniel—let the reader understand— 16 then <u>let those who are in Judea flee to the mountains</u>. 17 Let no one on the housetop go down to take anything out of the house. 18 Let no one in the field go back to get their cloak. 19 How dreadful it will be in those days for pregnant women ...**

Babylon could find identity as your city and my city and all cities. God is patiently holding back the hand of final judgment upon the earth.

Why the Name Babylon?

John has prepared us for this event. He has led us to understand that there is something inherently evil in the makeup of the place he refers to as Babylon. Babylon is mentioned 260 times in Scripture including 37 times in Jeremiah 50 and 51. The great city is representative of a world city. It could be Tokyo or London or New York, Paris or Moscow or Los Angeles. For John speaks not just of one city. Babylon represents all corrupt and evil cities.

We are witnessing the final act of God against the dominion of Satan. Everything and everyone associated with Satan is lost and doomed. Everything and everyone drawn to the blessed Christ is saved. There will never be another day for this day is the final day—the day of God's wrath. It is the day of God's judgment and wrath upon this wicked society. All activities of the great city cease instantly. It all goes up in smoke. Everything is concluded. There is no more opportunity for her. Her days of opportunity and her hope of salvation have ended.

The Tragic Suffering and Slaughter
of the Martyrs

We have seen how the prostitute city treated the martyrs. We have watched the battle between Satan and our great God. We have witnessed the rise of the Beast—the Antichrist. We have observed his reign, and his persecution of God's saints. Chapter 17 provides the basis for interpreting Chapter 18. There in 17 we saw the relationship to the prostitute city and the beast. In verse 17:3 she is seated on the beast. This shows the intimate relationship between antichrist and the harlot. They form a team to destroy the work of God in the world.

The Absolute End of the Great City

The **"great prostitute"** is the great city, here called Babylon. In verse 5 she is called **MYSTERY BABYLON THE GREAT.** As noted previously, I refer to her as "New Babylon."

18:6-7 Her Just Punishment

Text: Rev. 18:6-7
⁶ **Reward her even as she rewarded you, and double unto her double according to her works: in the cup which she *has* filled to her double. ⁷ How much she *has* glorified herself, and lived *luxuriously,* so much torment and sorrow give her: for she *says* in her heart, I sit a queen, and am no widow, and shall see no sorrow.** (EKJV)

What she has done to others will come back double upon her. It comes from her own cup (v. 6) which means she receives exactly what she dished out to others, only she receives a double portion. She rewarded herself with glory and luxury. She lived above the masses in poverty in her self-devoted opulence. She will receive an equal amount of **"torment and sorrow"** (v. 7). After she had consumed the wealth of the world there was scant amount left for all of the world's citizens. She piled wealth upon wealth while the world received immense pain and suffering. In her **"heart"** she is convinced that she sits on a throne as a **"queen"** (v. 7).

In a self image of royalty she feels invincible when, in truth, she has prostituted the earth. She makes her gain on illicit relations with the markets of the world. In the end, she controls the world and when she falls, every city will follow in a domino effect (See 17:1-5).

We know when John is carried away in the Spirit that is the beginning of a new vision. In this case, we have vision number three.

Seven Pronouncements of Her Doom in Chapters 18-19:

1. **Another Angel (18:1-3)**
2. **Voices from Heaven (18:4-8)**
3. **The Kings of the Earth (18:9-10)**
4. **The World's Merchants (18:11-16)**
5. **Every Shipmaster (18:17-20)**
6. **The Mighty Angel (18:21-24)**
7. **The Great Voice of a Multitude in Heaven (19:1-3)**

THE PORTRAITS OF HER GREATNESS

She Plots Great Seductions (18:3, 9; 17:2)
Text: Rev. 18:9-10
[9] **And the kings of the earth, who have committed *adultery* and lived *luxuriously* with her shall *wail over* her, and lament for her, when they shall see the smoke of her burning, [10] Standing far away for fear of her torment, saying, Alas, alas that great city Babylon, that mighty city! for in one hour *your* judgment *has* come.** (EKJV)

The kings of the earth committed adultery with her. She is the great seductress. Mankind marvels at her alluring attractions. They are drawn to her immorality and her illegitimacy. They are attracted to her other-worldliness.

She Commits Great Sins (18:5)
Her sins have reached up to heaven.
Text: Rev. 18:5
Rev. 18: 5 **...her sins have reached unto heaven, and God *has* remembered her iniquities.** (EKJV)

Her sins have accumulated. They have reached up to heaven. We are reminded of the tower of Babel when men were intent on building it to heaven. God remembers and He does not forget her abundant sins that have continued forever without repentance, remorse, or sorrow.

She Is Great in Scope (18:11-13)
The world pays homage to her and honors her as it would a queen.

Text: Rev. 18:11-13
[11] And the merchants of the earth shall weep and mourn over her; for no *one buys* their merchandise any more: [12] The merchandise of gold, and silver, and precious stones, and of pearls, and fine linen, and purple, and silk, and scarlet, and all *their* wood, and all *kinds of* vessels of ivory, and all *kinds of* vessels of *very* precious wood, and of brass, and iron, and marble, [13] And cinnamon, and *spices,* and ointments, and frankincense, and wine, and oil, and fine flour, and wheat, and *cattle,* and sheep, and horses, and chariots, and slaves, and souls of men. (EKJV)

The merchants of the earth weep—she had great international influence. The world comes together in her centers. But there will be no centers for the arts, business, technology or manufacturing. Her influence reaches the entire world. She sits on the waters and her goods are transported by ships to many ports. But, all of this will cease.

She trafficked in human slavery and misery (18:13). The last in the list of her wares is referred to as **"the souls of men"** (KJV; 18:13). Numerous versions follow the KJV with **"souls of men."** Christ died for the souls of men, but to her, humans are counted as worthless.

Because they bore witness even unto death, the servants of God will receive heavenly rewards and commendation. God does not forget their faithfulness and their sacrifices.

She Is Great in Worldly Splendor (18:14)

Text: Rev.18:14
Rev. 18:14 **"They will say, `The fruit you longed for has vanished. All your riches and splendor have vanished, never to be recovered.'** [15] The merchants who sold these things and gained their wealth from her will stand far off, terrified at her torment. They will weep and mourn..."**

The word **"splendor"** is usually referring to God and things holy (18:1; of God: 21:2; of the world: Mt. 4:8; Ps. 49:16, 17; 89:44; Is. 16:14 and other passages.) But splendor is in the eye of the beholder. We tend to worship something other than God unless our name is written in the Book of Life.

Matt. 4:8 **Again, the devil** *took* **him up into an exceeding high mountain, and** *showed* **him all the kingdoms of the world, and their** *splendor;* **⁹ And said to him, "***I will give you all these things,* **if** *you will* **fall down and worship me."** (EKJV)

The Devil offered Jesus this same splendor of the world (Mt. 4:9), but He adamantly refused. You show people your best, not your worst. Many people flatly fall for such attractive dressings. The trappings of her splendor vanish (18:14). The façade of splendor is removed and the foundation of filth and degradation is revealed for all to see.

She Brags of Her Great Sensuality
(18:16; also 17:4)
Text: Rev. 18:16

Rev. 18:16 **And saying, "Alas, alas that great city, that was clothed in fine linen, and purple, and scarlet, and decked with gold, and precious stones, and pearls!"**

Sensuous cities swallow the youth of our world. There is a dead give-away when you glance inside the gold cup in her hand. We see the seething evil and **"filth"** she has mixed for the world's consumption. Her seductiveness is a chief means of attracting the people of the world.

Rev. 17:4 **And the woman was** *dressed* **in purple and scarlet color, and decked with gold and precious stones and pearls, and she had a golden cup in her hand full of abominations and filthiness of her** *adulteries.* (EKJV)

Look at her decked in jewels. Glitter and splendor mark her. She glitters with gold, precious stones and pearls (17:4). People everywhere are intoxicated with her allure.

She Is Greatly Spoiled (ruined—18:19; 27:16)
"...she has been <u>ruined</u>" (v. 19).
Text: Rev. 18:19

Rev. 18:19 **Alas, alas, that great city, whereby all that had ships in the sea were made rich by reason of her costliness! for in one hour she became desolate.**

The kings are intoxicated with **"the wine of her adulteries"** (17:2). They became rich through their trading and business dealings with the prostitute city. As they see her sudden ruin they are crying in agony because she is the great port of the world's ships. **"In one hour she *has been ruined!*"** The hopes and imaginations of the merchants have come crashing down before their eyes. Their adulterous sins of collusion with the great harlot has left them hopeless.

She Is a Great Schemer (18:23)
"By *your magic* (or bewitching) were all nations deceived."
She has plotted and negotiated the control of the world's systems. She devises and plans a strategy to defy God and to destroy His people. She calls down wrath upon herself. She is universally against God and the Lamb. John says it is due to her **"magic"** (18:23; also see **"magic arts"** Rev. 9:21; 21:8; and 22:15). She cast a magic spell of wanton and tragic commitment to their false "god."

There Is Blood Beneath the Glitter (18:24)
"... **the blood of those who bore testimony to Jesus"** (cf. 16:6; 18:24).
The woman is drunk. The outward splendor and beauty is a mask for her inward depravity. To say that she is **"drunk"** is to say that she is satiated to overflowing. It is not the result of beverage alcohol, but her attraction to the slaughter of the saints. Did you ever watch a drunk? They are confused and irrational. The intoxication in this passage is because **"She was drunk with the blood of the saints, the blood of those who bore testimony to Jesus."**

The most godly and faithful of mankind have not fallen to her strategy without once denying the Savior. They are the true heroes of this account. God is avenging their unrelenting torture and vial treatment of His own dear saints. ^{Rev. 19:2} **"He *has* avenged the blood of his servants at her hand..."**

She Is a City of Incomparable World Glory
Her world is radically separated from God. She is oblivious to spiritual truth and spiritual views. There is no place for God in her systems. She opposes all relevant and authentic faith. The concepts of

the Lamb are foreign to her leaders. They are embarrassed by the shedding of the blood of the Savior. There is a liberal view prevalent in our national society that is dedicated to the removal of any and all references to God. The citizens of World City hate the church, and the truth and morality she stands for and preaches.

She disavows the true, holy and eternal God. Man does not want to be reminded of his sins. He is quite satisfied in them. If there is to be a church, man wants to control its message in order that he is not offended, and his sins are not revealed. You see this in sections of early America where once the issues of theology and of spiritual heritage were dominant. You see it where the love for missions began, but the mission heart is no longer prevalent. Today, many of those churches are old buildings. Some have been abandoned and turned into museums or government halls. There is a decline in evangelical witness.

She Is Part of the "Axis of Evil"
Who do you think authored such a concept? The domain of Satan is in power. Here we see the domain of evil inspired by its author. Sin flourishes. Evil is pronounced. President George Bush coined the term "Axis of Evil."

Her prostitution is evident in the unholy alliances she fosters rather than spiritual alliances. The beast that created the prostitute and the ten kings will actually hate and destroy her (17:16-17).
Text: Rev. 18:3
Rev. 18:3 **For all nations have drunk of the wine of the wrath of her *adultery,* and <u>the kings of the earth</u> have committed *adultery* with her, and the merchants of the earth are *made* rich through the abundance of her *luxuries.* (EKJV)**

HE "D'S" OF THE FINALITY OF HER TRAGIC END
She Is <u>Diabolical</u> by Her Basic Nature
Rev. 18:2 **And he *shouted* with a *loud* voice, saying, Babylon the great is fallen, is fallen, and *has* become the *home* of demons, and the *lodging* of every *unclean* spirit, and *a roost for every unclean and detestable bird.* (EKJV)**
No evil is passed over in order to further her desires. Demons live in her and evil spirits are throughout her territory. We see her world influence in her position of greatness. She is called **"the Great**

266

City" (17:18; 18:2, 10, 16, 18, 19, 21). **The woman—the harlot is the great city** (17:18).

Rev. 17:18 "**18** And the woman *that you saw* is that great city, which *reigns* over the kings of the earth." (EKJV)

This is a striking illustration of what the city has become. We are told she sits on **"many waters"** (17:1). Her intended realm is the same as God's. It is a world of people without spiritual roots, and pulled down by unholy commerce in the market place. The waters represent according to 17:15-.

- **Peoples**—families/genetics
- **Multitudes**—cultures and diversity
- **Nations**—governments/kingdoms
- **Languages**—communications

This is not a city in isolation, but the network of the arts, commerce, technology and communication of the entire world.

She Is a Home for the <u>Demonic</u> (18:2; cf. 16:13)
She has **"become the habitation of *demons* and the *lodging* of every foul spirit..."** (EKJV)

Text: Rev. 18:2 Printed Above
The catalogue of spiritual atrocities has no limit. Her streets are filled with Satanic and demonic evil. Any new evil practice will find lodging in New Babylon. The demons are right at home in her environs. This is Satan's realm and it is what he offered Christ in the temptations (Mt. 4). He recognized it as his domain. He offered it to those willing to accept his call of surrender to his direction and authority.

She Is Abandoned in <u>Desolation</u> (18:2)
Two Women in the Desert
John was transported to a desert where he viewed the demonic woman in 17:1.
The woman who is the mother in Chapter 12 also fled to a desert for protection from the Devil. The streets of New Babylon were filled with merriment and song. People celebrated the city and what she could give them. They were drawn to the labyrinth and valleys overshadowed by buildings that reached to the heavens. Traffic

filled her streets. Crowds came by hundreds of thousands to her arenas. Bars and clubs were filled. Alcohol and drugs were readily available. The city was like a magnet as it drew and attracted the masses. Who could ever think of her as desolate, alone, abandoned and cast off? Yet, that is exactly what God will do to her.

She Is Completely Devastated (18:3-8)
Cf. Babylon (Isaiah 13:19-22)

Never again will she be populated. The prophet said: **"How desolate Babylon will be among the nations"** (Jer. 51:41). The territory of Sodom and Gomorrah (Isa. 13:19) is still largely abandoned to this day. The verses below were written over 800 years before the birth of Christ. In view of Revelation they are certainly living prophecies.

Isa. 13:19 **And Babylon, the glory of kingdoms, the beauty and *splendor* of the Chaldees shall be as when God overthrew Sodom and Gomorrah. 20 It shall never be inhabited; neither shall it be dwelt in from generation to generation: neither shall the Arabian pitch a tent there; neither shall the shepherds make their fold there. 21 But wild *animals* of the desert shall lie there; and their houses shall be full of *howling* creatures; and *ostriches* shall dwell there, and satyrs *(or goat-demons)* shall dance there. 22 And the wild *animals* of the islands shall cry in their desolate houses, and *jackals* in their pleasant palaces: and her time is *coming soon,* and her days shall not be prolonged.** (EKJV)

Jer. 51:41 **"How is Sheshach taken! and how is the praise of the whole earth surprised! how Babylon *has* become an astonishment among the nations!** (EKJV)

She Faces Immediate Death (18:8)
Text: Rev. 18:8
Rev. 18:8 **Therefore her plagues *shall* come in one day, death, and mourning, and famine; and she shall be utterly burned with fire: for strong is the Lord God who *judges* her.** (EKJV)

Death will overtake her. She is as dead as she can be. This takes place **"in one day."** Her life has been forfeited because of her rebellion, sin, and degradation. The funeral dirge is found in verse 8. We have her sad obituary. The evil city has experienced God's judgment of death.

God's Judgment upon New Babylon

✓ **Plagues**—rampant and unstoppable death-dealing disease
✓ **Death**—death by disease, famine and the sword
✓ **Mourning**—the horrible recognition that there is no hope
✓ **Famine**—starvation and complete physical deprivation
✓ **Destruction** (by fire)—a total cataclysmic conflagration of blazing fire

Remember **the four horsemen of the Apocalypse** (Rev. 6:1ff).

❖ The **white horse and the victorious conqueror on a mission of conquest**
❖ The **fiery red horse** whose mission was to engage mankind in war and cause them to slay one another
❖ The **black horse** and his rider who proclaimed famine
❖ The **pale horse** whose rider **was named Death and Hades followed behind** (death).

Rev. 6:8 "...**And power was given to them over *a* fourth of the earth, to kill with sword, and with hunger, and with death, and with the *wild animals* of the earth.**"

And then **the fifth seal** was opened and John saw "**under the altar**" of Almighty God.

Rev. 6:9 **And when he had opened the fifth seal, I saw under the altar the souls of *those* that were slain for the word of God, and for the testimony which they held:** [10] **And they cried with a loud voice, saying, How long, O Lord, holy and true, do you not judge and avenge our blood on *those* that dwell on the earth?** [11] **And white robes were given to every one of them; and *they were told,* that they should rest for a little while, until their fellow servants *who are* also their brothers, should be killed *even* as they were, *and their number completed.* (EKJV)**

When **the sixth seal** is opened: **Rev. 6:13** **And the stars of heaven fell to the earth, even as a fig tree *drops* her figs *before they are ripe,* when she is shaken by a mighty wind.** [14] **And the heaven de-**

parted as a scroll when it is rolled together; and every mountain and island were moved out of their places." (Rev. 6:13; see 20:11).

Then we have thoughts here as we read in Chapter 19:17-19.
Rev. 6:15 And the kings of the earth, and the *important* men, and the rich men, and the chief captains, and the mighty men, and every *slave* and every free man, hid themselves in the dens and in the rocks of the mountains; 16 And said to the mountains and rocks, Fall on us, and hide us from the face of *the one* that sits on the throne, and from the wrath of the Lamb: 17 For the great day of his wrath *has* come; and who shall be able to stand?" (EKJV)

Revelation 17-19 reveals God's response to the prayers of the martyrs. They were told to wait, and now they are seeing God's retribution on the wicked kingdom that slaughtered them. The Harlot stands for the evil city figuratively called Babylon. When she falls, all kingdoms fall. The economies of the kings of the earth are based upon her success. Now notice the extent of her fall.

She Is Hopelessly <u>Doomed</u> (18:10)
"In one hour your doom has come" (v. 10).
To be doomed is to be hopeless and destitute. One is denied everything that promotes life or leads to survival. God is not going to delay His total judgment on the rebellious wicked city.
Rev. 18:10 Standing *far away because of the terror* of her torment, saying, Alas, alas that great city Babylon, that mighty city! for in one hour *your* judgment has come. (EKJV)

They See the Smoking Ruins of the Once Great City
They can weep for the city, but not for the countless lives of those she has brought to ruin. The people who are part of her composition and cosmopolitan citizenry are led into sins of total destruction, and not a soul sheds a tear for them.

But in Revelation 19 we see the great hallelujah of the saints. They rejoice with exceeding joy because she has received her final retribution, and she is no longer there to bring suffering on God's people.

Rev. 19:1 And after these things I heard *the tremendous sound of a multitude of* people in heaven, saying, "Alleluia; Salvation, and

glory, and honor, and power, unto the Lord our God: ² For true and righteous are his judgments: for he has judged the *great prostitute, who corrupted* the earth with her *adulteries,* and *he has avenged the blood of his servants.*"(EKJV)

She Will Experience Her Everlasting <u>Departure</u>

Everything is gone—"never to be recovered" (18:14). Notice the time frame **"in one hour your doom has come"** (v. 10). It is as if she never existed. Not just the World Trade Center Towers vanished in an overwhelming blow to the United States; but smoke rises from all the toppled complexes of the world. The destruction is of total and of enormous proportions, and the kings and merchants stand far away in grief and despair. There are no life boats and no rescue helicopters. There is no help coming for these who were so involved. They reaped just as they sowed.

Text: Rev. 18:21-24
Rev. 18:21 **And a mighty angel took up a stone like a great millstone, and *threw* it into the sea, saying, Thus with violence shall that great city Babylon be thrown down, and *shall never be found again.* ²² And the voice of harpist, and musicians, and of pipers, and trumpeters, shall *never be heard in you;* and no craftsman, of *any* craft shall be found *in you ever again;* and the sound of a millstone *shall never be heard in you again;* ²³ And the light of a candle shall *never shine in you again;* and the voice of the bridegroom and of the bride shall *never be heard in you again:* for thy merchants were the great men of the earth; *and* by their sorceries and *magic* they deceived all nations.** (EKJV)

²⁴ **And in her was found the blood of prophets, and of saints, and of all that were slain upon the earth.**

She Is Swept Away in Sudden <u>Destruction</u>
(17:8, 11; 18:9)

Text: Rev. 18:9
Rev. 18:9 **And the kings of the earth, who have committed *adultery* and lived *luxuriously* with her, shall *wail for* her, and lament for her, when they shall see the smoke of her burning.** (EKJV)

The smoke of blazing fires within all of her structures testifies to the totality of her destruction.

For the **"kings of the earth"** (v. 9), see Rev. 1:5; 6:15; 16:14 (KJV); 17:2, 18; 18:3, 9; 19:19; 21:18. The NIV has **"kings"** alone in Rev. 16:14. (There is a violent overthrow) Revelation 14:8 and 16:19 Announce Babylon's Doom

It happens suddenly: in one **"one day"** (v. 8)

Rev. 18:8 "**Therefore her *plagues shall come in one day...*"** There is no hope and no escape. She has brought this all on herself, and as God has promised through His prophets say that her punishment will be meted out with no delay. Perfect justice requires no appeal. Consider the reports of her judgment:

> ➤ **"Smoke"** (18:9, 18; 19:3)
> ➤ **"Where there's smoke there's fire."**
> ➤ **"Fire"** (17:16; 18:8)
> ➤ **Spontaneous**—**"one hour"** (vs. 10, 17, 19)

The Suffering and Pain of Her Sudden <u>Demise</u>
She Is Tortured (18:7)

As much glory and luxury as she gave herself, give that much <u>torture</u> and grief to her... (EHV)

In her destruction she receives the judgment, and thus the torture promised her for many centuries. What she gave herself in glory is paid back in **"torture."** In Rev. 9:5 those people who do not have the seal of God are tortured for **"five months"** by the creatures from the abyss.

Text: Rev. 18:7

Rev. 18:7 **How much she has glorified herself, and lived *luxuriously*, so *give her that* much torment and sorrow: for she says in her heart, I sit as a queen, and am not a widow, and shall see no sorrow.** (EKJV)

She Is Tormented (18:10, 15, 20)

Text : Rev. 18:10

Rev. 18:10 **Standing *far away for* fear of her torment, saying, "Alas, alas that great city Babylon, that mighty city! for in one hour *your* judgment has come!"** (EKJV)

Notice: "In one hour your doom has come." The phrase **"in one hour"** is found in vs. 10, 17 and 19. There is no time to even think. Her end comes suddenly, swiftly and without additional warning.

The Earth's Kings Are Terror Stricken (18:10, 15)
Their Just Punishment Is at Hand

Text: Rev. 18:15

Rev. 18:15 **The merchants of these things,** *that* **were made rich by her, shall stand** *far away* **for fear of her torment, weeping and wailing.** (EKJV)

The world is terrified at her destruction. Terrified at her torment, they will stand *"far away"*. There are two thoughts here. The merchants are terrified because their source of material gain is gone, but also because with her destruction, their great merchandise centers are eliminated. Can they be far behind? They sold out body and soul to the Great City. All that they call theirs is gone with her.

The Awful Fate of New Babylon

With the appearance of the **"mighty angel"** (v. 21) the destruction is finalized. The great city is **"thrown down"** violently **"never to be found again."** The musicians, the players of instruments will never be heard again; the tradesmen and manufacturers will never be found again; the sound of the mills will cease; the lights will never be turned on again. Rather perpetual darkness will reign. The bride and the bridegroom will never celebrate the beginning of life together there. When she is exposed the **"blood of the prophets and of God's holy people"** is revealed.

1. The end of **the arts**—music ceased (18:22).
2. The end of **commerce** (trades)—the merchants weep and mourn (18:22; cf. 18:9, 15, and 19).
3. The end of **manufacturing**—symbolized by the millstone (18:22)
4. The end of **light**—there is a reversion to primeval darkness (18:23).
5. The end of **relationships** and the home—symbolized by marriage, a joyful celebration of the new relationship (18:23) These mark the end of civilization. Tragically, it is all gone before the passing of an hour.

THE MOURNERS (GRIEF-STRICKEN)

They mourn because her destruction marks the end of their liveli-hood. They truly thought it would never end. The day of reckoning is coming.

- **MOURNERS**—Those who grieve at the fall of the great city
- **MONARCHS** (Kings)(18:3, 9; 17:18)
- **MERCHANTS** (18:11-17a)
- **MARINERS** (18:17b-19)—Includes sea captains, travelers and sailors. It is impressive to watch the great ships of the world lift their anchors and set out for their destination.

THE RIGHTEOUS (Rev. 19:8); REDEEMED (Rev. 14:3)
The Blood of the Saints

These are God's people (18:4). **The blood of the saints has been shed.** The righteous are called **to rejoice** (18:20). The slain includes **saints and prophets** (18:20). The blood of the saints and prophets is unassailable evidence of her rejection of and rebellion against God (18:24).

The Bride of Christ Receives the Promised Reward

The bride is not a woman. She is the redeemed body of God's peo-ple washed in the blood of the Lamb. The slaughtered saints be-come the bride of Christ, the Lamb (19:7; 21:2, 9; 22:17). In Rev. 22:17 they join with Christ in offering the invitation. She is dressed in **"fine linen, clean and white"** (19:8). The **"armies of heaven"** follow their Lord in bringing judgment and justice. (19:14). As God remembered the harlot city, He remembers His holy people.

The Beast and the False Prophet meet their fate—the Beast and the deceivers of the world are thrown into the lake of fire.

Rev. 19:20 **And the beast was taken, and with him the false prophet that *worked* miracles with which he deceived *those* that had re-ceived the mark of the beast, and *those* that worshiped his image. These both were cast alive into a lake of fire burning with brim-stone.** (EKJV)

What Appropriate Judgment!

Revelation portrays the final assault of those of the earth against the Lamb and their **instantaneous defeat.** Jesus warned us not to mislead a little child. So much more the multitudes mentioned here. The fate of the devil and the beast and his followers **is fully appropriate.** The prayers of the martyred saints **have been answered**. Evil has been destroyed.

Those who chose the way of the devil have met their fate. We see this coming as far back as the words of Moses. God is going to avenge the blood of his servants.

God's Vengeance Against Evil
From The Song of Moses
Deut. 32:43 **Rejoice, O ye nations, with his people: for he will avenge the blood of his servants, and will render vengeance to his adversaries, and will be merciful unto his land, and to his people.** (KJV)

A Day of Vengeance and a Year of Retribution
Isa. 34:8 **For it is the day of the LORD's vengeance, and the year of *retribution* for the *cause of God's people* Zion.** (EKJV)

Psalm 149 – A Psalm of David
Ps. 149:5 **Let the saints rejoice in this honor**
and sing for joy on their beds.
6 **May the praise of God be in their mouths**
and a double-edged sword in their hands,
7 **to inflict vengeance on the nations**
  and punishment on the peoples,
8 **to bind their kings with fetters,**
their nobles with shackles of iron,
9 **to carry out the sentence written against them.**
This is the glory of all his saints.
  Praise the LORD. (KJV)

Chapter 19

HEAVEN VERSUS EARTH: ARMAGEDDON
(AND THE GREAT HALLELUJAH)

> ### *Snapshot of Chapter 19*
> Chapter 19 begins with the glorious Hallelujah chorus of the redeemed saints as they rejoice over the punishment of the great prostitute. It concludes with the capture of the beast and the false prophet and the resounding and total defeat of the kings in the Battle of Armageddon. In verses 7-8 John is shown the redeemed in Christ made ready for the celebration of the Lamb. Then we see the Lamb coming with His mighty army and we learn His names that reveal His power and might as the Son of God. Finally, the battle is over instantly, and Christ is the Victor, and we are prepared for the glorious reign and resurrection of the saints in Chapter 20.

h1>THE VICTORY CELEBRATION (19:1-8)</h1>

19:1-2 "Salvation and glory and power belong to our God."

Text: Rev. 19:1-2

Rev. 19:1 **And after these things I heard a** *roar of an enormous multitude* **in heaven, saying, Alleluia; Salvation, and glory, and honor, and power, to the Lord our God:** [2] **For true and righteous are his judgments: for he has judged the great** *prostitute, who corrupted* **the earth with her** *adulteries,* **and has avenged the blood of his servants at her hand.** (Easy KJV)

Hallelujah is only found in Revelation 19 in the New Testament. The first two verses of Revelation 19 reflect back on Chapters 17 and 18. John heard the sound as of **"the roar of a great multitude in heaven" shouting over and over: "Hallelujah!"** (19:1). In this enormous roar we take note that they are not singing, but shouting because it is a victory celebration. The shouts grow louder and louder until they create a deafening roar. The multitude of the **"redeemed"** testify to the justice of God's judgments when He **"has judged the great prostitute who corrupted the earth..."** The sentence of God is always appropriate and true. His justice cannot be questioned because it is perfect, correct, and always consistent.

19:3-6 The Hallelujah Chorus

They are shouting **"Hallelujah! Hallelujah! Hallelujah! Hallelujah! Hallelujah!"** The great **"Hallelujah Chorus"** in Handel's *Messiah* is based on this passage. The Greek is **Alleluia.** The term occurs only here in the entire New Testament. In the Psalms the words are rendered **"praises the LORD"** (see Psalm 146:1, 10 for example. The Hebrew is *Hallelu Yah* **("praise ye Jahweh").** Psalms 113-118 contain the first group of **Hallel Psalms** and are known as The Egyptian Hallel psalms. The other two collections are the **"Great Hallel"** (Ps. 136); and the final Hallelujah psalms (146-150). Beginning with Psalm 146 we find the five hallelujah psalms that bring us to the end of the hymnal of Israel. These psalms are filled with praise to the Lord. Psalm 146 continues the praise we noted in Psalm 145. The word **"praise"** is found 150 times in Psalms. (For more see my *Psalms: Fresh Hope for Today, Vol. 2* for commentary on the above listed Psalms). God prepared his people for this ultimate day of praise as the kingdom becomes the kingdom of our Lord Christ. In John's vision the heavenly temple is alive with praise, just as God was praised in His earthly temple in Jerusalem. The hallelujahs have filtered into some of the great hymns of the church.

They are shouting in response to God's judgment on the great harlot. If you sin, you will be judged. There is no escape. We observe that the redeemed of the Lord are made ready for the **"wedding of the Lamb** (which) **has come"** (19:7-8). Here we have mention of the banquet (19:9) such as Christ spoke of in His earthly ministry (see Jesus' parables: Luke 12:36; and 14:13f for example).

The Universal Hallelujah

In this enormous heavenly multitude all creatures join in the chorus including the twenty-four elders (19:4), the four living creatures (19:4), the servants of God (19:5), and all people **"small and great"** (19:5). We are reminded of the "Lamb's Coronation Anthem" in Revelation 5:11-13 where every creature in heaven and on earth and in the sea, etc., breaks out in praise to the Lamb. It is like the roar of a great waterfall or the sound of ceaseless thunder.

The shouts grow louder and louder as we are prepared for the Lamb's final victory against the enormous evil army led by the earth's kings. Notice the redeemed of God (19:7-8). Jesus said: **"Rejoice and be exceedingly glad for great is your reward in heaven"** (Mt. 5:12).

Text: Rev. 19:3-5
Rev. 19:3 **And again they said, Alleluia. And her smoke rose up forever and ever. ⁴ And the twenty-four elders and the four creatures fell down and worshiped God that sat on the throne, saying, Amen; Alleluia. ⁵ And a voice came out of the throne, saying, Praise our God, all his servants, and you that fear him, both small and great.** (EKJV)

The reason for such glorious praise is due to the fact that "**the smoke from her goes up forever and ever" (v. 3).** For more scripture relating to **"Smoke—Forever"** see Isaiah 34:10; Joel 2:30; Acts 2:19; Rev. 14:11; 18:9, 18; 19:3. There follows the universal **"hallelujah"** as the redeemed of the Lord praise him for vindicating them and establishing the justice due them.

19:7-8 The Wedding Celebration of the Lamb and His Bride

Text: Rev. 19:6-7
Rev. 19:6 **And I heard the voice of a great multitude, and as the voice *like rushing* waters, and a sound *like* mighty *claps of thunder,* saying, Alleluia: for the Lord God omnipotent reigns. [7] Let us be glad and rejoice, and give honor to him: for the marriage of the Lamb *has* come, and his wife *has* made herself ready. [8] And it was granted to her that she should be arrayed in fine linen, clean and white: for the fine linen is the righteousness of saints.** (EKJV)

In the previous chapter we saw the grossly adulterous harlot (18:3), but in Chapter 19 we see the spotless bride of Christ. Christ is now forever in union with His eternal church. This union will never be dissolved. He purchased His people with His own blood. The theme of marriage of God with His people is found throughout the scriptures.

The book of Hosea highlights this relationship (Hos. 2:19). The church has become the bride of Christ and her deeds of works and ministry have become her wedding dress (v. 8). For the marriage motif regarding the **"bride"** of Christ see: Rev. 21:2, 9; 22:17. For the marriage of the land (**Beulah**) see Isa. 62:4. The great fear of the church was that on this day she would appear **"naked"** (2 Cor. 5:3; Rev. 3:17; 16:15). But **"his bride has made herself ready"** (v. 7-8). God has given her the proper dress for the wedding (v. 8); but now she is fully dressed for the banquet at God's table.

19:9 John's Fourth Beatitude in Revelation
Text: Rev. 19:9
Rev. 19:9 **And he *said to* me, Write, Blessed are *those who* are *invited to* the marriage supper of the Lamb. And he *said* to me, "These are the true sayings of God."** (EKJV)

This is the fourth of the seven beatitudes in Revelation all beginning with the word **"blessed"** (Rev. 1:3; 14:13; 16:15; 19:9; 20:6; 22:7, 14). The blessing here is upon **"those who are invited to the wedding supper of the Lamb."** This is the great invitation of the

Holy Spirit and the bride; but the final invitation of Christ excels in its reach to the masses of humanity:

Rev. 22:17 **And the Spirit and the bride say, Come. And let him that** *hears* **say, Come. And let him that is** *thirsty* **come. And whosoever will, let him take the water of life freely.** (EKJV)

19:10 The Deity of Holy God
Text: Rev. 19:10
Rev. 19:10 **And I fell at his feet to worship him. And he said to me,** *Do not do this.* **I am your fellow servant, and of** *your brothers* **that have the testimony of Jesus: worship God: for the testimony of Jesus is the spirit of prophecy.** (EKJV)

At this point John attempts to worship the angel, but is halted before he can do so. John is caught off guard. He surely knows better. But angels are glorious, beautiful creatures of God, and it should be noted that John is overwhelmed at the beauty, wisdom and understanding of the angel.

He certainly knew Christ in a personal and intimate manner, but in this moment following the great hallelujah, John is just inspired to do something then and there. The angel was his first thought, but the angel stopped him in an instant and reprimanded him: **"Worship God,"** he commanded.

Ps. 99:3 **Let them praise <u>your great and</u> *<u>awesome</u>* <u>name—it is holy</u>.**

Heb. 12:28 **Since** *we are* **receiving a kingdom that cannot be moved, let us have grace, whereby we may serve God acceptably with reverence and godly fear: [29] For our God is a consuming fire.**

THE GREAT BATTLE OF ARMAGEDDON
Rev. 19:11-21
Text: Rev. 19:11
Rev. 19:11 **And I saw heaven opened, and** *I saw* **a white horse; and the one that sat on him was called Faithful and True, and in righteousness he judges and makes war.** (EKJV)

Without warning the scene flashes from the bride—the church prepared for the wedding to the fearful sight of the Warrior from heaven followed by a magnificent army all on white horses. We have waited for the vengeance of God to come upon the willfully evil and rebellious multitudes. His righteous wrath will fall upon this enormous multitude of the ungodly from the nations. We are not forced to accept that there are no righteous people in these nations, but the kings who rule have dedicated themselves to a coalition of nations who follow the lead of the antichrist. We must not surrender the term "Armageddon". It has become the title of useless movies and television shows. The name is tossed about in political circuits by uninformed politicians who have no knowledge of the purpose of consequences of the battle of Armageddon in God's plans.

Before us is the final battle of history and the catastrophic end of the evil and rebellious nations that have opposed our God. John **"saw heaven opened"** (V. 11), and the approach of the Lord Christ in His triumphant role. The hosts of heaven follow Him to the awesome Battle of Armageddon. Paul is correct that the **"saints"** will come with Christ. Paul looks forward with desire to **"The coming of our Lord Jesus Christ with all his saints** (1 Thes. 3:13; cf. Jude 1:14; Ps. 149:9 KJV).The end comes suddenly, quickly and almost soundlessly. In one violent moment it is all over.

19:11-16 Christ the Conqueror
Text: Rev. 19:12
Rev. 19:12 **His eyes were *like* a flame of fire, and on his head were many crowns; and he had a name written, that no man *knows*, but himself.** (EKJV)

This is the second time John has observed heaven open (cf. 4:1). The first occasion allowed him to view the throne in heaven. On the second occasion he sees the coming of Christ the Victor for the great battle. **He rides a white horse—the symbol of victory in battle (v. 11).** There follows the great hosts including the martyrs and the angels. He rides in majesty. He is identified by four names: **"Faithful and true"** (v. 11; also 3:14)—He keeps His promises; **"A name...which no one knows but himself"** (cf. Luke 10:22)—this is the mystery of His divine being (v. 12); and **"the Word of God"** (v. 13). He is **"faithful," "true,"** has an unknown name, and is called **"the Word of God."**

John is shown the characteristics of His eternal reign. First, His **"eyes are like blazing fire"** (v. 12; cf. 1:14. 2:18). Upon His head are **"many crowns"** (v. 12). The crowns signify His universal rule and reign about to begin. He stands vindicated. What He refused from Satan, God has granted. God rewards every sacrifice with glory.

19:11 He Fulfills His Mission: He Comes as Judge
"...in righteousness he judges and makes war."
The Jesus that God raised from the dead is coming to judge the world.

Acts 17:31 For <u>he has set a day when he will judge the world with justice by the man he has appointed</u>. He has given proof of this to all men by raising him from the dead. (KJV)

Vengeance on the part of God lies in the hand of the Son who shall execute justice in accordance with the will of God.

19:11 He Comes to Confront and Eliminate Evil (v. 11; cf. Jude 14-15)
Jude points to the armies of heaven. They will accompany Christ when He comes to victoriously overcome in the battle of Armageddon.

> **Jude 14 Enoch, the seventh from Adam, prophesied about these men: "<u>*Look*, the Lord is coming with thousands upon thousands of his holy ones</u> 15 to judge everyone, and to convict all the ungodly of all the ungodly acts they have done in the ungodly way, and of all the harsh words ungodly sinners have spoken against him." (EKJV)**

19:13 He Conquers by His Blood
"And he was clothed with a *robe* dipped in blood..."

We contrast the blood of Calvary with the blood of the winepress (cf. v. 15; Rev. 14:19-20). The crimson flow of Calvary removes the sin of the world, but the robe of the Savior gives evidence of his role as judge.

19:13 He Conquers by His Word of Truth
"... his name is the Word of God."
Scripture is clear and consistent regarding the word of God as the passages below show together with many other passages. The very name of Christ here is **"the Word of God."** The Gospel of John

tells us so much about the Word of God. It is John who first revealed that Christ **"was God."** Therefore, in the current passage Johns tells us that "**his name is the word of God.**" This One is our mighty Savior and Redeemer. In John 1:1 we read: "**In the beginning was the Word, and the Word was with God, and the Word was God.**"

19:14 He Is Accompanied by the Armies of Heaven Riding on White Horses
"And the armies *that* were in heaven followed him upon white horses".

The saints also are on white horses. They will follow Him anywhere He leads. Look at these magnificent troops arrayed for battle. The **"armies of heaven"** include the saints and the innumerable angels that surround the throne of God. Note that they follow Him. They do not precede Him.

The Lord says in Jeremiah 23:5
"**... I will raise unto David a righteous Branch, and a King *who* shall reign and prosper, and shall execute judgment and justice in the earth.**"
It is clear by reference to the **"righteous Branch"** and the **"King (who) shall reign...and execute judgment and justice..."** that Christ is meant.

19:15 The Iron "Scepter" of Universal Divine Rule Is His
"**... he shall rule them with a rod of iron** *(or scepter)."*
The scepter is the emblem of the divine rule of Christ and is a major prophecy of Holy Scripture. Jacob initiated the prophecy at the time of his approaching death:
Gen. 49:10 **The scepter shall not depart from Judah, nor a *rod* from between his feet, until *the one comes to whom the people will be gathered*.** (EKJV)

The **"sceptre"** (KJV) belongs to Christ as the scriptures make clear. Hebrews quotes from Psalm 45.

> **Ps. 45:6** **Thy throne, O God, *is* forever and ever: <u>the scep-tre of your kingdom *is* a right sceptre.</u>** (EKJV)

> **Heb. 1:8** **But to the Son *he said,* Thy throne, O God, *is* for-ever and ever: <u>a sceptre of righteousness *is* the scep-tre of your kingdom.</u> ⁹ You have loved righteousness, and hated iniquity; therefore God, *even* your God, has anointed you with the oil of gladness above your fel-lows.** (EKJV)

Both Psalms 45 and 110 are beautiful and inspired passages pointing to the finished work of the Messiah and His universal rule as God's eternal Redeemer.

Ps. 110:2 **The LORD shall send the rod of your strength out of Zion: *you will rule* in the midst of *your* enemies.** (EKJV)

John in Revelation clearly refers to the role of Christ as seen in Psalm 2:9. In Revelation the prophecies of Jacob and David are re-vealed in their ultimate fulfillment.

> **Rev. 2:27** **And he shall rule them with <u>a rod of iron</u>; as the vessels of a potter shall they be broken to shivers: even as I received of my Father. ²⁸ And I will give him the morn-ing star.** (KJV)

Rev. 12:5 **And she brought forth a man child, <u>who was to rule all nations with a rod of iron</u>...** (KJV)

> **Rev. 19:14** **And the armies *which were* in heaven followed him upon white horses, clothed in fine linen, white and clean. ¹⁵ And <u>out of his mouth *there comes* a sharp sword</u>, that with it he *will* smite the nations: and <u>he shall rule them with a rod of iron</u>: and he *treads* the winepress of the fierceness and wrath of Almighty God. ¹⁶ And he has on *his clothing* and on his thigh a name written, KING OF KINGS, AND LORD OF LORDS.** (Also see Rev. 2:27; and 12:5 above). (EKJV)

At the occurrence of the Battle of Armageddon the absolute rule of Christ is realized. It is in this moment that the everlasting promise of God and the prayers of His people are fully accomplished in the universal rule of God's Son and our eternal Savior. The sword and the scepter belong to Christ the Victor and the conqueror over Satan and his evil domain.

19:15 He Conquers by His Weapon—"a sharp sword" (cf. 1:16; 2:12, 16)

Text: Rev. 19:15
Rev. 19:15 **"And <u>out of his mouth *there comes* a sharp sword</u>, that with it he *will strike down* the nations..."**
The term **double-edged sword** is specifically mentioned four times in prophetic scripture. See the following scriptures for mention of this sword and/or the double edged sword specifically: Psalm 149:6; Heb. 4:12; Rev. 1:16; Rev. 2:12; and the **"sword,"** but the double-edge is omitted: Rev. 19:15, 21. The sword in Psalm 149:6; Rev. 1:16 and 2:12 is the same sword we encounter in Rev. 19:15, 21. It is only referred to specifically as a **"double edged sword"** in four of the above, but implied in all. In the three references in Revelation, the sword is coming out of the mouth of the victor Christ. The prophecies of the iron scepter and the double-edged sword both are rendered in the prophecies of David given him by the Lord.

Rev. 1:16 **In his right hand he held seven stars, and <u>out of his mouth came a sharp double-edged sword</u>. His face was like the sun shining in all its brilliance.**

Rev. 2:12 **"To the angel of the church in Pergamum write: These are the words of <u>him who has the sharp, double-edged sword</u>."**

Rev. 2:16 **"Repent therefore! Otherwise, I will soon come to you and <u>will fight against them with the sword of my mouth</u>."**
The same sword is indicated here as in verse 12.

The Sword, the Saints and the Savior in the Judgment

David is credited with writing Psalm 149 (see my commentary on Psalms, vol. 2). The sword is **"in the hands of the saints"** (in

Psalm 149, KJV only). This is the only mention of the double-edged sword used for battle in the Old Testament. It is a clear prophecy of the final battle. Christ, the Victor, wields it on behalf of God the Father and His saints. He will **"execute"** (or) **"carry out the sentence"—RSV)"** <u>**vengeance upon the heathen"**</u> (or) **"nations"**), **"and punishments upon the people"** (v. 7). He is: **"To execute upon them the judgment <u>written</u>"** (v. 9).

19:15 He Treads the Winepress of the Fury of the Wrath of God

Text: Rev. 19:15
^{Rev. 19:15} <u>**He treads the winepress of the fury of the wrath of God Almighty.**</u>

The Treading of the Winepress in Isaiah and Revelation

Isaiah gives us the full picture in the prophecy of the winepress (Isa. 63:2-6). ^{Isa. 63:6} **And <u>I will tread down the people in my anger, and make them drunk in my fury...</u>**

Isaiah 63:2-6 describes the <u>Christ completing the wrath and vengeance of God</u> upon the wicked and fulfilling the prophecy of Ps. 58:10. ^{Ps. 58:10} **"he shall wash his <u>feet in the blood of the wicked</u>."**

In Revelation 14 the grapes are gathered, thrown into the winepress and trampled so that the **"blood"** runs out for 200 miles as deep as the horses' bridles. What is the meaning of treading the winepress? Who treads the winepress? How does this fit into the final eschatology of the Scripture?

The Winepress Prophecy in Isaiah
^{Isa. 63:2} **Why *is* your apparel red, and your garments like him that treaded in the wine vat? ³ I have trodden the winepress alone; and of the people *there was* none with me: for I will tread them in mine anger, and trample them in my fury; and their blood shall be sprinkled upon my garments, and I will stain all my raiment. ⁴ <u>For the day of vengeance *is* in mine heart, and the year of my redeemed has come</u>. ⁵ And I looked, and *there was* none to help; and I wondered that *there was* none to uphold *me*: therefore my own arm brought salvation to me; and my fury upheld me. ⁶ <u>And I will</u>**

> tread down the people in my anger, and make them drunk in my fury.
> The Scene of the Final Judgment of the Wicked
> Rev. 14:19 And the angel thrust his sickle into the earth, and gathered the vine of the earth, and cast *it* into the great winepress of the wrath of God. 20 And the winepress was trodden outside the city, and blood came out of the winepress, even unto the horse bridles, by the space of a thousand *and* six hundred furlongs.

19:15 He Treads the Grapes of God's Wrath

The one who will tramp the grapes is none other than Christ, the Lamb of God.

Text: Rev. 19:15-16

Rev. 19:15 And out of his mouth *comes* a sharp sword, that with it he should *strike down* the nations: and he shall rule them with a rod of iron: and he *treads* the winepress of the fierceness and wrath of Almighty God. 16 And he has on his vesture *(or his robe)* and on his thigh a name written, KING OF KINGS, AND LORD OF LORDS. (EKJV)

Take note of the specific prophecy of Isaiah:

> Isa. 63:3 ...I trampled them in my anger   and trod them down in my wrath; their blood spattered my *clothing*.   (Also see: Rev. 14:19)

The Old Testament Describes the Final Battle

> Isa. 34:9 Edom's streams will be turned into pitch, her dusts into burning sulfur; her land will become blazing pitch! 10 It will not be quenched night and day; its smoke will rise forever. From generation to generation it will lie desolate; no one will ever pass through it again.

> Daniel prophesies of God's eternal kingdom "that *(it)* will never be destroyed...." And he says: Dan. 2:44 "In the time of those kings, the God of heaven will set up a kingdom that will never be destroyed, nor will it be left to another people. It will crush all those kingdoms and bring them to an end, but it will *certainly* endure forever" (Also: Daniel 7, 9, and 11).

In Zechariah we are told of the battle of God against the nations:
Zech. 14:3 <u>Then the LORD will go out and fight against those nations, as he fights in the day of battle.</u>

Then the Lord will return: **Zech. 14:5 "Then the LORD my God will come, and all the holy ones with him"**
Rev. 11:15 The seventh angel sounded his trumpet, and there were loud voices in heaven, which said: "<u>The kingdom of the world has become the kingdom of our Lord and of his Christ, and he will reign forever and ever</u>."

Rev. 14:17 Another angel came out of the temple in heaven, and he too had a sharp sickle[19] <u>The angel swung his sickle on the earth, and gathered its grapes and threw them into the great winepress of God's wrath.</u> [20] <u>They were trampled in the winepress outside the city, and blood flowed out of the press, rising as high as the horses' bridles for a distance of 1,600 stadia.</u>

We are told that the Kings from the compass points will assemble at Armageddon with 200 million troops. The first mention of a mammoth army is in Rev. 9:16-
[16] And the number of the army of the horsemen were two hundred thousand thousand: and I heard *their* number.

The four angels that had been kept ready are released at the **"great river Euphrates."** We saw the four angels that were kept ready in Rev. 7:1-3. The troops are gathered for battle (Rev. 16:12-16). In Rev. 16:16 we hear the name **"Armageddon."**
Rev. 16:16 <u>Then they gathered the kings together to the place that in Hebrew is called Armageddon.</u>

The Day of the Lord and the Wicked (19:17-18)
Text: Rev. 19:17-18
Rev. 19:17 And I saw an angel standing in the sun; and he *shouted* with a loud voice, saying to all the fowls that fly in the midst of heaven, Come and gather yourselves together *for* the supper of the great God;

[18] That you may eat the flesh of kings, and the flesh of captains, and the flesh of mighty men, and the flesh of horses, and of *the ones* that sit on them, and the flesh of all men, both free and *slaves*, both small and great.

(Note the resemblance of these groups with those in Rev. 6:15 who also face punishment).

The Great Supper of God (19:17)

The angel summons the vultures before it begins. This is a way of saying it is going to be a total slaughter. Every rebellious soul is included and not one escapes. Kings and slaves meet their punishment together. All classes and ranks die together, and are left lying in the open for the consummation of their bodies by the scavengers. The Battle of Armageddon is over before it began.

THE CAPTURE OF SATAN'S EVIL ASSOCIATES (19:19-21)
They Meet Their End in the Lake of Fire
The Defeat, Capture and Destruction of Antichrist
Text: Rev. 19:19-20

Rev. 19:19 **Then I saw the beast and the kings of the earth and their armies gathered together to wage war against the rider on the horse and his army. [20] But the beast was captured, and with it the false prophet who had performed the signs on its behalf. With these signs he had deceived those who had received the mark of the beast and worshiped its image. The two of them were thrown alive into the fiery lake of burning sulfur.**

This is the climactic moment of victory over the Antichrist (here referred to as the **"beast"**). In contrast to Christ and the armies of heaven the beast is accompanied by **"the kings of the earth and their armies."** In Rev. 16:13 we read how demons like frogs were vomited up by the three: the dragon (Satan), the beast from the sea (Antichrist), and the beast from the earth (the false prophet) in order that they might gather the kings and their armies. Remember how it was said: **"Who is like unto the beast? Who is able to make war against him?"** (13:4).

Here is the victory. Here Christ has triumphed as prophesied in scripture. The **"King of kings and the Lord of lords"** has returned in glorious victory as He promised, defeated His enemies and now assumes His rightful throne.

No record exists that the armies with the beast ever fire a shot. Who captured the beast? It is probably an angel (note the angel with the key in Rev. 20:1). The forces of Satan and the antichrist have come to the end. Judgment falls quickly upon the antichrist. We read **"...they were gathered together to make war..."** (v. 19). **"...But the beast was captured and with him the false prophet..." "The two of them were thrown alive into the fiery lake of burning sulfur"** (v. 20)—this punishment is beyond imagination.

Instantaneous Victory

Text: Rev. 19:21

Rev. 19:21 **And the *rest* were slain with the sword of *the one* that sat on the horse, *with the* sword *coming* out of his mouth: and all the fowls were filled with their flesh.** (EKJV)

We witness the death of the hosts of evil (v. 21). All of their converts throughout history are cast together with them into the lake of fire. Those who fight together fall together. Be careful where you stand. How surprised they were. Evil falls victim to its own false conceit. They never understand the truth until it is too late."

HISTORY'S FINAL EVENTS
(According to Revelation 19-22)
THE (PRE-MILLENNIAL) RETURN OF CHRIST

1. The Battle of Armageddon (19:11-21; 16:13-16).
2. The Binding of Satan (20:1-4).

THE FIRST RESURRECTION (20:4-6)

The first resurrection includes saints of the Old Testament age, the New Testament age, and those saved during the Great Tribulation.

THE MILLENNIUM (20:3, 4b)
The Thousand-Year Reign of Christ and His Saints

1. Satan is bound and thrown into the abyss.
2. Satan is loosed briefly after the millennium (a thousand years).
3. Satan deceives the nations once again (20:8).
4. The battle of Gog and Magog follows Satan's loosing (20:8b).
5. We are shown the destruction of the enemies of God's people (20:9).

6. The Devil is delivered to the Lake of Fire to join the beast and the false prophet (20:10).

THE SECOND RESURRECTION
(THE WICKED, 20:11-15)

1. The final judgment of the wicked takes place before the Great White Throne.
2. Death and Hades are thrown into the Lake of Fire.
3. Those not found written in the Book of Life are thrown in the Lake of Fire (20:15).

THE NEW JERUSALEM (21:9-22:5)

1. A new heaven and a new earth are presented (21:1).
2. New Jerusalem, the bride of Christ comes down out of heaven (21:9f).
3. John explains the measuring of the city of God (21:15-21).
4. The glory and blessedness of the city are revealed (2

Chapter 20

THE ONE AND FINAL JUDGMENT OF GOD

Revelation 20:1-15
The Thousand Years

Text: Rev. 20:1-3

Revelation 20:1 And I saw an angel *coming* down from heaven, having the key of the bottomless pit *(or the abyss)* and a great chain in his hand. [2] And he *grabbed hold of* the dragon, that old serpent, which is the Devil, and Satan, and bound him *for* a thousand years, and placed a seal upon him, that he should *no longer* deceive the nations till the thousand years *had been* fulfilled: and after that he must be loosed a little *while.* (EKJV)

Snapshot of Chapter 20

Chapter 20 reveals the ultimate gathering of the saints, and the ultimate wrath of God's justice upon the wicked, unbelieving, and non-repenting. Satan is confined in the Abyss for 1000 years before he is everlastingly thrown into the fiery lake. We will see the eternal joy and glory of the heavenly city in chapter 21.

Satan Sealed in the Abyss

Just imagine a thousand years with Satan out of commission. Now, Satan will finally be corralled. His days of freedom are coming to an abrupt end. It only takes one angel to take care of Satan.

Rev. 20:1 And I saw an angel *coming* down from heaven, having the key of the bottomless pit *(or the abyss)* and a great chain in his hand.

We are shown the "**Abyss**" (Gk.); God's impregnable and inescapable "**prison**" (20:7) where Satan (the devil) is held securely by the power of our God. The *Septuagint* renders the word in Gen. 1:2 which is often translated "**deep**" as "**abyss.**" The Abyss is first seen in Rev. 9:1 where a star falls from heaven, and he has the key to unlock the **Abyss** permitting all manner of evil to be loosed. In Rev. 11:7, the earth beast rises from the **Abyss** (cf. Rev. 17:8). So here in Rev. 20 an angel from heaven is given the key to lock the **Abyss** where Satan is imprisoned. This same angel brings with him a "**great chain**" for the purpose of "**binding**" Satan. This suggests that his thousand years in prison will have no reprieve and no escape. Rev. 20:2 says: "**...that he should *no longer* deceive the nations till the thousand years *had been* fulfilled.**"

The notable thing about true prophecy sent by God is the reality usually far exceeds the ability of earthly language and images to describe. Nevertheless, prophetic descriptions are graphic images of what God will accomplish. The thought of a bottomless pit into which one plunges indicates the truth that one so incarcerated is removed by distance and confinement an impossible distance from people on earth. God is completely able to place Satan as far from those he has tormented as earth is from heaven. We have an example of such limitations in Jesus' account of the rich man and Lazarus:

Luke 16:26 And beside all this, between us and you there is a great *chasm* fixed so that *those that* desire to *go* from *here* to you cannot; neither can anyone *come* to us *from where you are*. (EKJV)

We are not told the details of the "**chasm.**" Rather, we are shown the impossibility of passing from one sphere to another. God has set the limits and the boundaries. There are no passports from one place to another. To say that the angel possessed the key is to say

293

that he controls who comes and goes. No one can leave the Abyss once the angel has shut and sealed it. It is the abode of the devil for a thousand years. This is the most extensive "time out" ever recorded. Satan can consider his life of evil and rebellion. Could he change? Well he didn't, but you can't say that God did not give him the opportunity.

John says the angel **"grabbed hold of the dragon...."** (v. 2). He just took hold of him, and Satan was helpless to resist the angel's empowerment by God. The **"dragon"** was first seen in chapter 12 where he is called **"the great red dragon."** John explains the battle of Christ against the devil.

^{1 John 3:8} <u>He who does what is sinful is of the devil, because the devil has been sinning from the beginning</u>. The reason the <u>Son of God appeared was to destroy the devil's work</u>.

His angels are also held in **"tartarus"** (Gk. For **"hell"** in 2 Peter 2:4) until the final judgment.

> ^{2 Peter 2:4} **For if God did not spare angels when they sinned, but sent them to hell, putting them in chains of darkness to be held for judgment...**

^{Jude 6} **And the angels who did not keep their positions of authority but abandoned their proper dwelling—these he has kept in darkness, bound with everlasting chains for judgment on the great Day** (Cf. Rev. 12:7-9).

When we come to the **"lake of fire"** in the latter part of this chapter, we are reminded once again that God has prepared special confinement for the devil. However, those who follow him will share in his confinement and suffering. Both the **Abyss** and the **lake of fire** are first intended for Satan.

Punishment of the Wicked in the Lake of Fire

Later in Revelation 20, we are shown the terrifying and terminal **"lake of fire"** (20:14-15). This last extremity of the wrath of God for those who absolutely refuse to repent is also inescapable. Jesus spoke of such a fiery result:

Matthew 13:49-51

> [49] So will it be at the end of the world: the angels will come *down,* and *separate* the wicked from the just, [50] And will *throw* them into the *fiery* furnace: there shall be wailing and gnashing of teeth. [51] Jesus *said* to them, "Have you understood all these things?" They *replied,* "Yes, Lord." *(Cp. Mt. 13:41ff; Rev. 14:10)* — 'he shall be tormented with fire and brimstone in the presence of the holy angels, and in the presence of the Lamb."

> In Matt. 25:41 Jesus refers to **"everlasting fire"** and notes that it is primarily **"prepared for the devil and his angels."**
> [41] **Leave my presence, you who are cursed, into everlasting fire, prepared for the devil and his angels."** (S*ee Matt. 18:8 and Jude 1:7 for* 'everlasting fire*")*. Christ also used the term **"gehenna"** referring to the hell of fire. This reference comes from the days when Israel sacrificed their children in fire as a form of wicked pagan worship. The reference is to the place where garbage burned continually along with other refuse.

All of earth's fire departments would be like a drop of water in the desert. The fire cannot be extinguished. In Matt. 9:47-48 **"the fire is not quenched."** In Luke 16:24 the rich man cries out **"Father Abraham, have mercy on me, and send Lazarus, that he may dip the tip of his finger in water, and cool my tongue; for I am tormented in this flame..."**

In Jude 1:7 he states of Sodom and Gomorrah: **They "are *shown as* an example, suffering the vengeance of eternal fire."** So John reports: **Rev. 20:15 And *anyone who* was not found *recorded* in the book of life was *thrown* into the lake of fire.**

The Devil's Thousand Years in Isolation (20:1-3)

The angel has **the key to the "bottomless pit" (or abyss) and a great chain.** Remember in Luke 8:31 how the many demons **"begged him *repeatedly* that he would not command them to go out into the *abyss.*"** We see the Abyss three times in the New Testament (Luke 8:31; Rev. 9; and Rev. 20:1-3; cf. Rev. 11:7).

The Announcement at the Sounding of the Fifth Trumpet - Rev. 9:1

"And the fifth angel sounded, and I saw a star fall from heaven to the earth: and he was given the key of the bottomless pit (or abyss). [2] And he opened the *abyss*; and there smoke *rose* out of the pit, *like* the smoke of a great furnace; and the sun and the air were darkened *because* of the smoke from the pit." (EKJV)

Rev. 9:11 explains that – **"they had a king over them, which is the angel of the bottomless pit *(or abyss),* whose name in the Hebrew tongue is Abaddon, but in the Greek tongue his name *is* Apollyon.** (Both names mean **Destroyer**). (EKJV)
There is authority over those in the Abyss. Remember in Revelation 19 that the universal authority over every creature now belongs to Christ. In Revelation 11:7 (the account of God's two witnesses) it states:
Rev. 11:7**"When they have finished their testimony, the beast that** *ascends* **out of the** *abyss* **will make war against them, and will overcome them, and kill them."** (EKJV)

In Rev. 17:7 we saw the Woman, who was drunk with the blood of the saints, and she was sitting on the beast, and John is reminded of the fate of the beast **"that *ascends* out of the (*abyss)*"** (Rev. 17:8).

[7] **And the angel said to me, *Why did you* marvel? I will tell you the mystery of the woman, and of the beast that *carries* her, *that has* the seven heads and ten horns. [8] The beast *that you saw* was, and is not; and shall ascend out of the *abyss*, <u>and go into *destruction*."</u>** (See Rev. 17 for the explanation). (EKJV)

The earth's population who are not in Christ will be filled with astonishment because they have placed their allegiance in the wrong leader. They will suffer along with the one they chose to follow. It is, indeed, tragic and terrifying to discover that your hope is the wrong hope, and that you have chosen a way that leads to eternal doom and destruction.

The Urgent Need to Follow Christ
Without Delay

"It is a fearful thing to fall into the hands of the living God" (Heb. 10:31). Think about **a bottomless pit!** It is to fall farther, and farther, and farther away from God into eternal darkness and hell.

> **Ezekiel 33:11** **"Say to them (the house of Israel), As surely as I live, declares the Sovereign Lord, I take no pleasure in the death of the wicked, but rather that they turn from their ways and live. Turn! Turn from your evil ways! Why will you die, O house of Israel?"**

"Since then, we know what it is to fear the Lord; we try to persuade men..." (2 Cor. 5:11).

> **"As God's fellow workers we urge you not to receive God's grace in vain.** **²** **For he says, 'In the time of my favor I heard you, and in the day of salvation I helped you.' I tell you, now is the time of God's favor, now is the day of salvation"** (2 Cor. 6:1-2). Also see: Matthew 5:29-30.

Satan Alias "the Devil"

Notice: Satan's identify is fully given: **"the dragon, that old serpent, which is the devil (diabolos), and Satan (Satanas)"** (Rev. 20:2). As there is an eternal place (abode) for the saved, so there is an everlasting habitation for the damned. Only <u>one simple angel</u> takes Satan. The heavenly power that tosses Satan from heaven (Rev. 12) will overcome him and toss him into the bottomless pit, and finally into the lake of fire.

Satan Silenced, Shut Up, Sealed and Secured for a Thousand Years

Note the steps in binding Satan. **"Throw him into the bottomless pit," "shut him up" (chain him up), "set a seal upon him"** (as was set upon the tomb of Christ – Mt. 27:66). Hell is never called **"life"** in the scriptures. It is referred to as **"the second death."** Hell is nowhere called "annihilation."

God told Adam and Eve that if they ate of the forbidden fruit **they would die.**

- They died spiritually **the moment they ate of it.**
- God in effect asked: **"Where did you go Adam?"**
- **At that moment, they began to go away from God.**

The First Resurrection (20:4-6)

Text: Rev. 20:4-6

Rev. 20:4 **And I saw thrones, and they sat on them, and *authority was given them to judge*: and I saw the souls of those that were beheaded for the witness of Jesus, and for the word of God, and *that had not* worshiped the beast, *nor* his image, *nor* had received his mark on their foreheads, or *on* their hands; and they lived and reigned with Christ a thousand years. [5] But the rest of the dead *did not live* again until the thousand years *was ended.* This is the first resurrection. [6] Blessed and holy is *the one that has* part in the first resurrection: on such the second death *has* no power, but they shall be priests of God and of Christ, and shall reign with him a thousand years.** (EKJV)

There are two resurrections explained in Chapter 20. Also see Acts 24:15-16. The first resurrection is the great resurrection of all of the redeemed, but the martyrs have a special recognition.

There are very important thoughts: the first is in verse 4, and the second is in verse 6. To be sure, the entire passage is vital, more so, when we read verse 4 and verse 6 together. In verse 4 John says: **"[4] And I saw thrones, and they sat on them, and *authority was given them to judge*."** What does this mean? I have preached on this subject many times and what I am going to tell you, I have included in my books on the Psalms.

Matt. 19:28 **And Jesus said to them, *Truly* I tell you, That you who have followed me, in the *renewal of all things* when the Son of**

298

man shall sit in the throne of his glory, you also shall sit on twelve thrones, judging the twelve tribes of Israel. (EKJV)

And Paul says in 1 Cor. 6:2–"**Do you not know that the saints shall judge the world?**" Also look in the next verse: 1 Cor. 6:3– "**Do you not know that we will judge angels?**"

And now we have this verse from Rev. 3:21. It is a vivid statement of how things will be. "**To him that overcomes I will grant to sit with me in my throne, even as I also overcame, and sat down with my Father in his throne.**" What a magnificent passage! These verses point us to a role we will share with Christ. We are not the judge of men's sins. God has that responsibility. But we will have our assignments.

For a thousand years, Satan will be removed from the scene and this will be a time of peace and joy in all of the earth. At the beginning of this period, we have the first Resurrection (Rev. 20:5-6). Those raised at the time of the first resurrection will never face "**the second death.**" And here we finish what we began to say earlier: "**they shall be priests of God and of Christ, and shall reign with him a thousand years.**" (20:6).

Paul affirmed: [Acts 24:15] **And (I) have hope toward God, which they themselves also allow, that there shall be a resurrection of the dead, both of the just and unjust.**

- The redeemed reign with Christ fo a thousand years.
- The millennium is a period of time – A thousand years.
- It comes from the Latin; *Mille* (thousand) and *annus* (year).
- Every Jew and every Gentile who enters the millennium kingdom must come through faith in Christ as Lord and Savior.

The Martyrs Share in Christ's Thousand Year Reign (20:4-6)

The martyrs are "**The souls of those that were beheaded for the witness of Jesus.**" There is no greater allegiance to Jesus than to offer up one's life. John the Baptist comes to mind when we speak of having been beheaded.

> **Mark 6:27** And immediately the king sent an executioner, and commanded his head to be brought: and he went and beheaded him in the prison, ²⁸ And brought his head in a charger, and gave it to the girl: and the girl gave it to her mother.

Rev. 6:9 And when he had opened the fifth seal, I saw under the altar the souls of *those* that were slain for the word of God, and for the testimony *that* they held: ¹⁰ And they cried *out* with a loud voice, saying, How long, O Lord, holy and true, *until you* judge and avenge our blood on *those that* dwell on the earth? ¹¹ And white robes were given to every one of them; and *they were told that* they should rest for a little while, until their fellow servants and their brothers that would be killed as they were, should be fulfilled. (EKJV)

Rev. 12:11 And they overcame him by the blood of the Lamb, and by the word of their testimony; and *they did not love their lives* to the death. (EKJV)

Three Qualifications for Martyrs

- First — They had not worshipped the beast.
- Second — His mark (the mark of the beast) was not on their foreheads of hands.
- Third — They willingly gave their lives as a testimony of faith in Christ. These "came to life and reigned with Christ a thousand years."

The Three Principle Views of the Millennium

Here is a greatly simplified explanation of the various views on the millennium. We are not entering into detailed discussions of these views. Rather, these conclusions are based on a forthright understanding of Scripture. It is the belief of this author that God intended the message just as we see it, although there are passages from which interpreters can draw other ideas. The first and primary thought is what we read and clearly understand. Remember, those who lived in times long ago did not have libraries of books explaining the Bible. They could only take the truths at face value.

- **The Pre-millennial view**: Jesus will return prior to the millennium and at that point He will begin his glorious reign.

Dispensationalism is a sub-section of this view. There is a discussion as to whether the Second Coming takes place before or after the Great Tribulation. This book is based on the Pre-millennial view.

- **The Post-millennial view**: Men will bring in the reign of peace by their good works and social ministries for the betterment of mankind. When this is complete, Jesus will return.
- **The A-millennial View** is understood by many commentators as a non-millennial view, or as some claim, the millennium began with the resurrection of Jesus 2000 years ago, and therefore is not a literal thousand years.
-

John's Fifth Beatitude

(See: 1:3; 14:13; 16:15; 19:9; 20:6; 22:7 and 22:14).

Text: Rev.20:6
Rev. 20:6 **Blessed and holy is he that has part in the first resurrection: the second death has no power *over them*, but they shall be priests of God and of Christ, and shall reign with him a thousand years.** (EKJV)

There is a lot to consider in this beatitude. The passage is speaking o those who have a part in the **"first resurrection."** The ones so included are immune to **"the second death."** The second death follows the death of the body and means that one is forever separated from God and from heaven. However, these who share in the first resurrection are forever free from the second death's **"power"** over them. On the contrary, they will serve God as **"priests"** as we stated above.

In the Old Testament, priests were those who served in God's temple. These now have a place of divine and eternal service before God and Christ in heaven. More than that, they will share in the millennial reign of the Lord Christ. The temple in Jerusalem was symbolic of the heavenly reality, but at best, it was a shallow example of the true heavenly reality.

Satan's Temporary Freedom (20:7-9)

This wonderful and refreshing freedom from Satan's presence will come to an end during his brief release. We see the effect of unrelenting evil. Evil seizes the hearts of those who are initially receptive and it never wants to let go. Such is the heart of Satan himself. He hates God, Christ, and people of faith.

Text: Rev. 20:7-10

Rev. 20:7 And when the thousand years are expired, Satan shall *be set free from* his prison, [8] And shall go out to deceive the nations in the four quarters of the earth, Gog, and Magog, to gather them together to battle: their number is as the sand of the sea. [9] And they *traveled* across the breadth of the earth, and surrounded the camp of the saints, *the city God loves*: and fire came down from God out of heaven, and devoured them. [10] And the devil that deceived them was *thrown* into the lake of fire and brimstone, where the beast and the false prophet are, and shall be tormented day and night forever and ever. (EKJV)

Unchanged After a Thousand Years

Satan was set free after the thousand years. **Luo** (Gk.) means to loose, to set at liberty, to unbind, to destroy. We have the Greek word **lutheseti** (*λυθηεται*) meaning ***"will be loosed."***

For a thousand years Satan has anticipated this moment. A thousand years is more than two dozen biblical generations. Rather than becoming repentant, Satan has been laying future plans to continue his battle against God and His people. As he has always deceived people from the wonderful truth of God, he plans to continue to lure them by deception. He cannot and will not tell the truth!

He has been crafting his battle plans for a thousand years. He relies on his tool of choice: deception. God is not required to permit this. Rather, God chooses to reveal to the world that Satan is without repentance and remorse. He is everlastingly incorrigible.

The Amazing Battle of Gog and Magog

We will not find John applying the prophecy of Ezekiel 38-39 in Revelation. John is not speaking of the Scythian hordes from the north, from Magog. In Revelation, the names represent the great world hoard of enemies as seen in the final battle of Rev. 19. John sees two cities: the city of Satan in company with the beast and the harlot, and the New Jerusalem where Christ the Redeemer Lamb of God reigns with His people.

A great hoard starts toward the **"camp of the saints, the city he loves."** While the armies of the nations in the battle of Armageddon numbered 200 million, the number of this army is **"like the sand of the sea."** They march in an innumerable army bent on an evil victory against the very people who belong to God. They surround His people leaving no avenue of escape. Fear would rise to an overwhelming level in the average person. Satan is confident of success. He yet hopes to claim lasting victory over God and His people. Now we read God's answer: **"and fire came down from God out of heaven, and devoured them."** We are reminded of those who opposed Moses and were destroyed in a similar fashion. There were no bodies to bury. God will utterly destroy them. **"And the devil that deceived them was** *thrown* **into the lake of fire and brimstone..."** (Rev. 20:10). The three (Satan and his two beasts) share a common punishment. They are together and **"will be tormented day and night forever and ever."**

The Consequences of Following Satan

We continue the theme of punishment with reference to the scripture above. John means that there is no end to the consequences for one who rejects the Lord God and His anointed. You can't ever "die out" your responsibility to God. Those who die in the Lord do not go out into nothingness. They enter into the glory of the Lord. The "sonic boom" of His appearing is near. One man, Billy Graham, preached the gospel to every nation. Most of the nations of the world now have churches in them.

God's Awesome Great White Judgment Throne (20:11-15)

Text: Rev. 20:11-15

Rev. 20:11 **And I saw a great white throne, and him that sat on it, from whose face the earth and the heaven fled away; and there was found no place for them.**

12 **And I saw the dead, small and great, stand before God; and the books were opened: and another book was opened, which is the book of life: and the dead were judged out of those things which were written in the books, according to** *what they have done.*

303

¹³ And the sea gave up the dead which were in it; and death and hell delivered up the dead which were in them: and *each one will be judged* according to *what they have done.* ¹⁴ And death and hell were *thrown* into the lake of fire. This is the second death. ¹⁵ And whosoever was not found written in the book of life was *thrown* into the lake of fire. (EKJV)

At the appearance of the **"great white throne and him who was seated on it"** a great phenomenon took place. **"Earth and sky fled from his presence, and there was no place for them"** (v. 11).

At the moment of judgment, the consummation of the universe and the cosmic disintegration takes place. We saw the prophecy of this moment and this event in Rev. 6:12ff that occurred with the opening of the sixth seal. (We treat this completely in our discussion along with Rev. 6:12ff). When John says "there was no place for them" (20:11), we understand that the path and design of the heavenly constellations will be eliminated. As we saw in Rev. 6, God has "rolled up" the heavens.

The Judgment Seat

Paul made it clear that everyone must appear before the judgment seat of Christ. **2 Cor. 5:10 For we must all appear before the judgment seat of Christ, so that each of us may receive what is due us for the things done while in the body, whether good or bad.** The reality of recompense, judgment, and accountability has arrived. Everyone will receive just what they desired, and in effect planned for through their life choices.

Hindsight is better than foresight. Someone looking back at this old world from God's grand and endlessly desirable heaven would never consider mediocre commitment. Christ called for total commitment. John describes the new heaven of God. He does so with neither Satan nor sin present. Satan has already been cast into the lake of fire.

Many people are unsure if they will go to heaven. They are pretty satisfied with the world we have. Others have dabbled in the church, but never experienced a life-changing relationship with Christ. If Christ is in one's heart, that person has a deep-seated and permanent longing to serve and please God. Can you imagine the suspense when the great **"book of life"** is opened? Many people just assume they are going to heaven, but they can give no reason for their assumption. What if my name is not included? They have relied on a last minute reprieve. And it is truly a terrifying experience to find that your name is not written down. These stand speechless before the **"great white throne"** (vs. 11-12) in a judgment without hope.

God Is No Respecter of Persons

God does not play favorites. He treats the **"great and small"** alike (v. 12). John saw them standing side by side before the throne of God. **"The books are open."** One set is referred to as **"books."** These are the books wherein the record of all persons is recorded. But also, there is the **"book of life."** There is going to be separation between the saved and those who rejected Christ. Remember the Rich Man and Lazarus? How far is Hell from Heaven? So far that none shall ever pass between the two. Such people are truthfully terrified when God opens the eternal record books.

Both the redeemed and the unrighteous will stand in the judgment. The book of life contains the full list of those who will enjoy the blessings of heaven and eternal life. Those who are redeemed have the assurance that their names have been recorded and are kept safely. Rev. 21-22 explains these rewards. Rev. 21:1-8 and 22:1-6 reveal the significant relationship to God and his blessings.

The first mention of the book of life in Revelation is in Revelation 3:5. Jesus is speaking of the one who is **"victorious,"** and he says of such a person: **"I will never blot his name out of the book of life."** What a great promise! But names are missing from the **"book of life."** In Revelation 13:8 Jesus is speaking of those who give their worship and allegiance to the beast. He identifies these people as those **"whose names have not been recorded in the Lamb's book of life."** The next mention of the book of life that we should consider is found in Rev. 21:27. **"And *by no means* shall anything that is *impure* enter it, or *whatever is an* abomination, or *deceives:* but only those that are written in the Lamb's book of life."**

The books (distinguished from the book of life) contain all of the deeds of mankind. It is all recorded there. And the judgment is issued. There is no appeal. There is no reprieve. Just as it was for Satan and his associates, these are cast immediately into the lake of fire. The scripture says that it doesn't matter how or where one dies, he will not escape this judgment. The dead will be summoned from **"death and Hades." "Each one will be judged according to *what they have done*"** (v. 13). Failure to have one's name recorded in the **"book of life"** meant that **"he was thrown into the lake of fire"** (v. 15). Thus, chapter 20 closes with this terrifying thought.

THE MEANING OF THE SECOND DEATH
Regarding Those That Experience the Second Death

1. Their **names are not in the Lamb's Book of Life.**
2. They **do not eat of the Tree of Life.**
3. They **do not eat of the Bread of Life.**
4. They **do not drink of the Water of Life.**
5. They **do not receive immortality.**
6. They **do not live forever in the presence of God and His holy angels.**
7. They **do not share in the eternal Holy City!**

CHAPTER 21

A MARRIAGE MADE IN HEAVEN
A New Heaven and a New Earth

Text: Rev. 21:1-2
Rev. 21:1 **And I saw a new heaven and a new earth: for the first heaven and the first earth were passed away; and there was no more sea. ² And I John saw the holy city, New Jerusalem, coming down from God out of heaven, prepared as a bride adorned for her husband.**

Snapshot of Chapter 21

This thrilling chapter takes us from the Lake of Fire to the New City of God. Although John mentions the city in the first verse, he regresses to explain how God will be with us in every way, and that all sorrows, pain and grief are gone while God wipes away all of our tears. In verse 9, the fourth and final vision is begun and it carries over into chapter 22. John will see and explain the details of the New City of God—the Bride of Christ (the church). Before we get to the end we are told that the kings of the earth have submitted their authority to the authority and rule of God. This results in great happiness and joy.

The Earth Will Have Been Dissolved

In this chapter we find that **"the first earth has passed away"** (21:1). The earth was disintegrated, dissolved and destroyed (Isa. 34:4 KJV; Rev. 6:12-14). In both passages the sky is said to be **"rolled up like a scroll."** The heavens are put away like a scroll that has been read to completion. In Rev. 20:11 the word states: **"the earth and the heaven fled away; and there was no place found for them."**

In Isa. 51:6, we read of these heavenly objects **"the heavens shall vanish...like smoke, and the earth shall** *wear out like clothing*, **and they that live there shall die in like manner: but my salvation shall be forever, and my righteousness shall not be abolished.."** The destruction to come is further explained in 2 Peter.
2 Peter 3:10 "The heavens will disappear with a roar; the elements will be destroyed by fire, and the earth and everything in it will be laid bare." Peter continues:
2 Peter 3:12 "That day will bring about the destruction of the heavens by fire, and the elements will melt in the heat."

Every creature will be removed by the great calamity (Isa. 65:17; 66:22; 2 Peter 3:7-13). Imagine that everything you know about earth is now without meaning. The earth has been dissolved and no longer exists. Every creature you have ever known, every city ever built, every continent, every sea, every towering mountain, and even the heavenly bodies we see when we scan the sky—all have vanished. More than that, we are in a new world, a new heaven. And this is just the beginning of our trip with God. You haven't seen anything yet because the best is ahead. The universe of stars and planets that we view in our heavens will all be completely destroyed. Isaiah 65:17 says: **Isa. 65:17 "Behold, I will create new heavens and a new earth..."**

Isa. 66:22 "As the new heavens and the new earth that I will make will endure before me," declares the Lord, **"so will your name and descendants endure"**

It staggers our imagination to think of two heavens and two earths. The first will be dissolved and God will create the second. God is not going to remodel earth as some think. He is going to create a new earth and a new heaven. The new is not a continuation of the former. Rather, the old creation is replaced with a totally new creation.

Jesus told us that those who enter heaven **"can no longer die; for they are like the angels"** (Luke 20:36). But those who are resurrected are a higher form of creation than the angels. ^{Heb. 1:14} **Are not all angels ministering spirits sent to serve those who will inherit salvation?"**

Thank God for a World Without Tears!

Text: Rev. 21:3-4

^{Rev. 21:3} **And I heard a great voice out of heaven saying, Look, the tabernacle of God is with men, and he will dwell with them, and they will be his people, and God himself will be with them, and be their God. ⁴ And God will wipe away all tears from their eyes; and there will be no more death, neither sorrow, nor crying, neither will there be any more pain: for the former things are passed away.**

^{Rev. 7:17} **For the Lamb which is in the midst of the throne shall feed them, and shall lead them unto living fountains of waters: and God shall wipe away all tears from their eyes.**

John unveils a revealing portion of God's master plan for His redeemed children. Before he begins the description of heaven, he explains the greatest benefit of living with God. This benefit is that God comes to dwell in His people, and He will be their God forever with a perfect relationship unaltered by any distraction (21:3). Pay attention to what God is going to do. God is going to wipe away all the tears in the eyes of His people yet glistening from their suffering on earth (cf. Isa. 25:7-9). It is as if He will dab each eye to dry up the tears of great suffering and pain as experienced by the martyrs. From this moment on, there will never be a death, a heartache, mourning, or pain. There are no deaths in heaven.

^{Isaiah 25:8} **He will swallow up death in victory; and the Lord GOD will wipe away tears from all faces; and the *disgrace* of his people shall he take away from off all the earth: for the LORD has spoken.**

No one will ever leave a cemetery in unrequited sorrow. All grief is vanquished by the eternal joy of God's full and overflowing presence holding His people for eternity.

Our past pain is difficult to forget. As much as we try, there are things we would like to forget, but they rise up in our memory without warning, and they disturb us. But in heaven we have the assurance of God's finished plan: **"For, behold, I create new heavens and a new earth: and the former <u>shall not be remembered, nor come into mind</u>"** (Isa. 65:17b). They are forever gone from our memory. While we believe that we will certainly recognize our former loved ones, in heaven we will be eternally sheltered from even remembering our own sins, and the tragic and depressing experiences of life on planet earth.

We have one of the greatest promises in God's word. It is the promise that we will not remember what has taken place in the past. Some people have great memories and never forget anything. I have to make a list of things I want to remember, but no matter. In regard to our former life on earth, our memory banks will be erased. Even Paul, on earth, worked hard at forgetting unprofitable thoughts. He said:

Phil. 3:13 "...**I do not consider myself yet to have taken hold of it. But one thing I do: Forgetting what is behind and straining toward what is ahead, [14] I press on toward the goal to win the prize for which God has called me heavenward in Christ Jesus.**"

It is not clear in what ways we will remember those we loved on earth (1 Cor. 13:11-12). Our knowledge of them will be appropriate for life in heaven. We don't need to remember earthly things when we get to heaven. This will be very encouraging for those who struggled to remember dates, places and events in history classes.

In heaven our memories become new as we gather around God the Father, and Christ, the Lamb of God. Sometime ago, a young wife was talking on Skype (where you can see each other via the computer and internet) to her husband who served in the military in Afghanistan when in her full sight he was killed. It will be hard for her to ever forget what she witnessed. But it was reported that despite the terrible scene, she was also grateful to have, in a sense, been with him when death came. Thank the Lord that He will remove all painful thoughts from our heavenly memory.

In Chapter 21 he leads us to the gates of the new and eternal City of God. **In Chapter 22** we are shown the Paradise of God. **The first** presents the city of God's perfection which the earthly Jerusalem could never become. **The second** reveals the perfect paradise of God without the sin and failure of Eden—the first Paradise. God is fulfilling His intention of life without sin or suffering in a place of indescribable and endless beauty and purity.

The Great Impossibility

How can John possibly translate his vision of heaven so that we on earth can understand? God is going to bestow upon His redeemed children a creation so spectacular that it can never be described by earthly words. The great impossibility is in describing the glory and grandeur of heaven. What words, symbols, and pictures might you use? How could you take a thing or place that man cannot conceive and explain it to a person's ability to understand? You stretch yourself far beyond any previous life experience in order to grasp God's eternal truth. For example, how could you tell someone how chocolate tastes? You could say it is delicious or sweet, or sometimes bitter. Or how could you explain the sunset to someone who cannot see? Paul explained it this way:

1 Cor. 2:9 **"... as it is written, Eye has not seen, nor ear heard, neither *has it* entered into the heart of man, the things...God has prepared for *those* that love him.** (EKJV)

In describing heaven, you explain the greater creation in terms of the lower examples found on earth. So John will give it his best. Diamonds or gold are precious on earth; but what is greatest on the earth is inadequate to portray the greater form in heaven. John relates that the golden streets of heaven are transparent. You can see right through them. How do you explain the building materials of God's infinitely greater creation in heaven? Everything in heaven is perfect and beyond decay. John announces the new reality:

Rev. 21:1 **And I saw a new heaven and a new earth: for the first heaven and the first earth were passed away; and there was no more sea.**

It seems somewhat strange to add **"and there was no more sea."** On Patmos, John was surrounded and imprisoned by the sea. The sea insured that the Island would remain a prison without reasonable hope of escape. On earth there are walls and barriers. Now John sees that there are no separations, hindrances, or barriers to complete freedom in the eternal realm of God. He is forever set free to receive the endless joy of heaven.

But also, we must understand what he means when he says **"no more sea."** We cannot know for sure, but the waters covered the earth before there was land (Ps. 104). The waters covered the earth prior to the creation of the firmament, and in the destruction that accompanies the end time, the sea will be removed.

In the moment when John is writing down these sights, he is distracted by a shout—a loud cry from the throne in heaven: *"Look! the tabernacle of God is with men, and he will dwell with them..."* (EKJV) God has removed the creation of earth, and now He has given Himself to His people. How can John possibly inform his readers of this awe-inspiring, divine vision?

All human languages of earth are totally inadequate to describe even the threshold of heaven. Yet, John is enabled to describe what he saw using the most beautiful descriptive images available to him. While he recognized the vast difference in his description and the reality of heaven, he yet conveyed to the minds of his readers the beauty and grandeur using the most glorious words in his vocabulary.

The Holy City, New Jerusalem: Prepared as a Bride

Text: Rev. 21:2
^{Rev. 21:2} **And I John saw the holy city, new Jerusalem, coming down from God out of heaven, prepared as a bride adorned for her husband.**

A marriage will take place. We saw the bride ready for the marriage in Revelation 19. In this chapter, John sees the bride in verses 2, 9 and 22:17. God will be forever united with the redeemed church of the earth and of all history. John is captivated by the majestic pageantry. Rather than walking down an aisle, the bride descends **"from God out of heaven."** She is **"prepared as a bride."** There is no mistaking what she represents. And she is **"adorned for her husband."** She is holy, pure, cleansed, and chaste because Christ has redeemed her. Her husband is the Lamb of God.

Nothing of the sin and shame previously wiped clean by Christ is now visible. None of the ravages of life's troubles, torture and tragedy remain. Many believers have been cruelly tortured and slaughtered for their faith. But nothing of that past suffering remains. The tears are gone. The celebration of a marriage is taking place. And the wedding feast is about to begin (Rev. 19:7, 9).

Transformed in an Instant

We know and we tell people that when we die, if we are saved and faithful, we go to heaven. Yet we have sought intimate knowledge of how things will be. We have difficulty envisioning a new body in a new creation. Jesus told us many wonderful things about His true home; and His followers gazed into heaven as he ascended back into the presence of the Father.

But they stood longing and wondering to know more. And John captures that first moment for the saved in heaven, and he explains that everything is transformed in an instant. Everything God has promised will become a reality in the twinkling of an eye (1 Cor. 15:52).

A Heavenly Voice Certifies the Vision's Validity

Text: Rev. 21:5
Rev. 21:5 **And he *who was seated* on the throne said, Behold, I make all things new. And he said unto me, "Write: for these words are true and faithful."** (EKJV)

We may love the smell of a new car, or the thrill of moving into a new home with new furnishings, but now everything is new. Nothing of the old past remains. We hear the voice of the one **"who was seated on the throne..."** (Compare: Rev. 1:4; 4:2, 9-10; 5:1, 7, 13; 6:16; 7:9-11, 15, 17; 12:5; 19:4-5; 20:11-12; 21:3, 5; 22:1, 3). In Rev. 19:9 we read: **"These are the true sayings of God."** A number of other verses indicate thoughts concerning the throne of God without so stating the fact. The throne of God is central to this book.

Therefore, it is God who speaks from His throne: **"I make all things new."** He continues speaking: **"Write this down, for these words are true and faithful."** The angel affirms this truth with identically the same words in Rev. 22:6. You can take them into your heart and know that they are the words of God. Eleven times in the Revelation John is instructed to **"write."** Once in Rev. 10:4 he is instructed **"do not write it down,"** but to **"seal it up."** We actually have the prophecy of Revelation 21:5 in Isaiah.

Everything Begins and Ends in Christ
Text: Rev. 21:6-7
Rev. 21:6 **And he said to me, It is done. I am Alpha and Omega, the beginning and the end. I will give to *the one* that is *thirsty to drink from* the fountain of the water of life freely. ⁷ He *who* overcomes shall inherit all *these* things; and I will be his God, and he shall be my son.** (EKJV)

"I am the Alpha and Omega..." first spoken by Christ in Rev. 1:8 where He is called **"the Lord God..."** and **"the Almighty."** In Rev.21:6 the Alpha and Omega quenches His people's thirst forever. And in 22:13 He rewards people **"according to what they have done"** (2 Cor. 5:10).

Christ, the Lamb of God, precedes all things, exceeds all things, sustains all things, and finishes all things. Even as Jesus spoke on the cross and said in regard to His offering for salvation **"It is finished,"** He also says here **"It is done."** God's eternal plan for His creation is completed. And He adds, **"I am the beginning and the end."** Alpha is the first letter of the Greek alphabet, and Omega is the final letter. Here again, it is affirmed that everything is completed and finished.

When we built our home many people would see us and ask "Is it finished yet?" I would always answer: "I think it is finished, but there are always touches to add." But in the case of the New Jerusalem, nothing remains to be accomplished. **"It is done!"**

Those who belong to Jesus will walk with Him in a city and a home that lacks nothing. Nor will it ever require remodeling, repair, or upkeep.

The Victorious Ones
The one **"who overcomes will inherit all these things..."** (Rev. 21:7). The victory belongs to those who have trusted Christ and who live in faith of eternal life. The inheritance God has laid up for

us is greater than the wealth of any king. Yet, the poorest beggar saved by Christ receives God's greatest blessings forever more.

Again God continues speaking: **"I will be their God and they will be my children..."** (Rev. 21:7). They have lived by faith in His forgiveness and His promises. Now He fulfills those promises. Imagine this! You will **"inherit *all this.*"** What John sees and relates is beyond our mind's conception. No treasure on earth compares to the unfolding inheritance, and the benefits. He returns to the provisions for his children.

Rev. 21:6 **"I will give to *the one* that is *thirsty water freely from* the fountain of the water of life."** (EKJV)
Imagine drinking from **"the fountain of the water of life."** For more information see commentary on Rev. 22:1-3: the River of the water of life. David was in the Judean desert apparently dying of thirst; yet he cried out to God, for whom his greatest thirst was felt.

Psalm 63:1 **O God, you are my God; early will I seek you: my soul thirsts for you, my whole body longs for you in a dry and thirsty land, where there is no water.** Compare Isaiah 44:3; 48:21; 49:10; and 55:1.

Jesus conversed with the woman at the well in Samaria:
John 4:13 **Jesus answered...her, Whoever drinks of this water shall thirst again: **14** But whoever drinks of the water that I shall give him shall never thirst; but the water that I shall give him shall be in him a well of water springing up into everlasting life."** See Jn. 6:35; 7:37; and Rev. 7:16; also 22:17.

Thirst is one of life's great pains. Unfulfilled thirst will eventually result in dehydration and death. The body requires constant and regular hydration, but there is a spring of water that unceasingly supplies needs. God promises that our greater need for Him will be supplied to the full. In the next verse, however, we encounter those who never knew this thirst for God.

Eternal Separation

Text: Rev. 21:8
Rev. 21:8 **But the fearful, and unbelieving, and the abominable, and murderers, and adulterers, and sorcerers, and idolaters,   and   all**

liars, shall have their part in the lake which burns with fire and brimstone: which is the second death."
As in chapter 20:11-15, John explains the terrible penalty for those who reject Christ, and the eternal separation experienced by faithless, sinful, and evil unbelievers. The exclusion clause is found in Rev. 21:8. The evil and immoral multitudes of this world have no place in heaven. They have forfeited all rights and privileges to residence in God's beautiful eternal city. It is their choice and their eternal loss. They are lost forever. There are no second chances! Families, loved ones, and friends will be everlastingly separated in the extremes of God's magnificent reward for His children, and the estate of the wicked. These persons in Rev. 21:8 have rejected the love, redemption and saving power of Jesus—the name above all names.

The Bride Is Ready
Through John's eyes we see the wonderful unity of the bride with the Lamb. The angel of the **plagues** (Rev. 15) is now the angel of the **promise.** The angel has a new and far-reaching role assigned by the Father. John is permitted a view of the **bride** and **wife** of the Lamb (v. 9; also 19:7).

What a magnificent sight he beholds. In Isaiah 62:4 God says of His nation: **"She will be called Hephzibah and Beulah."** **"Hephzibah"** is only found twice in Scripture and it means **"My delight is in her..."** In 2 Kings 21:1 it is the name of King Hezekiah's wife. In Isaiah 62:4 it is a message of hope to the nation of Israel. God plans to change her name from **"Deserted"** and **"Desolate"** to **"Hephzibah"** and **"Beulah." "Beulah"** means **"married."** When God changes a name in the Bible, it conveys transformation, a second chance, and a new beginning.

The Church is the Bride
In Revelation 21 a marriage is taking place and they will have a new name. Isa. 62:5 **"...as the bridegroom rejoices over the bride, so shall your God rejoice over you."** Remember Rev. 19:7.
"Let us be glad and rejoice, and give honor to him: for the marriage of the Lamb *has* come, and his wife has made herself ready."

God rejoices because His church, the bride, has made herself ready. God will rejoice in His people because there is no spirit of disobedience and no act of unrighteousness in them. Every one of them is a redeemed saint. His first creation brought Him endless grief (Gen. 6:6; Psalm 78:40; Ezek. 6:9, etc.) It has caused Him unrelenting pain because He must bring punishment and destruction on His beloved nation. We can't really imagine how we have grieved God. He came to bear our grief, and yet we grieve Him. ^{Isa. 53:4} "**Surely he took up our infirmities and carried our sorrows**" (NIV).

Characteristics of the New Jerusalem
John Used Three Old Testament Terms to Explain Heaven

The first two existed in a period of the Old Testament from Moses to the Babylonian Captivity. The third, of course, is the glorious and final city of our God. As one of my professors would often say:

- ❖ **The Tabernacle** – If you are in the tent, **you are in the presence of God.**
- ❖ **The Temple** – If you are in the Temple, **you are in the presence of God.**
- ❖ **The City** – If you are in the city, **you are in the presence of God.**

Note: The temple was destroyed by the Babylonians and not rebuilt until after the Captivity. Even then, it was a shallow structure compared to Solomon's Temple. We have the city: Jerusalem and the new city of God from heaven.

God's Dwelling Place

A Tabernacle–Rev. 15:5ff, 21:3; **A Temple**–21:22; **A City**–21:2; 10-21. To be in any of them is to be in the presence of God. The first two were part of the period of the first covenant, and are no longer needed because God will bring us into His new city. In the city the Lamb provides all the light you will need (21:23).

We translate the Greek *skene* in Rev. 21:3 to mean exactly what it does mean: a tent, tabernacle, temporary dwelling-place, or home. John first says that God is going to **"dwell"** with His people. He is going to **"tabernacle,"** or He will make His **"home"** with them (2 Cor. 5:1-9).

317

In John 1:14 John writes: **"the word (***logos***) became flesh and dwelt among us..."** or tented with mankind. Revelation 21:3 is not a picture of us going to God. Rather it is a view of God gathering His people to Himself, and abiding or making His home with them, and taking away all pain, suffering and grief (Isa. 25:8).

After the tabernacle, the next place the people met God was in the Temple in Jerusalem. The city, as was the temple, is considered the place where people met God (Ps. 122:1-4). But there were remarkable exceptions to what God required in both. John says in Revelation 21 that in the new city there will be no need of a temple for God will be all they need. The city is perfect in every way, and it is in the new city where they will dwell with God in perfect joy.

The Builder Is the Owner
It is a **new** world (a new earth and a new heaven) - **"...a city whose builder and maker is God"** (Heb. 11:10). As God created all things in our universe, His new creation will be from His own power, strength and glory.

God's Three New Creations
❖ A **New Heaven** (cf. 2 Peter 3:13; Isa. 65:17; 66:22; 2 Cor. 5:1).
❖ A **New Earth** (Isa. 65:17; 66:22; 51:6; Rev. 21:1; 2 Peter 3:13).
❖ A **New Jerusalem** (cf. Heb. 11:10; Rev. 3:12) – **"...a city whose builder and maker is God."**
It is important to read Rev. 21-22:5 as a single unit to capture the total vision of heaven.

Everything Is New
Καινοσ (Greek) means **"new"** and suggests **fresh life rising from the wreck and decay** of the world. In Heb. 8:13 the writer speaks of **"a new covenant."** The first covenant is obsolete.

> **Hebrews 8:13** **"In *calling it,* A new covenant, he has made the first old. Now *anything that* decays and *becomes old* is ready to vanish away."**
>
> **Hebrews 9:1** **Then *it is true* that the first covenant *also had* ordinances of worship and *for an earthly* sanctuary.** (EKJV)

Remember: There Are Four Visions in Revelation
- 1st – 1:9-3:22
- 2nd – 4:1—16:21
- 3rd – 17:1—21:8 (Note: 21:9.)
- 4th – 21:9—22:5

The fourth vision begins at Rev. 21:9 and continues through chapter 22:5.

THE FOURTH VISION Rev. 21:9-22:5
THE NEW JERUSALEM
Each vision begins with "I was in the Spirit..."
(cf. 1:10; 4:1; 17:3; and 21:10)

The New Jerusalem, the Bride of the Lamb
Text: Rev. 21:9-10
Rev. 21:9 **And one of the seven angels which had the seven vials full of the seven last plagues came to me, and talked with me, saying, Come here, I will show you the bride, the Lamb's wife. 10 And he carried me away in the spirit to a great high mountain, and showed me that great city, the holy Jerusalem, descending out of heaven from God,**

There Are Two Cities in These Visions
The Harlot City and The Holy City
Are Contrasted (Rev. 21-22:5)

- The Harlot City represents **man's ultimate work.**
- The Holy City represents **God's ultimate work**
The Parallels of the Two Cities
(Rev. 17:1-2 and 21:9-14)

- Both were marked by the **angel of the bowls.**
- Both times John is **carried away in a trance.**
- Both times John is **shown a bejeweled woman** who was actually a city.
- Babylon is the **earthly travesty.** The bride is the **heavenly reality.**

319

The vision is introduced by one of the angels who held the seven bowls of plagues which I now call the angel of promise. In the prior appearance of this angel in Rev. 16-17 where the Seven Bowls are revealed we are told by John:

> **Revelation17:1** And one of the seven angels which had the seven *bowls*, came and talked with me, saying, Come here; I will show you the judgment of the great prostitute that sits on many waters.
>
> [3] So he carried me away in the spirit into the wilderness: and I saw a woman sitting on a scarlet colored beast, full of names of blasphemy, having seven heads and ten horns.

Remember: We Said the Church Is the Bride

On this occasion, however, the angel transported John to an exceedingly high mountain peak where he saw a vision of heaven in all of its glory. The invitation from the angel is accompanied by the reason for taking John to the mountain peak. The angel said: **"Come here, I will show you the bride, the Lamb's wife."**

John was caught up in the moment. He flashes forward to the scene of the Holy City descending. It is his primary thought, but he also knows that he must answer some questions in the minds of believers on earth. And he draws a picture of a wedding and a beautiful bride. In this marriage, which was introduced in Revelation 19, John says the bride is the church.

This is not what we think of when we say we are going to the church. This is the enormous body of Christ made holy, cleansed and purified by the blood of Christ in order that she may become this radiant, glorious, beautiful bride dressed for an immortal occasion. She is prepared to be joined with holy God.

We have been holding our breath since Revelation 19:7 when the bride was introduced, but not identified. We were left anticipating a beautiful wedding. Indeed we seem to have been invited to the privileged **"wedding supper of the Lamb"** (19:9).

The bride is the church of our Lord, and the city is the home of the redeemed of all time (cf. Rev. 19:7-9). The bride—the **church** was born out of the suffering of Christ. The church's life came from the sacrifice of Christ. Here are all those converted in all ages. The **redeemed** of all the ages are gathered (21:2). The expected and anticipated glory of God becomes a reality (Cf. Isaiah 2:2-3; Ezek. 28:12-16; Micah 4:1-2; Zech. 8:23; 14:16).

John Relates the Details of the Eternal City

What a marvelous, transforming vision! But John is shown much more! He sees the details and limits of the city. The city is astronomically more than he could ever imagine. I don't know what John expected, but he is shown a city like no other. There is no comparison to anything else in the universe. Previously, we have spoken of the two cities.

From the high mountain John sees the New Jerusalem. It is coming down from God (out of heaven – Greekk= *ex tou ouranou*). Cf. Ezek. 28:12-16; also Isa. 2:2-3 (the same in Micah 4:1-2); Zech. 8:23; 14:16).

Isaiah 2:2 **And it shall come to pass in the last days, that the mountain of the LORD's house shall be established in the top of the mountains, and shall be exalted above the hills; and all nations shall flow unto it.** (Micah is identical to this passage). *See comments on verses 23-24.*

Zechariah 8:23 **Thus says the LORD of hosts; In those days it shall come to pass, that ten men out of all languages of the nations, shall take hold of the skirt of him that is a Jew, saying, We will go with you: for we have heard that God is with you.**

Zechariah 14:16 **And it shall come to pass, that every one that is left of all the nations which came against Jerusalem shall even go up from year to year to worship the King, the LORD of hosts, and to keep the feast of tabernacles.**

When we die, those who are saved and faithful will go to heaven. That is the scene of the wedding feast. The whole city is aglow with God's glory. This city reflects the divine nature in every part. Paul said it is **"better by far"** to depart and be with Christ for he would be **"at home with the Lord"** (cf. 2 Cor. 5:8; Phil. 1:23).

> 2 Cor. 5:8 **We are confident, I say, and would prefer to be away from the body and at home with the Lord. ⁹ So we make it our goal to please him, whether we are at home in the body or away from it. ¹⁰ For we must all appear before the judgment seat of Christ, that each one may receive what is due him for the things done while in the body, whether good or bad.**
>
> Phil. 1:21 **For to me, to live is Christ and to die is gain. ²² If I am to go on living in the body, this will mean fruitful labor for me. Yet what shall I choose? I do not know! ²³ I am torn between the two: I desire to depart and be with Christ, which is better by far...**

How Will We Be Known?

We will recognize our loved ones. Moses and Elijah were recognized at the Transfiguration. The spiritual resurrected body is a real body—a literal body. But it is not a flesh and blood body that is subject to pain, death and decay. It is an eternal body made to live with God. Our likeness will be evident, but our body will not be subject to decay or ruin. Christ, in His resurrected body, could move back and forth between the crucified body and the new spiritual body. When he appeared to His disciples in the days between his resurrection and His ascension, He appeared as they had last seen Him with nail prints and the spear gouge. Even in Revelation, John says that He appeared as a lamb that **"had been slain"** (or slaughtered, Rev. 5:6, 9, 12; 6:8-9 the souls of the slain under the altar; 13:8).

The Exterior of the City ---Transparent Quality of Light and Beauty

Text: Rev. 21:11-13
Rev. 21:11 **Having the glory of God: and her light was like a *very precious stone, just* like a jasper stone, clear as crystal; ¹² And it had a *great high wall* with twelve gates, and at the gates twelve angels, and names written on them. *These* are the names of the twelve tribes of the children of Israel: ¹³ On the east three gates; on the north three gates; on the south three gates; and on the west three gates.** (EKJV)

The first view that you observe is its transparency. The outside is an array of light, beauty and wonder. John relates: **"It shone with the glory of God..."** He adds: **"...and her light was like a very precious jewel, just like a jasper, clear as crystal..."** (v. 11). A jasper stone is a diamond. John finds the brilliance astonishing. We can only imagine its brightness. Three times in John's visions he records that a thing is clear as crystal: first in Rev. 4:6 the **"sea of glass before the throne"** of God. Then in this passage he says the same of the holy city, and finally of the river of the water of life (Rev. 22:1) **"flowing from the throne of God and of the Lamb."**

It has what John calls **"a *very* high wall."** The wall is so high that a man could not scale it. But there are twelve gates so there is no need to worry. These twelve gates are **like great pearls,** (Rev. 21:21; cf. Ezek. 48:30ff) **"and on them are written the names of the twelve tribes of Israel"** (21:12). They represent the redeemed of the Old Testament age. John says rather matter-of-factly that there are twelve angels stationed one at each gate.

We should pause and consider Ezekiel's views of a city. There are differences: Ezekiel's gates are **exits** (Ezek. 48:30-35).

Text: Rev. 21:14
Rev. 21:14 **And the wall of the city had twelve foundations, and in them the names of the twelve apostles of the Lamb.**

Twelve foundations represent the twelve apostles, and all those saved in the age of Christ and His church (21:13). It is built upon the gospel as transmitted through the apostles (Eph. 2:19-20).

"THE LORD IS THERE"
Ezekiel 48:35

- John's gates are **entrances. (These are *going in places*).**
- The twelve tribes **represent the saints of the Old Testament.**
- There are **twelve foundations** (v. 12).
- The **twelve apostles represent the saved in this age** – the New Testament age.
- The total of 24 represents all of God's redeemed.

No connection with astrology is intended.

A City Perfect in Symmetry

Text: Rev. 21:15-17
^{Rev. 21:15} **And (the angel) that talked with me had a golden reed to measure the city, and the gates, *and the wall.* ⁶ And the city *lies* foursquare, and the length is as large as the *width*: and he measured the city with the reed, twelve thousand furlongs. The length and the *width* and the height of it are equal. ¹⁷ And he measured the wall...and it was a hundred and forty four cubits, according to the measure of a man—of the angel.** (EKJV)

Everything is precise. The angel who guided John took a measuring rod and measured the entire city. The entire city is in perfect symmetry. Many people can appreciate symmetry. John viewed the interior of the city (21:21b.) There are wide avenues (streets), and the city is transparent like golden glass. There is no physical temple, but the presence of God is there. John saw no artificial light or heavenly bodies (21:23). We note the exclusion of everything that defiles (21:27).

The City Is Four Square
All Dimensions Are Equal

Ezekiel's city is also four square (Ezek. 45:2f; 48:20). There are similarities between this great Old Testament prophet and John, the author of five books of the New Testament.

> ^{Ezekiel 45:2} **Of this, a section 500 cubits square is to be for the sanctuary, with 50 cubits around it for open land.**
>
> ^{Ezekiel 48:20} **The entire portion will be a square, 25,000 cubits on each side. As a special gift you will set aside the sacred portion, along with the property of the city.**

The new celestial city is 1500 miles long, by 1500 miles wide, by 1500 miles **high**. The distance **from Maine to Florida** is 1500 miles. Some believe that the 12,000 furlongs relates to the 12,000 out of each of the 12 tribes (Rev. 7) but we cannot know this. Here is a city where there is room for all. While we are here on earth, Jesus is doing two things. He is making intercession (Heb. 7:25).

And He is preparing a celestial city. He is building a city for eternity (cf. John 14).

The Foundation Contains Twelve Precious Stones

Text: Rev. 21:18-21

Rev. 21:18 **And the building of the wall of it was of jasper: and the city was pure gold, like unto clear glass. ¹⁹ And the foundations of the wall of the city were garnished with all manner of precious stones. The first foundation was jasper; the second, sapphire; the third, a chalcedony; the fourth, an emerald; ²⁰ The fifth, sardonyx; the sixth, sardius; the seventh, chrysolyte; the eighth, beryl; the ninth, a topaz; the tenth, a chrysoprasus; the eleventh, a jacinth; the twelfth, an amethyst. ²¹ And the twelve gates were twelve pearls: every gate was of one pearl: and the street of the city was pure gold, as it were transparent glass.**

The material of the New City of God is perfect in every way and lacks nothing. Each of the twelve stones is perfect in color. Each is exquisite in beauty. The color excels anything known on earth. Look at their beautiful hues as John explains. But the most thrilling part is that the Lord is there (Ezek. 48:35). God is all in all, and there is no need of a temple in this city. Everything and every part, and every citizen of this city possesses an everlasting relationship to the heavenly Father—the Lord of all.

Text: Rev. 21:22-27

Rev. 21:22 **And *I did not see a temple* in it: for the Lord God Almighty and the Lamb are its temple. ²³ And the city had no need of the sun, *or* the moon, to shine in it: for the glory of God *is its light* and the Lamb is the light of it. ²⁴ And the nations of *those* that are saved shall walk in its light: and the kings of the earth will bring their glory and honor into it. ²⁵ And the gates of it shall never be shut by day: for there shall be no night there. ²⁶ And they shall bring the glory and honor of the nations into it. ²⁷ And *not one single thing* shall enter it that *is impure or defiles* or anything *that is an* abomination, or *deceives*: but only those that are written in the Lamb's book of life.** (EKJV)

When we see a temple, church or religious gathering place we cannot know if the Lord is in that place, but in this city, the Lord is there. **"God Almighty and the Lamb are its temple"** (v. 22).

The Approaching Everlasting Day

Text: Rev. 21:23

Rev. 21:23 **The city does not need the sun or the moon to shine on it, for the glory of God gives it light, and the Lamb is its lamp.**

We love lights of all kinds. They are used for visibility, security and beauty. Billions of dollars the world over are spent for light to penetrate the darkness of night, to illuminate our surroundings, and to bring us comfort and security from what we are unable to see. But in heaven, the Lord will be our everlasting light. Heaven's light is beautiful, glorious and always shining with the brilliance of our God. There are people that trudge into the coal mines before daylight and emerge after the sun has set and never see the light of day. Often we are frustrated because we do not have time to finish what we start in a day. But a brilliant and endless day is coming.

In these final chapters we see the fulfillment of Isaiah 60:19-20 that darkness will end and the glory of God and the Lamb will illuminate the eternal world with everlasting brightness.

> Isaiah 60:19 **The sun will no more be your light by day, nor will the brightness of the moon shine on you, for <u>the LORD will be your everlasting light</u>, and your God will be your glory. ²⁰ Your sun will never set again, and your moon will wane no more; <u>the LORD will be your everlasting light, and your days of sorrow will end</u>.**

The city is built on the Apostles and on the apostolic tradition as its foundation. Where do we get such an idea? We find it in the scriptures.

> Eph. 2:19 **Consequently, you are no longer foreigners and aliens, but fellow citizens with God's people and members of God's household, ²⁰ <u>built on the foundation of the apostles and prophets</u>, with Christ Jesus himself as the chief cornerstone.**

The Light of the City Shines to the Nations (Isa. 60:3)

Text: Rev. 21:24-26

Rev. 21:24 **The <u>nations will walk by its light, and the kings of the earth will bring their splendor into it.</u> ²⁵ On no day will its gates** ever be shut, for there will be no night there. ²⁶ <u>The glory and honor of the nations will be brought into it.</u>

The Prophecy of the Final Submission of the Nations
(Psalm 138:4)

^{Psalm 138:4} **All the kings of the earth shall praise thee, O LORD, when they hear the words of thy mouth. ⁵ Yea, they shall sing in the ways of the LORD: for great is the glory of the LORD.**

First of all, we need to note that this is a psalm of David, and God revealed great truths and prophecies of world-wide events to His anointed king. The psalms do foresee the rebellion of the kings of the world against God. They take note of the wrath of God that will fall upon all who reject Him and who live in disobedience. But especially, we are led to see, in the writings of David, Isaiah, the minor prophets, as well as the New Testament, that a day is coming when there will be world-wide submission to the Lord and Savior Jesus Christ and to God the Father.

The term **"The kings of the earth"** is found nine times in the Revelation of John (NIV) if you include 16:14 **"the kings of the whole earth"** which carries the same meaning. In all cases, the meaning is: all the rulers who have sinned, rebelled against God, fought against God, including those who have ultimately brought glory into the new heaven (Rev. 21:24). Rev. 1:5 announces **"Jesus Christ, the first begotten of the dead, and prince of the kings of the earth."**

How Will This Prophecy Be Fulfilled?

There are two questions. First, how shall this be since the kings of the world are living, even today, in notorious rebellion against God? And in the second place: when shall this world-wide event take place?

To understand the revelation of divine scripture, we need to think in the terms used in scripture. The scriptures speak in terms of kings, nations, Gentiles, kingdoms, and a general term including all of the above: **"the ends of the earth."** In regard to **the ends of the earth**, we are led to see two great movements. First the church must do what David could not do. She must take the gospel to the ends of the earth. Never mind the difficulty of the task, or the slowness of the response. The church is planting the seeds of world redemption, and the seeds will sprout and burst into faith and praise to our God and His Son.

Secondly, we should see that we are in the age of the gospel, but the final acts of God are going to be magnificent beyond comprehension. Thus, there will be a day when the eternal harvest of the nations will become a reality, and God will be eternally praised by those nations who have, thus far, rejected Him. And while the rulers stand against God, in every country there are people of genuine repentance, love and faith for Jesus the Savior.

The Nations Rebel Against God and His Anointed

The same David to whom God granted this wonderful understanding was also greatly disturbed by the rebellion of the nations against God (see Mt. 27:35; refers to Ps. 22 as a prophecy; Acts 2:30 where it is written: **"...David, being a prophet"**).

How do we identify these kings? First, John has already stated in Revelation 20 that the resurrection has taken place and all people have been judged. But what we see here is the fulfillment of the many prophecies that every knee shall bow before the Lord. In John's mind, these kings, not to be confused with the wicked kings who died in the battle of Armageddon, now fall on their knees before the Lamb, the King of kings, and the Lord of lords.

Even though these wicked kings were destroyed, there were still people residing in these countries, and their new rulers are now coming before the risen Christ. Also, for a thousand years during the Millennium, people resided on the earth. Some of them fell under the leadership of Satan once he was released. Others had become believers during this unprecedented period of peace under the reign of Christ. No matter their identity they all fall in submission and honor before Christ.

> **Isa. 60:3 Nations will come to your light, and kings to the brightness of your dawn.**

It is certainly easy to reconcile these words from the prophet Isaiah around 800 years before Christ. God is the Master of long-range planning. All of His prophecies are fulfilled exactly as they are spoken or written. If a prophecy never comes true, it is not from God. If you have watched the opening ceremony in the Olympics you have witnessed the vast array of nations parading into the Olympic stadium. We shall witness, and perhaps participate, in the parade of nations entering the holy city bringing their allegiance to the Lord of lords, and the King of kings, for there is only one king over the citizens of heaven. Just imagine what a glorious parade that will be as the nations come not for war, but for worship falling before their Lord.

Now we continue in the final chapter—chapter 22. The first six verses are a continuation of the description of the new city. The river, shade, fruit and park atmosphere is not separate from, but is an inclusive part of the new city of God. Verse 6 is a transition with the angel speaking.

CHAPTER 22

"RETIRING" IN PARADISE

THE CONCLUSION

THE GARDEN OF EDEN RESTORED IN THE NEW PARADISE

Text: Rev. 22:1-2

^{Rev. 22:1} And *the angel showed* me a river of the water of life, clear as crystal, *coming* out of the throne of God and of the Lamb. ² In the midst of *its street,* and on either side of the river, *was* the tree of life, *that produced* twelve kinds of fruits, and yielded her fruit every month: and the leaves of the tree were for the healing of the nations. (Easy KJV)

---

napshot of Chapter 22

This final chapter of the prophecy of God recorded by John in the Book of Revelation continues describing the New City of God with details of the river of the water of life flowing from the throne and down the middle of the great street. The Garden of Eden is lost, but there is a paradise in the New City. After verse 6 we find commands from the angel, and the risen Christ, and responses by John. These are diverse but very important. Read this final chapter with an open and clear mind and heart to God speaking in various ways.

Our focus regarding paradise centers on 22:1-6. The word **"para-dise"** only appears two times in Scripture: first in Luke 23:43 when Jesus says to a thief on a cross next to His, **"today you will be with me in paradise."** The next occurrence of the word is in Rev. 2:7 when Jesus said: **"To him who overcomes, I will give the right to eat from the tree of life, which is in the paradise of God."** In Revelation 22 we are brought to; the paradise of God—the new Eden so to speak. Imagine for a moment that you were allowed to walk in the Garden of Eden at the creation with Adam and Eve.

In Rev. 21:1-6 we find the description of the paradise which Jesus spoke of in these two passages. Why was the original paradise denied, and why must God wait until the conclusion of human history to restore that glorious and wonderful life? Look at what God intended. There are some timeless truths that never change.

God planned for man to be happy. Eden means a **"pleasant place."** The word **"garden"** in the **LXX** (the Septuagint, the Greek version of the Old Testament) is borrowed from the Persians and means paradise. We are meant to know peace and fellowship with God. The Hebrew greeting usually translated peace is **"Shalom."** It is the presence of everything God can give.

God Established Boundaries to
the Garden of Eden

The Tree of Life (Gen. 2:9; Gen. 2:15-17) was the tree of the knowledge of good and evil. We are to trust God first. If faith comes first, the knowledge can be taken by degrees. Man was disqualified and, therefore, lost that inner quality of life in the garden.

What did God do with **the Tree of Life**? He placed cherubim with a flaming sword to guard the entrance. Why? In case someone comes along with the right qualifications to enter. Everlasting life isn't lost forever. God sent His Son to restore the right to enter heaven for those who receive Christ as Lord. This privilege is through faith in Him and His resurrection from the dead by God's power. Through Him, death is ended. There is no **second death** for those who are redeemed **by the blood of the Lamb**.

God Gives Us a New Body in His Eternal Paradise

We need to step aside and consider what kind of body we will possess in heaven. When Jesus was resurrected there was no physical body left behind. God is going to fashion a new body from the essence of the old (cf. Phil. 3:21; cf. 1 Jn. 3:2). We have tremendous symbols for eternal life as the following explains. Paradise means: Our name is in **the Lamb's Book of Life** (Ps. 69:28; Phil. 4:3; Rev. 3:5; 13:8; 17:8; 20:12, 15; 21:27). We eat of **the Tree of Life** (Gen. 2:9; 3:17, 22, 24; Rev. 2:7; 22:2, 14, 19). We drink of **the Water of Life** (Jn. 4:14; Rev. 21:6; 22:1, 17). We eat of the **Bread of Life** (Jn. 6:35, 48, 51). We **receive immortality** (Rom. 2:7; 1 Cor. 15:53, 54; 2 Tim. 1:10). Rev. 22:1-2 parallels Genesis Chapters 1-2. God's Word is a balanced book. *(See "**the River of the water of Life**"– Rev. 22:1).*

This River of the Water of Life Flows from the Throne of God and the Lamb

Text: Rev. 22:1

Rev. 22:1 **And *the angel showed* me a river of the water of life, clear as crystal, *coming* out of the throne of God and of the Lamb.** (EKJV)

The Psalmist said: **"There is a river, the stream whereof makes glad the city of God"** (Ps. 46:4). In Eden, the River had four branches. There is nothing as refreshing as cool, clear water. John saw this beautiful stream in the heavenly paradise of God where the redeemed may drink and live forever.

God is the source of all life. Every day the gaping grave swallows up the dying. Grief overwhelms the bereaved. Jesus promised **"Living water"** – (Jn. 4:10, 14; Cf. Ezek. 47:1, 12; Zech. 14:8; Jn. 7:38). The Dead Sea takes all and gives nothing back, but the River of Life never ceases in providing what mankind needs.

The Tree of Life Is Eternally Available

Text: Rev. 22:2

Rev. 22:2b **...on either side of the river *was* the tree of life that *produced* twelve kinds of fruits, and yielded her fruit every month: and the leaves of the tree were for the healing of the nations.** (EKJV)

The way to the tree of life is no longer blocked. It sounds as if we are going to eat fruit in heaven. Angels ate when entertained by Abraham. Our Lord ate following His resurrection. Jesus said He would drink of the fruit of the vine in heaven (Mt. 26:29). **The Tree of Life** is on **"either side"** — therefore it offers unlimited access.

Rev. 2:7 **"To him who conquers I will grant to eat of the tree of life, which is in the paradise of God."**

The Curse is Forever Ended

The curse that came upon Adam and Eve and their descendants is done away with (cf. Gen. 3:17).

Text: Rev. 22:3-4
Rev. 22:3 **And there shall be no more curse: but the throne of God and of the Lamb shall be in it; and his servants shall serve him: 4 And they shall see his face; and his name shall be in their foreheads.**

To be marked with the name of God is the ultimate right of entrance into heaven. No flaming sword bars the way as was the case with the Garden of Eden. We shall see His blessed face for we are His forever more.

We need to be reminded in the midst of the scene of paradise that we are still in the city and **"the throne of God and of the Lamb will be in the city, and his servants will serve him"** (v. 3). We are not on vacation. We are in the garden, but we will have definite responsibilities. Nothing is more tiring than finding that you have nothing to do, and that no one needs you to serve any purpose. God will have need of your services and you will have a place to serve. But, also, note that we will **"see his face."** That is the blessed face of Jesus our Savior. You may imagine what His face looks like, but you will see Him and know Him, and rejoice in Christ your Savior. Further, His name will mark you! **"His name will be on** (your) **forehead"** (cf. Rev. 7:3; 9:4; 14:1; 20:4). It has been our expectation, in the journey through Revelation, that our foreheads will be marked with His name.

No More Night

Text: Rev. 22:5

Rev. 22:5 **And there shall be no night there; and they need no candle, neither light of the sun; for the Lord God gives them light: and they shall reign forever and ever.** (See Rev. 7:3; 9:4; 14:1).

We will have no need of a lamp. Our light will be furnished by **"the Lord God"** (v. 5; see Rev. 21:24-25). The sun will have been destroyed along with the heavenly bodies, but the light will be abundant and glorious as God provides everything we need.

We Enter the Eternal Reign of the Lamb

Rev. 22:5b **"...They shall reign forever and ever."** We share the royal office (Rev. 5:10; 11:15, 17; 20:4, 6; 22:5). The eternal reign makes the 1000-year reign look insignificant. We are not born sinners. A sinful nature will begin to assert itself. Adam and Eve were innocent, but not sinlessly perfect in the beginning. We are inclined toward evil. It took an act of God to bring about forgiveness and redemption.

The Angel Certifies the Message

Text: Rev. 22:6

Rev. 22:6 **The angel said to me, These sayings are faithful and true: and the Lord God of the holy prophets sent his angel to show his servants the things *that must soon take place.*** (EKJV)

The words of the Paradise Prophecy are certified by the angel (22:6). The angel explains the **"...things that must soon take place"** (22:6). John experienced the things that explode the mind. They are almost beyond comprehension. The angel gives him a pause. **"These words are trustworthy and true..."** In other words, "John, you can rest assured that everything you have seen and experienced is valid. You can trust your visions."

I Am Coming Soon

Text: Rev. 22:7

Rev. 22:7 **"Look, I am coming soon!"** This is repeated in Rev. 3:11; 22:12, and 20. And John adds at the final statement: **"Amen. Come, Lord Jesus"** (v. 20). But it is much more than that. Verse 7 sets the tone for what follows: Rev. 22:20 **He who testifies to these things says, "Yes, I am coming soon." Amen. Come, Lord Jesus.** (See additional commentary under verse 20.)

John, the Last Prophet

Text: Rev. 22:7
Rev. 22:7 "...blessed is he *who* keeps the sayings of the prophecy of this book."

Revelation is called a prophecy six times in Revelation 1:3; 19:10; 22:7, 10, 18, and 19. The first and last chapters contain five of the six references. John is definitely a prophet. The first beatitude contains the initial reference. The second reference is in Rev.19:10. This is the sixth beatitude in the book.

Rev. 1:3 **Blessed is he that reads, and those that hear the words of this prophecy, and keep *those* things which are written in it: for the time is at hand.**

Rev. 19:10 "...worship God: for the testimony of Jesus is the Spirit of prophecy." Cf. 2 Pet. 1:12, 20, and 21.

Rev. 22:10 **And he *said to* me, *Do not seal up* the words of the prophecy of this book: for the *time is near (or at hand)*.** (EKJV)

Rev. 22:18 **For I testify to every*one* that hears the words of the prophecy of this book, If any man shall add to these things, God shall add unto him the plagues that are written in this book: ¹⁹ And if any man takes away from the words of the book of this prophecy, God shall take away his part out of the book of life, and out of the holy city, and from the things which are written in this book.**

Revelation 1:3 and 22:10 have an important key. Both contain the phrase **"...the time is near."** Jesus used similar expressions, but in this case they add significant meaning to the message of the passage. In Rev. 1:3 they are to hear the prophecy and keep what is written because the time is near or at hand: **"those that hear the words of this prophecy, and keep those things which are written therein: for the time is at hand..."** As we know, many people were under persecution and the pains of death already. The time of the writing of Revelation was a time of significant persecution and execution of believers. In Rev. 22:10 the same thought follows the command: **"..."Do not seal up the words of the prophecy of this scroll, because <u>the time is near</u>."**

335

Revelation 22:8-21– Summary and Conclusion
John's Compelling Desire to Fall Down and Worship the Angel

Text: Rev. 22:8-9

Rev. 22:8 **I John saw these things, and heard them. And when I had heard and seen, I fell down to worship *at* the feet of the angel *who showed them* to me. ⁹ Then *he said* to me, *Do not do this*: for I am your fellow servant, and *I am among your* brethren the prophets, and those that keep the sayings of this book: worship God!"** (EKJV)

John attempts to worship the angel and is rebuffed (vv. 8-9). John testifies that he both heard and saw the events and scenes in the four visions. His senses of hearing and sight were called into constant use. John is moved to fall down and worship the angel who had guided him through this final vision. After all, the scenes of the eternal city of God were perhaps the most moving and inspiring of all. But the angel sharply forbids his attempt to worship him. Angels are not meant to be worshiped. They are servants of God to do what pleases Him.

The angel stated the fact that, like John's fellow prophets throughout history, he is a **"fellow servant."** John is commanded to **"Worship God!"** John was slow to pick up on this. He experienced exactly this same scene with an angel (Rev. 19:10). Throughout the book the twenty four elders and others fell face down before God in His infinite glory and worshiped Him (Rev. 4:10; 5:14; 7:11; 11:16; 14:7; 15:4; 19:4).

A Command to Not Seal the Book

Text: Rev. 22:10

Rev. 22:10 **Then he told me, "Do not seal up the words of the prophecy of this scroll, because the time is near.**

John is forbidden to seal the book. It is the end. Why not seal the book? In the earlier portion of Revelation, there was a scroll sealed with seven seals, and there was great weeping and shedding of tears because the meaning and message could not be read. But then, the Lamb of God came upon the scene, and He alone could open the seals, and He did so one by one. But here the command rings out: **"Do not seal up the words of the prophecy..."** Leave it so that all those of the world can read God's final plans for His creation. Leave it so that they can understand the final choices between eternal life and the second death. Leave it in order that under the Holy Spirit men and women can find their way to heaven through faith in the Christ who died for them. God is still at work until the end when Christ appears. We have not been relieved of our calling to take the gospel to the world on behalf of Christ Jesus (Mt. 28:19-20).

The time is always imminent for the return of Christ. **"...the time is near"** (Mt. 24:32-33; Lk. 21:31; James 5:8; Rev. 1:3; 3:11; 22:7, 10, 12). Time is not in God's mind. There are no clocks or calendars in heaven. A thousand years is of no particular meaning to the Father (2 Peter 3:8). We grow impatient, but God is patient in order that many may be brought into His kingdom.

2 Peter 3:9 **The Lord is not slow in keeping his promise, as some understand slowness. Instead he is patient with you, not wanting anyone to perish, but everyone to come to repentance.**

What is it that should not be sealed? The message is **"the words of prophecy."** Prophecy is always God's guidance to His people. In His prophecy He reveals the future for His church, for judgment upon the wicked, for salvation for the righteous that come to Him by faith. He reveals what will happen to this earth and to the solar system.

He reveals the climax of the cosmos—the calamities that will return these bodies to chaos and destruction. The world is spinning toward its own oblivion. Millions die without the hope of heaven. Each day that God delays provides an additional opportunity for the prophecy to be shared and explained, and for people to embrace Christ as Lord. By all means **"do not seal up the words of prophecy"** for in them is life and blessing and truth and salvation.

But there is also this perplexing verse that follows immediately. Rev. 22:11 **He that is unjust, let him be unjust still: and he who is filthy, let him be filthy still: and he who is righteous, let him be righteous still: and he that is holy, let him be holy still."** We have this word **"let."** Four times he uses this word in this single verse. **"Let"** means to permit or allow. God will never force us. He will show us the way. He will give us a wonderful prophetic preview of eternity, of the eternal city, of paradise, of saints in His presence

337

and sinners in the judgment. But then He will speak out of the sadness of His heart. Let them continue as they are.

The angels are saying, "Can't something be done to remove the blazing lake of fire and keep people from facing that judgment?" And He will answer, "I have done all that I can. I sent my Son to die on a cross. I have given them hundreds of prophecies. I have revealed to My servant John these terrible pictures of what is coming upon the world, and the glorious pictures of what I have planned for the saved. But in the end, they have a free will. They will have to choose. And to honor their free will I must let them follow the choices they make. Heaven would not be heaven if I forced them to choose Me."

Christ's Wonderful Promises
Text: Rev. 22:12-14
^{Rev. 22:12} "*Look, I am coming soon*; and my reward is with me, *to* give to every man according to his *works.* (EKJV)

We see the rewards of the risen Christ (vv. 12-17). The rewards are separated by a passage describing those outside the grace of God. The positive blessings of Christ are explained in vs. 12-14 and 16-17.

I Am Coming Soon

^{Rev. 22:12, 20} "*Look, I am coming soon*!
(See the commentary under verse 20).

My Reward Is with Me
Rev. 22:12
^{Rev. 22:12b} "*...my reward is with me, to* give to every man according to his *works.*"
His reward should not be confused with salvation. Salvation has nothing to do with works. But we have already seen the precious promises to the martyrs, for example. Observe the reason: "**...we must all appear before the judgment seat of Christ, so that each of us may receive what is due us for the things done while in the body, whether good or bad**" (2 Cor. 5:10).

This judgment, however, is the final great white throne judgment. It is not an occasion of rewards, but of separating the righteous from the wicked, and the believers from the unbelievers. In Titus 3:5 "**he saved us not because of righteous things we had done...**" So we see the connection of the first reference to this passage in Revelation. Rev. 20:13 "**...and each person was judged according to what they had done.**"

The Alpha and the Omega

Jesus identifies Himself in three references as "**the Alpha and Omega**" (Rev. 1:8; 21:6; and 22:13). It is in the third location that Jesus fully identifies the meaning.

Text: Rev. 22:13
Rev. 22:13 **I am the Alpha and the Omega, the First and the Last, the Beginning and the End.**

Every child who memorized the alphabet knew the first and the last letters. **Alpha and Omega** are the first and final letters of the Greek Alphabet, and therefore Jesus says He is "**the first and the last**" (22:13), but in this verse He further clarifies the meaning by adding "**the beginning and the end.**" Each of the three phrases equals the same: the start of something and the ending.

This leads us back to one of John's initial phrases in John, Chapter 1. "**In the beginning was the word, and the word was with God, and the word was God.**" Jesus was in existence prior to the creation, and when the creation is removed and destroyed (the end) He is still here. When the earth is destroyed, the sun and planets go dark, and the heavenly bodies collide, Jesus will still be here and He is God.

Blessed Ones Who Wash Their Robes

Text: Rev. 22:14
Rev. 22:14 "**Blessed are those that do his commandments that they may have the right to the tree of life, and may enter in through the gates into the city.**"

Rev. 7:14 **... And he said, "These are the ones who have come out of the great tribulation; they have washed their robes and made them white in the blood of the Lamb.**"

Rev. 12:11 **And they overcame him by the blood of the Lamb, and by the word of their testimony; and they loved not their lives unto the death.**

Rev. 22:14 is the last of the seven beatitudes in Revelation. The emphasis is not upon the washing as if it were something we had accomplished. It is on the **"blood of the Lamb."** It is inexplicable that washing in blood could make a robe white. But through the power of the blood of Christ we are seen in the purity and whiteness of one who is without sin because He took our sins upon Himself. When we come to Christ, we receive His cleansing, washing, forgiveness, and righteousness. In no way do we deserve this grace.

The People Who Miss Paradise
Text Rev. 22:15

Rev. 22:15 **For outside are dogs, and sorcerers, and the *immoral,* and murderers, and idolaters, and whosoever *delights in a lie.*** (EKJV)
On the outside, the vision pictures people who are likened to dogs perhaps covered in sores and mange, howling to be admitted. In Rev. 22:15 and 21:8 we see the fate of those who are rejected for heaven. The two lists are very similar.

In this passage we have five major sins: (1) magic arts, (2) sexual immorality, (3) murders, (4) idolaters, and (5) those who love and practice falsehood. The first and last are wanton and deliberate deception. The second and third are acts against fellow humans: the act of practicing sexual immorality and of taking the life of another human being. The fourth is against God. Idolatry is in this and the first two lists below. Idolatry breaks the commandment. It is to have another god rather than holy God.

They are rejected because they have rejected Christ, God's Son. It is those who have washed their robes in the blood of the Lamb that have the right to enter the city. We have another list from Paul in Col. 3:5. Notice the consistency of those who are **"cast outside"** in the additional verses below.

Rev. 21:8 " But the fearful, and unbelieving, and the abomina-ble, and murderers, and adulterers, and sorcerers, and idolaters, and all liars, shall have their part in the lake which burns with fire and brimstone: which is the second death." *Note: the fiery lake is outside.*

Colossians 3:5 "**Put to death, therefore, whatever belongs to your earthly nature: sexual immorality, impurity, lust, evil desires and greed, which is idolatry. [6] Because of these, the wrath of God is coming...**"

Rev. 14:20 "**They** (the grapes) **were trampled in the wine-press <u>outside</u> the city...**"

Matt. 8:12 "**But the *subjects* of the kingdom shall be cast out in-to outer darkness: there shall be weeping and gnashing of teeth.**

Matt. 22:13 "**Then the king said to the servants, *Tie* him hand and foot, and take him away, and *throw* him into outer darkness, *where* there shall be weeping and gnashing of teeth.**"

Matt. 25:30 "**...throw the unprofitable servant into outer dark-ness: there shall be weeping and gnashing of teeth. [31] When the Son of man shall come in his glory, and all the holy an-gels with him, then shall he sit upon the throne of his glo-ry...**"

Luke 13:25 **Once the master of the house *rises up*, and *shuts the door*, and (then)*you begin to stand outside, and knock at the door*, saying, Lord, Lord, *let us in*; and he shall answer and say to you, *I don't know you or where you have come from!***

The Certification and Authority of Jesus

Text: Rev. 22:16

Rev. 22:16 "**I Jesus have sent mine angel to testify these things *to you* in the churches. I am the root and the offspring of David, and the bright and morning star.**"

We have two powerful thoughts in these verses. The first is: **"I Je-sus have sent mine angel to testify these things to you in the churches."** It sounds as if this is addressed to John. "John, I Jesus have sent my angel to you..." I am authenticating the angel's mes-sage. **"I Jesus have sent..."** him. All that you have heard and seen is from me. And John, I have sent him as a testimony **"to you in the churches."**

In the earlier chapters we were introduced to seven representative churches. Each had some problems, and we were shown Christ walking among them and taking note of their sins and their obedience. He warned them, He challenged them. He called them out on the wrongs they were guilty of, and He praised them for acts of obedience and faith. But there are hundreds of thousands of churches the world over. Jesus says that this message is for the churches. Through the angel and then John, Jesus has sent this message.

The second thing that comes out of this verse is His self-identification. **"I am the root and the offspring of David, and the bright and morning star."**

He traces His human genealogy back to David, the chosen servant of God and the king of the Jews. **"I am the Root and offspring..."** "I am descended from David as My genealogy in Luke and Matthew testifies. I am who I claim to be, and I am the one spoken of in scripture as Messiah." We see this same thought in Rev. 5:5.

Rev. 5:5 **"And one of the elders *said* to me, Weep not: see, the Lion of the tribe of Judah, the Root of David, has prevailed to open the book *and the* seven seals."**

In the magnificent prophecy of Isaiah we see this prophecy. Jesse was David's father. So now we see Messiah listed, just like David as a son of Jesse.

Isa. 11:10 **"And in that day there shall be a root of Jesse, *that will stand as a banner for* the people; the Gentiles shall be drawn to it, and *his resting place* shall be glorious."** (EKJV)

But He continues: **"I am...the bright Morning Star."** In a dark night, people the world over looked for the brightest star before dawn: **"the bright morning star." God tells Job of the glory of the creation and how "the morning stars sang together."** God's celestial creation joined together in an anthem of rejoicing as they watched God set the **"footings"** and lay the **"cornerstone"** of the earth. He says **"all the angels shouted together."** The words here translated **"angels"** is literally "the sons of God," for indeed God had long ago brought the angels into being.

Job 38:6-7
⁶ Upon what are the foundations of it fastened? or who laid the corner stone; ⁷ When the morning stars sang together, and all the sons of God shouted for joy?

Peter knows that Christ is the **"morning star"** in prophecy.
2 Peter 1:19 We also *have a very sure word* of prophecy; and *you should pay attention*, as to a light that *shines brightly* in a dark place, until the day dawns, and the day star arise in your hearts.

He passes on the prophetic message that he says **"We also have..."** His readers should heed the message. The morning star rises in hearts where Christ is Savior and Lord. In Rev. 2:28 Jesus promises the morning star to one of His churches. He will give Himself to His church.
Rev. 2:28 I will also give that one the morning star.

The Great and Final Invitation
to Eternal Life in Christ
Text: Rev. 22:17
Rev. 22:17 And the Spirit and the bride say, Come. And let *the one* that *hears* say, Come. And let *the one* that is *thirsty* come. And let *the one that desires* take the water of life freely. (EKJV)

The invitation becomes somewhat universal as voices join together crying **"Come."** The promise is the gift of eternal life without cost. But the cost to Jesus was enormous. All who hear are to join in the universal cry to ask the world to come to Christ. Faith comes by hearing. First, the Holy Spirit and the bride—the redeemed church shout **"Come!"**

Every day this cry of invitation is sent out into the world in the ears and hearts of people who have never believed. Once these have heard, they can believe and join in and they too will say **"Come!"** Then Christ issues the appeal and He cries **"Let the one who is thirsty come..."** Finally He says **"And let *the one that desires* take the water of life freely."**

It was the prophet Isaiah who brought God's prophecy with the invitation to **"come…"**

Isa. 55:1 **"*Everyone that is thirsty*, come to the waters (and drink), and he that *has* no money; come, buy, and eat; *yes*, come, buy wine and milk without money and without price."** (EKJV)

The gift of salvation is free. Jesus promises that they will never be thirsty again because He will be in them.

John 4:14 **But whosoever drinks of the water that I shall give him shall never thirst; but the water that I shall give him shall be in him a well of water springing up into everlasting life."**

He repeats the promise coupled with an **"I am"** saying: **"I am the bread of life."** He will fill the needs of those who both hunger and thirst.

John 6:35 **Then Jesus declared "…whoever believes in me will never be thirsty."**

John 7:37 **"Jesus stood and cried *out*, saying, If any man is *thirsty* let him come unto me, and drink. ³⁸ The one that believeth on me, as the scripture has said, rivers of living water *shall flow from within him*."** (EKJV)

He makes this promise again in Rev. 21:6. Every day in every city and countryside the message should ring out. "Come today to the Savior for His gift is free," but it is eternal in nature.

Rev. 21:6 **He said to me: "It is done. I am the Alpha and the Omega, the Beginning and the End. To the thirsty I will give water without cost from the spring of the water of life."**

The Terrible Penalty for Distorting the Message
Text: Rev. 22:18-19

Rev. 22:18 **For I testify to every*one* that hears the words of the prophecy of this book, If any man shall add to these things, God shall add unto him the plagues that are written in this book: ¹⁹ And if any man takes away from the words of the book of this prophecy, God shall take away his part out of the book of life, and out of the holy city, and from the things which are written in this book.**

It is a terrible act to alter the prophecy. **"If anyone adds anything to them, God will add to that person the plagues described in this scroll."** And on the other hand, to remove or take away any words is sufficient to cause that person to forfeit **"any share in the tree of life and the Holy City."** We must carefully teach these scriptures under the leadership of the Holy Spirit. We dare not take it upon ourselves to distort the inspired prophecy of God.

The Promise of the Imminent Return of Christ
22:7, 12, 20

Text: Rev. 22:20
Rev. 22:20 **He which testifies these things** *says,* **Surely I come quickly. Amen. Even so, come, Lord Jesus.**

Christ is coming again gloriously, outwardly visible, fully in keeping with His promise. He is coming accompanied by all of His angels. Over 300 verses speak to the second coming of Christ. The Bible warns us again and again to be ready. Our world is defiant toward the authority of God. They live under the domination of Satan. Their way is chosen out of selfish desire, but Christ is coming and the Day of Judgment approaches. I do not know when, but all signs point to the end of this world in a relatively short time. The scriptures printed below very clearly affirm the fact that we should be ready and waiting.

Rev. 3:11 **"I am coming soon."**
Matt. 24:30 **"Then will appear the sign of the Son of Man in heaven. And then all the peoples of the earth will mourn when they see the Son of Man coming on the clouds of heaven, with power and great glory."** Cf. Mt. 26:64; Mark 14:62; Dan. 7:13.
Matt. 24:37 **"As it was in the days of Noah, so it will be at the coming of the Son of Man."**
1 Thes. 4:15 **Concerning: "we who ...are left until the coming of the Lord..."**
Matt. 24:39 **"...and they knew nothing about what would happen until the flood came and took them all away. That is how it will be at the coming of the Son of Man.**
Matt. 24:43 **"If the owner of the house had known at what time ...the thief was coming..."**
Matt. 25:5 **"The bridegroom was a long time in coming, and they ... fell asleep."**
Matt. 26:64 **"...you will see the Son of Man...coming on the clouds of heaven."**

> John 5:25 "..."I tell you, a time is coming ... when the dead will hear the voice of the Son of God and those who hear will live."

Benediction

Rev. 22:20 He which *testifies* these things *says* Surely I come quickly. Amen. Even so, come, Lord Jesus.

Revelation closes with a simple benediction—a prayer that [21] **"The grace of our Lord Jesus Christ be with you all. Amen."**

But, oh what sufficiency to have the grace of God in our earthly life! The Garden of Eden was a paradise where **no sin separated** man from God. God is preparing paradise in the **future** where everything will be **in perfect harmony with the Father.** His first intention will be realized. Heaven and earth will be **one**—no longer will there be a cleavage or separation. Isaiah referred to this place as **Beulah Land** (62:1-5). Beulah means married. Heaven and earth are married. This thought is expressed in the old hymn **"Beulah Land."**

> **"O Beulah Land, sweet Beulah Land,**
> **As on the highest mount I stand,**
> **I look away beyond the sea**
> **Where mansions are prepared for me,**
> **And view the shining glory shore,**
> **My heaven, my home forever more."**

> *–Edgar Page Stites , 1875*

Appendices

The Seven Testimony Statements of Jesus in Revelation

Prologue
First – Rev. 1:1– **"the testimony of Jesus Christ"**
Second – Rev. 1:9– **"the testimony of Jesus"**
Third – Rev. 12:17–**"their testimony about Jesus"**
Fourth –Rev. 17:6– **"who bore testimony to Jesus"**
Fifth and Sixth–Rev. 19:10
    "who hold to the testimony of Jesus."
    For **"the testimony of Jesus is the spirit of prophecy."**
Sixth– Rev. 20:4–"I saw the souls of those who had been
    beheaded **because of their testimony about Jesus and
    because of the word of God."**
Seventh–Jesus Gives His Testimony to the Churches
Rev. 22:16–**"I, Jesus, have sent my angel to give you this
testimony for the churches."**

The Seven "I Am" Sayings of Jesus in the Gospel of John

1. John 6:48 <u>I am the bread of life</u>.
2. John 8:12 "<u>I am the light of the world</u>. Whoever follows me will never walk in darkness, but will have the light of life. (Also: Jn. 9:5).
3. John 11:25 "<u>I am the resurrection and the life</u>. The one who believes in me will live, even though they die;
4. John 10:9 "<u>I am the gate...</u>"
5. John 10:11 "<u>I am the good shepherd</u>. The good shepherd lays down his life for the sheep. (Also: v. 14).
6. John 14:6 "<u>I am the way and the truth and the life</u>. No one comes to the Father except through me.
7. John 15:1 "<u>I am the true vine</u>, and my Father is the gardener.

The Ministry of the Angels

Revelation is a book filled with angels. They are everywhere. Below is our attempt to show how the Lord has used angels in the past.

> Ps. 91:9 Because you have made the LORD, *which is* my refuge, *even* the most High, your habitation; [10] There no evil shall befall you neither shall any plague come nigh your dwelling. [11] <u>For he shall give his angels charge over you, to keep you in all your ways</u>. [12] They shall bear you up in *their* hands, lest you dash your foot against a stone. (KJV)

Matt. 4:6 And said unto him, If you be the Son of God, cast yourself down: for it is written, <u>He shall give his angels charge concerning you: and in *their* hands they shall bear you up, lest at any time you dash your foot against a stone</u>. (KJV)

The Marvel of the Angels

Ps. 103:20 Bless the LORD, <u>you his angels that excel in strength, that do his commandments, hearkening to the voice of his word</u>. [21] Bless you the LORD, <u>all *you* his hosts; you ministers of his, that do his pleasure</u>. [22] Bless the LORD, all his works in all places of his dominion: bless the LORD, O my soul.

The Mandate to the Angels

Ps. 148:1 Praise the LORD. Praise the LORD from the heavens: praise him in the heights. [2] <u>Praise him, all his angels: praise him, all his hosts</u>. [3] Praise him, sun and moon: praise him, all stars of light. [4] Praise him, heavens of heavens, and the waters that *are* above the heavens. (KJV)

> Matt. 16:27 For the <u>Son of man shall come in the glory of his Father with his angels</u>; and then he shall reward every man according to his works. (KJV)

Matt. 24:31 <u>And he shall send his angels with a *deafening* sound of a trumpet, and they shall gather together his elect from the four winds</u>, from one end of heaven to the other.

Matt. 26:53 *Do you* think that I cannot *in this moment* pray to my Father, and <u>he shall give me more than twelve legions of angels</u>? (KJV)

The Multitudes of Angels

Ps. 68:17 <u>The chariots of God *are* twenty thousand, *even* thousands of angels</u>: the Lord *is* among them, *as in* Sinai, in the holy *place.* [18] You have ascended on high, you have led captivity captive: you have received gifts for men; yes, *for* the rebellious also, that the LORD God might dwell *among them.* (KJV)

> Heb. 12:22 But you have come to Mount Zion, and to the city of the living God, <u>the heavenly Jerusalem, and to an innumerable company of angels</u>. (KJV)

> Rev. 5:11 And I looked, and I heard the voice of many angels round about the throne and the *(four) creatures* and the elders: and the number of them was ten thousand times ten thousand, and thousands of thousands; [12] Saying with a loud voice, Worthy is the Lamb that was slain.

The Military Angels

Michael leads the military. He and his angels succeeded in casting Satan, the old dragon, down from heaven.

> Rev. 12:7 And there was war in heaven: <u>Michael and his angels fought against the dragon; and the dragon fought and his angels,</u> [8] And prevailed not; neither was their place found any more in heaven. (KJV)

The Messenger Angel

Gabriel is the angel of the message (Daniel 8:16; 9:21; Luke 1:19, 26). In life, we may come to realize that angels have come to help us in our time of unprecedented need.

While we could speculate endlessly as to the identity of the angel that delivered the message of Revelation to John, and we might even speculate that it was Gabriel, the chief messenger angel of the Lord, our consideration would be useless. Revelation overflows with angels and not one of them, except Michael, is identified. The angels stress that they are not important. John is forbidden to worship them. What is important is God's message of His final wrath upon the earth including the blessed preservation of His saints to enter the New Jerusalem.

349

THE ANGELS OF REVELATION

In Revelation we are always expecting a pattern of seven or three.

The Angels of the Seven Churches
(Actually Pastors/Messengers—Rev. 2-3)
The First Mighty Angel of the Mystery (Rev. 5)
The Angel of the Seal of God (Rev. 7)
The Angel Bearing the Golden Censer (Rev. 8)

The Seven Angels with Trumpets (Rev. 8-11)
The Second Mighty Angel Interjects (Rev. 10:1ff)
The Angel of the Eternal Gospel (Rev. 14)
The Angel Proclaiming Babylon's Fate (Rev. 14)
The Angel Who Commands the Harvest (Rev. 14:14ff)
The Angel with the Sickle of Wrath (Rev. 14:17)
The Angel of the Altar Reappears and Casts Fire on the Earth
(Rev. 14:18)

The Seven Angels of the Last Plagues
The Seven Angels of the Last Plagues (Rev. 15-16)
The Angel in Charge of the Waters Interprets (Rev. 16:5)
The Narrating Angel (One of the Seven Plague Angels) (Rev.
17:1ff; 21:9ff; 22:6)
The Angel with Great Authority (Rev. 18:1ff)
The Third Mighty Angel with the Boulder (Rev. 18:21)
The Angel of World-wide Carnage (Rev. 19:17ff)
The Angel Who Unlocks the Abyss and Binds Satan (Rev.
20:1ff)
The Narrating Angel Reappears and Transports John in the
Spirit (Rev. 21:9-22)

- The Angel Measures the Eternal City of God (Rev.
  21:15ff)
- The Angel Guides John to the River of the Water of Life
  (Rev. 22:1).

The Narrating Angel Certifies the Vision (Revelation 22:6)

- John Is Instructed Not to Seal the Book (Rev. 22:10ff)
- Jesus Has Commissioned the Angel's Message (Rev.
  22:16)

Jesus Offers the Invitation to Life (Rev. 22:16-17)

The Wonderful Themes of Revelation
Subjects are for chapters. Key Verses are supplied where appropriate.

Chapter 1—the Alpha and the Omega (Rev. 1:12-18)

Chapter 2—the Living Christ "Knows" Me (Rev. 2, 9, 19)

Chapter 3—the Church Must Repent (Rev. 3:2-3; cf. Rev. 9:20ff.)

Chapter 4—Heaven's Open Door (Rev. 4:1)

Chapter 5—the Complete Worthiness of the Lamb (Rev. 5:1-14)

Chapter 6—God's Approaching Judgment, The End of Planet Earth (Rev. 6:9-17)

Chapter 7—the Great Tribulation; or Redeemed by the Blood (Rev. 7:13ff)

Chapter 8-10—the Work and Ministry of Angels; the Onslaught of Evil from the Abyss

Chapter 11—the Perseverance of the Covenant, or God's Two Courageous Messengers (Rev. 11:19)

Chapter 12—the Providence of God for His Church or Satan's War against the Church (Rev. 12:13ff)

Chapter 12-14—the Ultimate Overthrow of Evil

Chapter 13—Satan's Evil Duo or The Antichrist: His Assault on the World (Rev. 13)

Chapter 14—The Security of God's People (Saints), or The Final Harvest of the Earth

Chapter 15-16—the Wrath of God, or The Bowls of Wrath

Chapter 17-18—His Vengeance upon Earth's Kingdoms; The End of World City; or The Kingdoms in Flames

Chapter 19—The King of Kings and the Lord of Lords (Rev. 19:1ff); Endless Hallelujahs (19:1-6)

Chapter 20—The Glorious Rewards of God; There Really is a Hell

Chapter 21—Heaven's Eternal Blessings or The Eternal City of God

Chapter 22—the Paradise of God or Christ's Final Invitation

I BELIEVE!

Revelation Should Inspire Belief in Our Hearts

Chapter 1—I Believe in the Magnificent Risen Christ (1:9-20)
Chapter 1—I Believe in the Alpha and Omega (1:12-18)
Chapter 2—I Believe the Living Christ "Knows" Me (2:2, 9, 19)
Chapter 3—I Believe the Church Must Repent (3:2-3; cf. 9:20ff.)
Chapter 4—I Believe in the Wonder of Heaven (5:1-14)
Chapter 5—I Believe in the Worthiness of the Lamb (5:6)
Chapter 6—I Believe in God's Ultimate Judgment (6:9-17)
Chapter 7—I Believe in the Great Tribulation (7:13ff.)
Chapter 8—I Believe God Listens to Our Prayers (8:1-4)
Chapter 9—I Believe in the Reality of Evil (9:1-6; 20-21)
Chapter 10—I Believe in the Power of the Word (10:5-11)
Chapter 11—I Believe in Christ's Eternal Reign (11:15)
Chapter 12—I Believe in the Providence of God for His Church
        (12:13ff.)
Chapter 12—I Believe in Satan's War Against Believers (12:1-17;
        13:7)
Chapter 13—I Believe Satan Will Persecute Believers (13:1-9)
Chapter 14—I Believe in God's Provision for His Saints (14:1-3;
        12-16)
Chapter 14—I Believe Christ Will Resurrect the Dead (14:12-16
Chapter 15—I Believe There Is Celebration in Heaven (15:1-5)
Chapter 16—I Believe in the Wrath of God (16:15-21)
Chapter 17—I Believe in the Depravity Within Society (17:1-6; 12-
        18)
Chapter 18—I Believe God Will Destroy Evil (18:4-21)
Chapter 19—I Believe Christ is the King of kings and the Lord of
        lords (19:11ff.)
Chapter 20—I Believe in the Eternal Rewards of God (20:11-15)
Chapter 21—I Believe in the Place Called Heaven (21:1-4; 9-10)
Chapter 22—I Believe in I Will See God's Paradise (22:1-6)
Chapter 22—I Believe in Christ's Glorious Return (22:7; 12-17)

PLEASE CHECK OUT OUT WEB PAGE

<u>www.shufordjones.com</u>

If you enjoyed this commentary, may we suggest our two volumes on the Psalms.

Psalms Fresh Hope for Today
Vo. 1
The Life of David and
Psalms 1-72

Psalms Fresh Hope for Today
Vol. 2
Psalms 73-150

Thank You for Reading

Shuford Jones

CPSIA information can be obtained
at www.ICGtesting.com
Printed in the USA
FSHW011704091218
54303FS

9 781732 698703